D1571735

THEY WERE
PILGRIMS

THEY WERE
PILGRIMS

MARCUS L. LOANE

THE BANNER OF TRUTH TRUST

THE BANNER OF TRUTH TRUST
3 Murrayfield Road, Edinburgh EH12 6EL, UK
P O Box 621, Carlisle, PA 17013, USA

*

First published 1970
First Banner of Truth edition 2006

*

ISBN-10: 0 85151 928 8
ISBN-13: 978 0 85151 928 9

*

Typeset in 12/14 pt Galliard by
Initial Typesetting Services,
Edinburgh, U.K.

Printed in the U.S.A. by
Versa Press, Inc.,
East Peoria, IL

TO

PATRICIA

MY TRUE FELLOW-PILGRIM
TO THAT CITY WHOSE BUILDER
AND MAKER IS GOD

Lo, by slow small footsteps,
　　By the daily cross,
By the heart's unspoken yearning,
　　By its grief and loss,
So he brings them home to rest,
With the victors, crowned and blest.

So, O weary pilgrim,
　　'Tis the Master's way,
And it leadeth surely, surely,
　　Unto endless day.
Doubt not; fear not; gladly go –
He will bring thee homeward so.

Lilias Trotter

Contents

Foreword
to the Banner of Truth Edition

M any will ever be thankful that Marcus Loane not only loves history but believes the best way to make it live for others is to write in terms of *people*. When his *Masters of the English Reformation* was first published, in 1954,[1] I well remember the thrill of 'meeting' men such as William Tyndale and Hugh Latimer. The same author once commented with regard to past history that, while we know in advance how it ended, 'We can never perfectly recapture what it was like to stand at the start line when the future was all unknown.' Nonetheless, in a book such as the present one, we are brought near 'the start line'. It has been said of his biographical writings, 'In such studies, Loane identified himself so closely with his subjects that readers might suspect that he would have preferred to live in their days.'[2] That has not been my own impression; rather I would say he is so in sympathy with those of whom he writes that the difference in time begins to disappear.

[1] Sir Marcus Loane, *Masters of the English Reformation* (1954; repr. Edinburgh: Banner of Truth, 2005), ISBN 0 85151 910 5.

[2] J. R. Reid, *Marcus L. Loane: A Biography* (Brunswick East, Victoria: Acorn Press, 2004), p. 112.

Like his subjects, Marcus Loane has a cause in view in writing and he wants that same cause to live on in other generations. Such a motive is scarcely *de rigueur* in academic circles today, but happily this author has never bowed to the limitations that can impede writers who look for acceptance. To understand the purpose he keeps in view in his writing I would urge the reader not to pass over the two Prefaces in this book.

Many titles by Marcus Loane have appeared since his *Oxford and the Evangelical Succession* came out in 1950. But it is my impression that the present book is one of his favourites, and that because it lies close to what has been his special, life-long interest, namely, the preparation of young men for the Christian ministry, and the encouragement of young people to be out and out Christians. The South African missionary, John Smith Moffat, once commented: 'Many take religion as they take their bridge and tennis, when they have nothing more pressing to do. Religion ought to be a ruling passion.'

The young men in the following pages are eminent examples of what Christian passion means. In many respects the four were different. They belonged to different places and different eras. None of their lives overlapped. Yet one ambition moved them and, in all that is most important, their likeness to each other is convincing evidence of the reality of oneness in Christ.

On most of the men portrayed in this book a good deal has been written, and each has been the theme of at least one full biography. Marcus Loane brings to this book, not only a thorough acquaintance with these sources, but a wide background of reading that often throws light into unexpected corners. In addition there is the attraction that he has himself had the opportunity to visit the far-flung corners of the earth where his subjects served and often suffered.

In reproducing the likeness of a person, the success of an artist is not judged by the size of his canvas; a miniature can sometimes be more compelling and lifelike than a full-size portrait.

While these biographies are a good deal more than miniatures, it is the authenticity of portrayal, not their length, that gives them their special value. Here some readers will have a first meeting with Brainerd, Martyn, M'Cheyne and Keith-Falconer. And for other readers, who have long revered these names, there will be the pleasure of meeting them again, as true to life as any book can make them.

For us all there is the challenge to live with greater devotion to Christ. What follows in these pages aims to deepen what is a fundamental New Testament conviction, and it will surely help us to understand the prayer of Robert Murray M'Cheyne: 'I long for love without any coldness, light without dimness, and purity without spot or wrinkle. I long to lie at Jesus' feet, and tell Him I am all His, and ever will be.'

It remains for me, on behalf of the present publishers, to express our gratitude to the author for all the leadership he has given, and continues to give the Christian world in his books; and in being thankful to God for him, we would include thankfulness that Patricia Knox who, in 1937, became Mrs and now Lady Loane, remains beside him as his own special encourager and helper.

In a Foreword to one of his books Marcus Loane closed with words of testimony which we would repeat here:

'We would gladly subscribe to the dying words of Richard Hooker as told in his *Life* by Isaac Walton:

> Though I have, by His grace, loved Him in my youth, and feared Him in my age, and laboured to have a conscience void of offence . . . yet if Thou, O Lord, be extreme to mark what is done amiss, who can abide it? And therefore, where I have failed, Lord, show mercy to me; for I plead not my righteousness, but the forgiveness of my unrighteousness for His merits who died to purchase pardon for penitent sinners.'

IAIN H. MURRAY
Edinburgh,
January 2006

Preface
to the New (1984) Edition

S ince this book first appeared fifteen years ago, I have had various opportunities to learn a great deal more about David Brainerd and Henry Martyn, and to a lesser extent, about Ion Keith-Falconer. This has been due, at least in part, to the kind of information one can only derive from a visit to the sites where their life and work took place. This has left me with a special desire to revise each chapter in order to incorporate certain details which may otherwise easily be lost.

But the body of the work is the same. I was very taken with some remarks of Professor H. R. Trevor-Roper in the Preface to a new edition of his life of Archbishop Laud. He said that an author who sets out to revise one of his own books is bound to feel a tinge of regret. 'As he re-reads his old work, he finds so much that, if he were to write it now for the first time, he would write very differently, but which, once written, he cannot change. For unless a book is a mere compilation, its date is an essential part of it. A book expresses the author's mind at the time of writing, and that expression can not, by mere verbal changes, be brought up-to-date – that is, up to another date, at which it was not written.'

A book like this cannot replace the classical biographies or the personal records of the four men concerned. But there are such uncommon links between them, such remarkable affinities in spiritual aspiration and missionary vision, and such striking correspondence in the early age at which their work was done, that I believe there is special value in placing the record of their lives side by side. And I confess that for myself, so great is the impact each of these men has made that it is like trying to pay the debt I owe to tell again what God wrought in them and through them for his glory in the furtherance of the gospel.

MARCUS LOANE
1984

Preface
to the Original Edition

The men whose life stories are told in the course of this book left a mark on their own generation which still persists. Their lives cover the period of history from 1718 to 1887, and the secret force and driving motive in each case was identical. They were inspired by a passionate loyalty to the lordship of Christ and to the spread of the gospel. This found different forms of expression according to the emphasis of the age to which they belonged, but they were all at full stretch, as it were, for the goals of personal holiness and the salvation of men. They were all linked with the missionary movement which had its birth in the spiritual awakening of the eighteenth century, and they were all pioneers in the outreach of the gospel: David Brainerd with the Red Indians; Robert M'Cheyne with the Jews; Henry Martyn and Ion Keith-Falconer with the Muslim world in Persia and Arabia.

The death of those who are young and pure in heart may seem premature in the eyes of the world, but it can be glorious as well. Sorrow of such a kind is a necessary and precious element in God's over-ruling purpose of love.

These four men were to average a life span of only thirty years each. Henry Martyn was thirty-one when he died; Ion Keith-Falconer was thirty; Brainerd and M'Cheyne were twenty-nine. Theirs were short lives, but they crowded them with effort, and their very brevity was to add its special distinction. Henry Martyn's term of active service lasted a little less than nine years in all; Robert M'Cheyne's less than seven; David Brainerd's less than five; and Ion Keith-Falconer's but a few months. They lived as the children of time; they were pilgrims on the road to eternity.

These men whose life span was so short were all impelled by a sense of tremendous urgency. There are but twelve hours in the day, and they strove to complete their work while it was day; they knew that night was at hand when no man can work. They knew that they could not recall a lost moment; still less a lost life, a lost soul, a lost eternity. And this made them more than willing to act on the words of the Lord Jesus: 'Whosoever will save his life shall lose it; and whosoever will lose his life for my sake shall find it' (*Matt.* 16:25).

It is true that all men stand on the same level, and yet they do not all reach the same height. These were men of spiritual stature, and it was a stature which made them stand head and shoulders above many who had stood with them as equals in age or in ability. They were men who would have revelled in the burning passion of an ancient Hebrew for an earthly Jerusalem. They would have made their own the words in the metrical translation of one of those hymns of Zion:

> Thy saints take pleasure in her stones:
> Her very dust to them is dear.[1]

They had the same ardent, patriotic feeling for a kingdom which is not of this world, and their eyes were towards that great city whose builder and maker is God.

And we now look with the eyes of faith through the latticework of time and watch from afar as they vanish through the gates of eternity to stand before the King. It is with them in view that we hear the words of exhortation: 'Whose faith follow, considering the end of their conversation' (*Heb.* 13:7).

[1] Psalm 102:14

David Brainerd

A Guide to the Delawares
1718–47

North American Indians, from
an engraving by John Boydell, 1775.

Where the *safe* ways end,
Known and unknown divide,
God's great uncharted prairies upward trend,
Where the spirit of man, undaunted, is undenied,
And beyond the last camp fire, man has faith for friend.
And beyond all guidance, the courage of God for guide.

ANON.

Early Days and Conversion

David Brainerd[1] was born in the village of Haddam near Hartford in Connecticut on 20 April 1718, and grew up on a New England farm in a strong Puritan atmosphere.[2] His father held office as a deacon in the church at Haddam and was a member of the King's Council for the government of the colony. From his mother he would derive a rich family tradition of duty and ideal, for her forbears on each side had been men of mark as loyal Puritan ministers. Her father's father was Peter Hobart who had been a minister in Norfolk; her mother's father was Samuel Whiting who had been a minister at Boston. But the repressive government of that age in England had led them to cross the sea in the wake of the *Mayflower,* and their ministry had been continued among the settlers in Massachusetts. Four of Hobart's sons and three of Whiting's sons had become ministers in New England; Hobart's second son had married Whiting's daughter and had settled down as minister of the church at Haddam. When their daughter married Hezekiah Brainerd, she brought him a spiritual dowry better than gold or land. Five sons and four daughters were born to grace their home, and three of those sons were in due time called to the ministry. David was the third son of this spacious household, and his earliest memories were all imbued with the high-minded devotion of his parents. But his father died in 1727 when he was nine, and his mother in 1732 when he was fourteen years old. This meant that he passed through his teens as an orphan, and his boyhood was subdued with sorrow. He

3

was thoughtful beyond his years, conscientious in habit, introspective in spirit, with a growing concern of soul; and this concern was to provide the great master motive in his pursuit of the grace and glory of God.

Brainerd was to run the gauntlet of an experience which taught him to know his own heart in all its moods. He had little inclination for the social 'frolics' of those of his own age and would seldom take part in them. 'But this I know,' he wrote, 'that when I did go into such company, I never returned with so good a con-science as when I went; it always added new guilt and made me afraid to come to the throne of grace.'[3] This led him to devote himself to a ceaseless round of duty in the hope that it would wean his heart from the world, and this was the spirit in which, at the age of nineteen, he set his mind on the goal of ordination. He read the whole Bible twice in the year and spent much time night and day on his knees, stretching every nerve in constant effort to draw near to God in the name of Christ. He longed for true release from the rule of sin and the love of self so that he might belong wholly to God and be his for ever.[4] But a sense of guilt and lack of peace still haunted his mind, and he found that there was nothing stable in the inner world of private feelings. He would look with sensitive interest into the pools of his own heart, and he could see nothing in their troubled depths to reflect back the image of Christ. He was to drift on the starless waters of such moods and feelings until he stood on the rugged shore of manhood, and it was from the depth that his cry of need and longing went up to God. Here and there a rift broke through the clouds in momentary relief; then he was lost again in the darkness. 'I could not bear that all I had done should stand for mere nothing,' he wrote, 'who had been very conscientious in duty.'[5] But his cry had been heard, and the end was at hand. Light shone at last, and with that flash from the sun of glory, he caught sight of 'the King in his beauty' (*Isa.* 33:17).

This great change took place on 12 July 1739, a Sunday evening which followed a week of self-despair. He had gone out to a solitary haunt where he could release all the pent-up feeling of his troubled spirit in prayer. He spent half an hour in dull and lifeless efforts to pray, 'but found no heart to engage in that or any other duty'.[6] But while he was walking in thick woodland, conscious of the fact that he had reached the end of all his striving, God gave him a sudden revelation of his presence. 'Unspeakable glory', so he recalled, 'seemed to open to the view and apprehension of my soul . . . It was a new inward apprehension or view that I had of God, such as I never had before.'[7] It was as though some bright vision like that of one of the ancient seers had opened before the eyes of his soul, and he was allowed to taste the bliss of an absolute submission to the God of glory. 'Thus God brought me to . . . set Him on the throne,' he wrote, 'and . . . I felt myself in a new world.'[8] The whole record of his experience is so vivid that it deserves to be read in his own simple, graphic language. The man had met the Maker and Master of his inmost being, and his whole soul rose up in welcome and worship. It was so real and so profound that no occasional melancholy could in future shake his hold on God as his God or could rob him of his fundamental sense of pardon and peace. Jonathan Edwards testified that 'His experiences, instead of dying away, were evidently of an increasing nature. His first love and other holy affections even at the beginning were very great; but after months and years became much greater and more remarkable.'[9] It marked the great point of departure which led to an altogether exceptional career of personal holiness and Christian attainment.

A STUDENT AT YALE

Two months later, in September 1739, he enrolled as a student of Yale College in New Haven, though not without anxiety lest he should fail to lead as strict a life as was now his desire. But trial was not to come in the way he was inclined to fear, and he throve in spirit as he fed on the Word of God. 'One day I remember in particular,' so he recalled; 'I think it was in June 1740. I walked to a considerable distance from the College, in the fields alone at noon, and in prayer found unspeakable sweetness and delight in God.'[10] He gave himself up to hard and constant study, and made steady progress as a freshman. His health broke down twice in the course of 1740; the first signs of pulmonary tuberculosis had begun to appear. But his time was not yet, and he only felt a quickened desire for God. It was in this spirit that on 9 December 1740, he wrote: 'O! one hour with God infinitely exceeds all the pleasures and delights of this lower world!'[11]

His first two years at Yale coincided with the first tour of George Whitefield through New England, and a spiritual movement had been set on foot which would stir long-smouldering conviction in the hearts of thousands. In October 1740, Whitefield paid a three-day visit to New Haven and spoke to the students with all the force of his tremendous earnestness. 'It was no small grief to me,' he wrote afterwards, 'that I was obliged to say of your College that your light was become darkness.'[12] Then in February 1741, Gilbert Tennent paid a visit to New Haven and saw the dawn of a spiritual awakening. 'At New Haven', he told Whitefield, 'the concern was general, both in the College and town; about thirty students came on foot ten miles to hear the Word of God.'[13] Brainerd, worn with ill-health, hard study, and constant vigils, caught fire at this awakening in the College; he was more than ever resolved to live only for God.[14]

But there had been reason for George Whitefield's stricture on the College. It was an age when those who sat in the seat of academic authority viewed such movements with cold disapproval. They stood aloof and frowned disdain at the thought of religious revival, and a clash was bound to occur when the trustees of Yale passed a resolution to the effect that any student who engaged in criticism of College Tutors should be expelled.[15] Brainerd was the unfortunate student who gave offence and was singled out for rigorous discipline; but the offence was so trifling that the story of what happened now seems almost incredible. He was chatting in the hall with two or three friends when he made the remark that a certain tutor had no more grace than the leg of a chair.[16] This chance remark was overheard and repeated by a freshman to a certain woman who then in turn told the Rector of the College. Brainerd's friends were questioned by the Rector and were forced to admit what he had said and to whom it referred. Brainerd himself was then required to appear before the College and to make a public statement; but he would not demean himself by an apology in hall for a remark which had only been made in private conversation. This offence was aggravated by two other matters. Brainerd had gone to a meeting in New Haven in spite of the Rector's prohibition, and had then been accused of an intemperate criticism of the Rector who had imposed a fine on some students who followed Gilbert Tennent to Milford. As a result, he was expelled

from Yale in the winter term of 1742. Such a stringent
verdict can only be compared with the action of the Vice-
Chancellor of Oxford in 1768 when six students were
expelled on account of their Methodist sympathies. It
was blind and bitter judgment on the part of academic
authority at New Haven and at Oxford alike; but the
disgrace was nonetheless real for David Brainerd and the
six St Edmund students who found themselves expelled
from their College and denied their degree.

Brainerd knew that he had been wronged; he knew
that his treatment had been unfair and the verdict unjust.
There are passages in his Diary which show how much
this had to do with the melancholy which cast a long
shadow over his life. The whole situation preyed on his
mind because of the reproach which he thought it would
bring on the honour of Christ. But he never uttered a
word against the men who had done him this wrong,
and he never wrote a sentence which breathed other than
the spirit of charity and forbearance. On 12 April 1742,
he referred in passing to his 'great trial at College'.[17] On
14 May, he came before a Council of Ministers at
Hartford, and they agreed to ask for his reinstatement:
their request was refused.[18] On 3 July, he observed: 'My
heart seemed again to sink. The disgrace I was laid under
at College seemed to damp me, as it opens the mouths
of opposers. I had no refuge but in God.'[19] On 6 June
1743, he rode to New Haven in the hope that he could
effect a reconciliation with the Rector; a month later, he
renewed the attempt.[20] It was in vain. On 14 September,
he wrote: 'This day I ought to have taken my degree;
but God sees fit to deny it me . . . I have long feared this
season . . . but found much more pleasure and divine
comfort than I expected.'[21] The next evening, on the
advice of friends, he gave the Rector and Trustees a frank

written apology, and wrote in his Diary: 'Though what I said . . . was only spoken in private, to a friend or two; and being partly overheard, was related to the Rector, and by him extorted from my friends; yet, seeing it was divulged and made public, I was willing to confess my fault therein publicly.'[22] It was too late. The Rector and Trustees were willing to receive him back to the College, but they would not allow him to proceed to his degree for a further twelve months. The Diary never referred to the subject again, but the disappointment remained.

Spiritual Growth

One may watch the growth of his soul from the time when he left College through the open windows of his revealing Diary. It was written for his own eye alone as a daily record of all that passed within his heart; and he was most anxious that it should be destroyed when he knew that death was at hand. The first two books which had covered his days as a student were burnt at his request, but the rest were preserved intact and were published by Jonathan Edwards after his death. They show that he went to live with the Reverend Jedediah Mills at Ripton when he left Yale, and that he was engaged in a course of guided reading with a view to ordination. The first entry was for 1 April 1742, and it sounded the note which so often rang through the hours which he spent in soliloquy and prayer: 'Oh, if I ever get to heaven, it will be because God will, and nothing else; for I never did anything of myself, but get away from God!'[23] His deep sense of disappointment at the rebuff with which he had met at College may have given a fresh impulse to the intro-spective severity of his early training, but the entries for the months which follow gleam with the fire of a holy aspiration. He was possessed with a thirst for God that gave his words a compelling earnestness. Thus on 15 April 1742, he wrote: 'I know I long for God, and a conformity to His will in inward purity and holiness, ten thousand times more than for anything here below.'[24] And again on 20 April: 'I think my soul was never so drawn out in intercession for others as it has been this night ... I wanted to wear out my life in His service and for His glory.'[25] He felt that he would not mind what he had to pass through so long as his heart was on fire with love for God.[26] On 13 May, he wrote: 'O, the closest walk with God is the sweetest heaven that can be enjoyed on earth.'[27]

There were indeed days of rapture as well as of melancholy in his experience and it has been argued that his emotional fluctuations were 'pathological in origin'.[28] But he was cast in the mould of one whose life was controlled by an absolute devotion to his sense of God and duty. On 18 June 1742, he wrote: 'My soul seemed to breathe after holiness, a life of constant devotedness to God.'[29] And on 4 July, he hungered for the humility that is content 'to be little, to be nothing, and to lie in the dust.'[30] It may be true that the rigorous discipline of his Puritan character had a certain staid and joyless aspect; this is evident in his Diary. But it would be wrong to draw the picture from this record alone; he was never dull or morose in the eyes of his friends.[31] He was cheerful in society and pleasant in conversation; but his social pleasures would have been no pleasure at all if they were not centred in Christ. On 10 September, for example, he wrote: 'In the evening took leave of that house [in New Haven]; but first kneeled down and prayed. The Lord was of a truth in the midst of us; it was a sweet parting season; felt in myself much sweetness and affection in the things of God. Blessed be God for every such divine gale of His Spirit to speed me on my way to the New Jerusalem!'[32] He knew what it was to 'enjoy God', and yet to be kept still 'reaching forward'.[33] This is never clearer than in the cry which found its way into his Diary on 4 November, and which has the accent as well as the insight of a true saint: 'Oh for holiness! Oh for more of God in my soul! Oh this pleasing pain!'[34] Dr John A. Mackay quotes these words, adding the fine comment: 'God in the soul is life's supreme pleasure, for in the divine communion, every human longing is met. God in the soul is also life's most exquisite pain, for the soul in whom God dwells becomes a sharer in His love passion for men. The love of God is both rapture and suffering.'[35]

Ordained to Preach to the Indians

Meanwhile, though he hardly knew it, he was being prepared to take up the mantle of John Eliot as a missionary among the Red Indians. John Eliot was born in England in 1604 and took his degree at Cambridge in 1622. He followed the Pilgrim Fathers to Boston in 1631 and became the minister at Roxbury in Massachusetts in 1632. He exercised his ministry in that village until his death on 21 May 1690, and it was linked with a truly remarkable missionary outreach. He found himself in close contact with the Iroquois and the Mohicans, and he began to preach among them in 1646. He mastered their language and published a translation of the New Testament in 1661 and of the Old Testament in 1663. He travelled widely among the tribes of New England, and by 1674 he had established no less than fourteen towns as Christian settlements. In one memorable sentence, written in his own hand at the end of his Grammar, he has left the secret: 'Prayers and pains, through faith in Christ, can do anything.'[36]

Eliot was the first true English-speaking missionary since the Reformation, but the outbreak of war was to scatter his 'praying Indians' and to undo his work. His fourteen Christian settlements were reduced to four, and even these dwindled under hostile pressure.[37] When he died in 1690, little seemed to remain; many years were to pass before the next significant development. Then in 1734, the Society for the Propagation of the Gospel in London and the Commissioners for Indian Affairs in Boston appointed John Sergeant as a pioneer missionary at Stockbridge, near the north-west border of Massachusetts. And in 1740, the Scottish Society for Propagating Christian Knowledge was induced to provide grants for two missionaries to work among the Indians. The Society named certain persons as its Correspondents in New England: their task was to find the missionaries, handle the grants, and manage their affairs. The first missionary was Azariah Horton who began work on Long Island in August 1741, but a second missionary was not at once available.[38] Then a letter from the Correspondents reached David Brainerd on 19 November 1742, asking him to meet them in New York as soon as he could arrange to come.[39]

Brainerd was the right man for such a call, for months before, his spirit had begun to stir with an apostolic passion for the regions beyond. Thus on 2 April 1742, he had written: 'Some time past, I had much pleasure in the prospect of the heathen being brought home to Christ, and desired that the Lord would employ me in that work.'[40] And on 6 April: 'I then began to find it sweet to pray; and could think of undergoing the greatest sufferings in the cause of Christ with pleasure; and found myself willing, if God should so order it, to suffer banishment from my native land among the heathen, that

I might do something for their salvation.'[41] And on 8 April: 'Had raised hopes today respecting the heathen. O that God would bring in great numbers of them to Jesus Christ! I cannot but hope I shall see that glorious day.'[42] His thoughts were still running along this line some months later, when on 23 August he spent 'a sweet season in prayer'. 'O my soul tasted the sweetness of the upper world', he wrote, 'and was drawn out in prayer for the world, that it might come home to Christ! Had much comfort in the thoughts and hopes of the ingathering of the heathen.'[43] But though he wrote of 'the heathen' and felt a strong desire to be employed as a missionary, he made no reference to the Red Indians until he received the letter from the Correspondents. 'Received a letter from the Reverend Mr Pemberton of New York,' he wrote on November 19th, 'desiring me speedily to go down thither and consult about the Indian affairs in those parts.'[44] Such an invitation may not have been wholly unexpected; God had indeed prepared his heart. He gave himself to prayer and took counsel with friends, and then set foot in the stirrup to start the long eighty-five mile ride to New York. On 25 November, he had his first momentous interview with the Correspondents, and the result was a mutual agreement that he should take up the missionary burden as soon as the winter came to an end.

Brainerd had been examined by a group of ministers who met at Danbury in Connecticut, and was licensed as a preacher of the gospel on 29 July 1742. He preached his first sermon the next day at Southbury and was able to think of it with hope. 'I seemed to have power with God in prayer,' he wrote, 'and power to get hold of the hearts of the people in preaching.'[45] He had to preach in the presence of the Correspondents when he came to

New York at the end of the year. Then he entered on a round of farewell visits during the cold months of winter. His Diary on 23 December shows what this meant for him: 'My soul was refreshed and sweetly melted with divine things. Oh that I was always consecrated to God!'[46] He sold his small patrimony and arranged to devote what it had brought to the education of a candidate for the ministry. He preached for the last time at East Haddam on 1 February 1743, and then went to visit Azariah Horton's Indian settlements on Long Island. He was deeply conscious of the wrench with the past, but he rode on his way, laying hold on God as his strength. On 7 March he wrote: 'My heart ascribed glory, glory, glory, to the blessed God, and bid welcome to all inward distress again if God saw meet to exercise me with it. Time appeared but an inch long, and eternity at hand; and I thought I could with patience and cheerfulness bear anything for the cause of God.'[47]

The plan of the Correspondents had been to send him to the Forks of Delaware in Pennsylvania, but news had been received to the effect that there was strife between local settlers and the Redskins about their lands. As a result, the plan was changed and the Correspondents resolved to send him to start work among the Indians at Kaunaumeek, a place in the province of New York between Stockbridge and Albany. Therefore on 21 March, he took his seat in the saddle and turned his eyes towards the great unknown.

On 31 March, Brainerd travelled the last twelve miles through the valley from Sheffield to Stockbridge where he would be made welcome in the home of John Sergeant. Stockbridge was a frontier settlement on the Housatonic River in Western Massachusetts: 'beyond the line of the frontier, and a mere dot in the wilderness'.[48] In 1737, four white families were chosen to settle at Stockbridge in order to strengthen it as an outpost of civilisation. In 1739, Sergeant married and built a fine home which still stands with its three floors and two chimneys. It was a home in which Brainerd would always be welcome and where he was often to stay for a night or two in the months at hand. There was so much that he could learn from Sergeant who had already translated prayers and Scripture portions into the dialect of the Housatonics. But on this occasion, he did not linger. Stockbridge was 'the farther-most edge of civilised America',[49] and his destination lay twenty miles beyond in the uncharted wilderness. The next day he set out to ride over several ranges of heavily wooded hills – the Berkshire Hills – to a little Indian settlement known as Kaunaumeek. There must have been clearly defined tracks through the woods or he could not have found his way. The settlement at Kaunaumeek is now the site of a little village known as Brainard (spelt with an 'a'), but no trace of David's presence and no memories of the Indian settlement remain today.[50] Here he arrived on the evening of 1 April 1743, and lay down on a little heap of straw. Henceforth he would have to ride through forests where campfire and wig-wam were the only shelter, and where Pale-face and Red-skin were in frequent conflict. He was prepared to count all things but loss for Christ, but he could not tell what form that would take; and he did not know that he had entered on a pilgrimage of loneliness and an adventure of suffering whose end would be premature death and immortal glory.

But there was no glamour in mind as he lay down that night on the little heap of straw; rather he was assailed with the javelin-thrusts of deep-seated melancholy. 'In the evening,' so he confessed, 'my heart was sunk, and I seemed to have no God to go to. O that God would help me!'[51] There were hardships enough in this new way of life if he were to win the goodwill of the Red men: loneliness, frustration, meagre diet, language problems, and an ailing physique. 'My circumstances are such', he wrote on 18 May, 'that I have no comfort of any kind but what I have in God.'[52] But the only burden that could make such hardship seem too grievous to bear was want of that conscious comfort: 'That which makes all my difficulties grievous to be borne is that God hides His face from me.'[53] But he quickly found an answer to such melancholy in a ceaseless round of duty and prayer. On 4 August, he declared: 'Filling up our time with and for God is the way to rise up and lie down in peace.'[54] And on 15 August: 'In prayer I enjoyed great freedom, and blessed God as much for my present circumstances as if I had been a king.'[55] He built himself a hut among the wig-wams; he bent his mind to work upon the language. He was often in the saddle, and he had to ride out in all weathers; he was sometimes lost in the dark, and he knew what it was to spend the night in the forest. His Diary on 4 October provides a bare outline of his experience: 'I have been often exposed to cold and hunger in the wilderness where the comforts of life were not to be had; have frequently been lost in the woods and sometimes obliged to ride much of the night; and once lay out in the woods all night; yet blessed be God, He has preserved me.'[56] God had allowed him a vision of the heathen as his inheritance, and the idea of sacrifice had disappeared like a cloud from the sky.

Such work was not in vain, though it was to prove brief enough in point of time. God so laid hold on one woman when he began to preach on 10 April that her heart cried out for Christ from that day forward,[57] and God so spoke to them all at his last service on 11 March

1744 that he scarce knew how to leave off preaching.[58]
On 14 March he set out for New York where he was to
meet the Correspondents, and found himself besieged
on the journey with two pressing calls to the church at
East Hampton and to the church at Millington. He knew
that East Hampton had a large and wealthy congregation
in one of the most attractive settlements on Long Island,
and he knew that Millington was close to his home where
he would be in the midst of friends.[59] He was in a pre-
carious state of health at the end of twelve months of
constant hardship, and his shaken sources of strength
might have excused him from further hazard. But his
heart went out to the fields that were white for harvest,
and he turned his eyes to the wild forest country 'where
the safe ways end, known and unknown divide'.

On 6 April, he was ready for fresh orders from the
Correspondents; he was to leave Kaunaumeek and go to
the Indians at the Forks of Delaware in Pennsylvania.[60]
He had arranged for his congregation at Kaunaumeek to
take up new land at Stockbridge where they would come
under the care of John Sergeant. There he took leave of
them in two final sermons on 29 April, and then rode to
Kaunaumeek on 30 April to pack his books and clothes.[61]
The next day, in spite of severe pain and weakness, he left
on the first stage of his journey. On 12 May, he came to
a little outpost of Dutch and Irish settlers some twelve
miles above the Forks of Delaware near the modern town
of Easton, and the very next day began to preach both to
red and to white.[62]

He had hardly begun his work when he received a fresh
summons from the Correspondents, and he set out on
the four-day journey from the Forks of Delaware. He
reached New York on 31 May in a state of utter fatigue;
he was 'exceedingly tired and worn out'.[63] But the object

of this journey was his ordination by the Presbytery of New York, whose leading members were Ebenezer Pemberton, Jonathan Dickinson and John Pierson. Brainerd had been closely identified with them ever since he had been expelled from Yale, and they were men of the highest spiritual stature, moderate, irenic, and wise.[64] On 11 June, he met them at Newark and preached a trial sermon in their presence. The next morning he was ordained, and his feelings were well summed up in his entry at the close of the day: 'I was affected with a sense of the important trust committed to me, yet was composed and solemn, without distraction; and I hope that then, as many times before, I gave myself up to God to be for Him and not for another.'[65]

He was so ill that he could not return at once, and it was 19 June before he set out for the Forks of Delaware. He was hardly able to walk when he reached the wig-wams, and his heart was burdened with the problems which he now had to bear. But he went on in the strength God gave him and wrote on 25 June: 'In evening prayer, my faith and hope in God were much raised. To an eye of reason, everything that respects the conversion of the heathen is as dark as midnight; and yet I cannot but hope in God for the accomplishment of something glorious among them.'[66] The ordination at Newark could not add to the grace that was his in the Son of God, but it had stirred his whole being to a yet more profound passion for self-surrender and self-sacrifice. On 1 July this desire found its expression in his Diary: 'My whole soul cried, Lord, to Thee I dedicate myself! O accept of me, and let me be Thine for ever. Lord, I desire nothing else, I desire nothing more. Whom have I in heaven but Thee? And there is none upon earth that I desire besides Thee.'[67]

AMONG THE DELAWARE INDIANS

It was in this spirit that he entered upon his work with the Delaware Indians, and it pervades all the ensuing entries in his Diary. But there were great difficulties in the way of this work, and the situation in which he found himself must be taken into account. He was not a fluent linguist, and the language which he now had to learn was split into the most intricate dialects. The slight knowledge of the dialect which he had built up at Kaunaumeek was of no real value at all with the Delaware Indians, and he had to rely on the service of an interpreter who was much more concerned with the white man's liquor than with the love of God. His health was now in a state of serious disorder; he was in the grip of a disease whose real nature was not understood and for which no cure and little treatment was known. He had probably contracted tubercular trouble during childhood; he had certainly developed it by the time he entered College. He now had all the signs of this illness in the weakened state of his lungs, but he could pay little regard to the fundamental laws of rest and diet. He had to deal with a tribe which was so debased through ignorance and drunkenness that it was hard to know how to begin. They had been so often deceived by the white man that they could not be blamed for a spirit of deep mistrust. But on 6 July, his longings found utterance in his Diary: 'Last year I longed to be prepared for a world of glory and speedily to depart out of this world; but of late all my concern almost is for the conversion of the heathen; and for that end I long to live.'[68] He had begun to share in the passion of Christ for the outcast, and it filled his thoughts by day and his dreams by night. He had work to perform, and was straitened until it was complete. Thus on 21 July, he wrote: 'While I was asleep, I dreamed of these things, and when I waked ... the first thing I thought of was this great work.'[69]

He was soon faced with a crisis which was to guide his whole attitude to the Indians. He heard that an idolatrous feast was to take place in circumstances that filled him with dismay. 'Then I began to be in anguish', he wrote. 'I thought I must in conscience go, and endeavour to break them up; and knew not how to attempt such a thing.'[70] He spent that night on his knees in such a conflict of prayer that it was as if he strove to take the kingdom of God by storm. 'When I rose from my knees', he wrote, 'the sweat ran down my face and body, and nature seemed as it would dissolve.'[71] But he felt that he had prevailed, and that the God who had heard would arise and act. On Sunday 22 July, he awoke and withdrew into the woods for one last hour of prayer before he rode away to the Red-skin revels. 'I had a strong hope', he wrote, 'that God would bow the heavens and come down, and do some marvellous work among the heathen.'[72] Then he went off in search of them with the sober expectation that 'God would make this the day of His power and grace'.[73]

He found them some three miles away in the full whirl of their idolatrous festivities, and he broke in among their pow-wows and dances without ado. God was with him, and the devil-worship stopped dead as he began to preach. But he could see nothing of a special work of grace in their midst, and he felt as though he had failed. He rode back to his camp in the evening, 'very weak and weary, and borne down with perplexity'.[74] He could review it all with a calm mind one day later, and he 'desired nothing so much as the conversion of the heathen to God and that His kingdom might come'.[75] Nor was it all in vain. He found that his hearers grew in number until there were sometimes more than forty at once, and when summer came to an end, some of them had renounced idolatry and had begun to seek the way of life.[76]

The next Sunday he was confined to bed, too ill to preach, and he spent the month of August in great weakness and pain. After the first few days he crawled outside, and twice made an attempt to preach. He was obliged to sit on the ground while he spoke, and the effort left him faint with pain and fatigue. He was indeed so weak that for some time he could not leave his bed at all; he felt as though he had no strength even to read or pray. He could only scrawl a few words now and then where he lay, and his cry of distress went up: 'O that God would pity my state!'[77] Strength did slowly return, and on 2 September he was able to preach once more with an ever-growing concern for his hearers: 'And I am persuaded God enabled me to exercise faith in Him while I was speaking to them.'[78] Most of this month was spent in New England where he hoped to recuperate, and he returned to the Forks of Delaware at the end of September with a new lease of health and strength.

But in July he had found a group of Indians some thirty miles west of the Forks of Delaware. They had heard him twice and had shown genuine interest, but they were just about to break camp and return to their home ground on the Susquehannah River. They gave him an invitation to pay them a further visit, and the Correspondents agreed to the journey.[79] Therefore on 1 October he set out on horseback through the roughest country in which he had ever travelled. His horse broke a leg, and he was forced to complete the one hundred and twenty mile journey on foot.[80] He reached Opeholhaupung (now called Sunbury), on 5 October, was well received, and preached freely in the presence of the Chief and his braves. On his return, he wrote in his Diary on 19 October: 'My soul was now tender, devout, and solemn. And I was afraid of nothing but sin; and afraid of that in every action and thought.'[81] This was but the first of many journeys, and he quickly learned to make the mountain forests his home. 'Such fatigues and hardships as these', he wrote on 22 November, 'serve to wean me more from the earth, and I trust will make heaven the sweeter.'[82]

Just before River Road reaches Martin's Creek, there is a side road which leads to a hill overlooking the Delaware. A monument in memory of Brainerd stands there and states that the hut which he built for his winter quarters, and in which he wrote a large part of his Journal in 1744, was a few roods away.[83] God was better to him than his fears and his ministry was not without encouragement. His Diary on 9 December refers to the presence and power of God during a visit to Greenwich in New Jersey: 'The effects were apparent, tears running down many cheeks.'[84] He was away for five weeks in March and April 1745, and rode some six hundred miles in the course of a journey whose main object was to secure support for a fellow missionary so that he would not have to live and work alone.[85] He had made up his mind to move to the Susquehannah, and he went to Philadelphia to obtain the consent of the chief of the Six Nations. On 8 May, he left the Forks of Delaware with his interpreter and rode along the banks of the Susquehannah for more than a hundred miles to seek out Indian settlements. He met seven or eight distinct tribes to whom he preached by means of interpreters, and some of the Kaunaumeek Indians met and heard him again with joy. He spent two weeks on this journey, and was eager to do yet more lest it should not be done at all. But hardship and fatigue brought on his old complaint, and he was racked with pain and fever, and a frightening haemorrhage. He had driven himself in body and spirit to a standstill, and was without food or suitable medicine. It was only after a week's rest in the hut of a friendly trader that he was able to ride home.[86] On 30 May, he was back in comparative comfort with the Delaware Indians, and soon resumed all his activities. Early in June, he rode fifty miles to assist at a sacramental service and the reference in his Diary is still remarkable. 'God gave me great assistance', he wrote on 9 June, 'and the Word was attended with amazing power; many scores, if not hundreds, in that great assembly, consisting of three or four thousand, were much affected.'[87]

SPIRITUAL AWAKENING AT CROSSWEEKSUNG, NEW JERSEY

Jonathan Edwards was to say that God had endowed Brainerd with 'very uncommon abilities and gifts of nature';[88] and in addition to this, his life was ruled by very uncommon devotion to Christ. He was keenly disappointed by the lack of response from the Delaware Indians, and for some time had been planning to move his base. It was on 19 June 1745 that he first visited the Indians at Crossweeksung (now called Crosswicks), in New Jersey, not quite eighty miles south-east from the Forks of Delaware.[89] He had come at last to the field where he was to reap the richest harvest, and the record has been doubly preserved. His own Diary for the period from 19 June 1745 to 19 June 1746 can now be read alongside the Journal which he prepared at the request of his Society. These two companion documents show how all the fires of spiritual longing were in fact fused in one bright flame, and the Red men could not resist the power of his prayers or the force of his preaching.

There were only seven or eight people present when he began to preach on 19 June, but they grew in number daily. On 22 June, there were thirty; on 27 June, forty; and on 1 July, nearly fifty hearers. The next morning he left for the Forks of Delaware, and on 21 July he baptized the interpreter and his wife as the first converts. On 26 July, he baptized their children, and his Diary indicates how this moved him to cry for the heathen: 'I could not but cry.'[90] On 1 August, he was back at Crossweeksung, and his heart was so drawn out in prayer that it drove sleep from his eyes. Those cries, which no ear heard except the ear of God, were to have power and to prevail, for on 6 August, his hearers were surprised to find themselves under tremendous conviction. It was the love of God of which he spoke, but the air was filled with their cries. 'There was scarce three in forty that could refrain from tears';[91] their hearts had been pierced and broken with the arrows of the love that has no equal.

Nor was this just the mood of a moment, for from all parts Indians came streaming in to hear the gospel; 'and it was remarkable', he wrote on 7 August, 'that as fast as they came . . . the Spirit of God seemed to seize them with concern for their souls'.[92] They would crowd round his horse and catch hold of the bridle, standing with speechless interest or stricken with searching conviction while he explained the Word of God. Those who had grown old in drunken squalor no less than those who were still in happy childhood were touched and drawn by the loving kindness of the gospel invitation.[93] The numbers still increased: on 8 August, there were sixty-five; on 9 August, seventy; on 25 August, ninety-five. It was not the terror of the law or the threat of judgment which had subdued their hearts; it was the love of God and the cross of Christ. He soon observed that the awakening was never more remarkable than when he was making Christ known as the only Saviour.[94] Yet there was a thoroughness in their conviction of sin which could not be denied. He was moved to write on 9 August: 'There was indeed a very great mourning among them, and yet every one seemed to mourn apart.'[95] The sight of these needy children of the forest, lately filling the air with shouts and yells at their idolatrous feasts and drunken revels, but now stretching out their hands in faith and finding their way to God with tears, filled him with a sense of profound wonder and awe,[96] and on 16 August he wrote: 'I never saw the work of God appear so independent of means as at this time ... I seemed to do nothing, and indeed to have nothing to do, but to stand still and see the salvation of God.'[97] As a result, on 25 August, he baptized fifteen adults and ten children,[98] and the whole camp was stirred either with joy in the Saviour or with utmost concern to obtain an interest in His salvation.[99]

On 26 August, he told them that the time had come to leave Crossweeksung for a further visit to the tribes on the banks of the Susquehannah. 'I asked them', he wrote, 'if they could not be willing to spend the remainder of the day in prayer for me, that God would go with me.'[100] They had caught the spirit of their shepherd; they gave themselves to prayer that night until the break of day. He reached the Forks of Delaware five days later, and on 1 September, preached both to Red men and to white. He spent nine days at this centre, and saw the signs of an awakening which was altogether new in their midst.[101] On 9 September, he set out on the long westward journey to the Susquehannah, and was soon in direct contact with the crudest rites of idolatry. He found himself in the midst of ritual sacrifice, and there was no escape from the dancing and the devil-worship which were kept up all night. He felt that he had come to a place where Satan had his seat in great strength, and his heart sank as he saw how the love of God was held in sheer contempt.[102] On 1 October, he was back at the Forks of Delaware, and some of the Indians undertook to come and see the work in New Jersey. On 5 October, he reached Crossweeksung, and his heart stood in awe at the change in men's lives.[103] On 3 November, he baptized six adults and eight children; and one of these converts was a woman nearly eighty years old.[104] On 5 November, he set out for New Town on Long Island where he took part in a meeting of the Presbytery and tried to raise funds for a school master.[105] On 10 December, he was able to occupy his own house at Crossweeksung, ready for the winter.[106] By the end of the year, he had baptized twenty-three adults and twenty-four children, thirty-five of whom came from Crossweeksung and twelve from the Forks of Delaware.[107] And the thirst of others for the waters of life was so intense that his days were filled in seeking to meet their need.

Power in the Midst of Physical Weakness

It is clear that Brainerd had been forced to sound the depths of his own weakness before the power of God revealed itself before his eyes. He was allowed to feel as though he had spent his strength for nothing, and the early dream of success had grown faint and distant. He knew that his inner vitality was a wasting factor, and he hardly dared to go on hoping. 'I had little reason', he wrote, 'so much as to hope that God had made me instrumental in the saving conversion of any of the Indians except my interpreter and his wife.'[108] He had almost resolved to give up his mission at the end of 1745 since there was so little to show for all his prayers and pains. 'I do not know', he wrote, 'that my hopes respecting the conversion of the Indians were ever reduced to so low an ebb since I had any special concern for them as at this time.'[109] This was the frame of mind in which he first came to Crossweeksung where God began to bless his work with the crowning joy of conversions. The strong reality of this awakening was proved by the decisive character of the change which was wrought; not one of those who were baptized failed to provide proof in their lives of the grace that was in their hearts.[110] Men who had been 'idle, immoral, drunkards, murderers, gross idolaters, and wizards' were brought to 'permanent sobriety, diligence, devotion, honesty, conscientiousness, and charity.'[111] On 20 November 1745, he summed up the situation in a memorable statement. 'As these poor ignorant pagans stood in need of having line upon line and precept upon precept in order to their being instructed and grounded in the principles of Christianity, so I preached publicly and taught from house to house almost every day for whole weeks together', he wrote. 'And my public discourses did not then make up the one half of my work while there were so many constantly coming to me with that important inquiry, What must we do to be saved?'[112] And their response was an abundant recompense for the lonely vigils, the suffering and privation, and the burden of mind and heart which he had to accept.[113]

Brainerd entered the new year with a fresh dedication of his remaining energies, and on 1 January 1746, he wrote: 'O that I might live nearer to God this year than I did the last . . . May I for the future be enabled more sensibly to make the glory of God my all!'[114] He had travelled some four thousand miles on horseback during the last twelve months: 'Almost the whole of it has been in my own proper business as a missionary.'[115] He had tried to provide for the support of a fellow missionary or of a school master, and though he could not get the one, he was now to have the other; and on 1 February, he was able to start a school with a master who was as like-minded as he could wish. He taught adults by night as well as children by day, and they had to learn the Shorter Catechism as well as the fundamentals of reading and writing.[116] On 2 March, he was able to write: 'I know of no assembly of Christians where there seems to be so much of the presence of God, where brotherly love so much prevails, and where I should take so much delight in the public worship of God as in my own congregation: although not more than nine months ago, they were worshipping devils and dumb idols under the power of pagan darkness and superstition.'[117]

On 16 March, he first described how his house was thronged with people, and then declared that such was their thirst for Christian instruction that he could not avoid working to the point of serious exhaustion.[118] He had paid a visit to the Forks of Delaware during February and had found some signs of encouragement. But it did not compare with the work at Crossweeksung, where on 20 April he wrote: 'God has caused this little fleece to be repeatedly wet with the blessed dews of His divine grace, while all the earth around has been comparatively dry.'[119] A week later, on 27 April, he administered the Lord's Supper for the first time; twenty-three Indians came forward to share in it. 'And never', he wrote, 'did I see such an appearance of Christian love among any people in all my life. It was so remarkable that one might well have cried with an agreeable surprise, Behold how they love one another!'[120]

On 24 March, Brainerd observed that where there had been ten hearers less than twelve months before, they had now grown to more than one hundred and thirty in number.[121] This led him to plan a Christian settlement similar to those established by John Eliot, and he persuaded them to go and clear new lands at Cranberry (now Cranbury), some fifteen miles to the north of Crossweeksung.[122] They moved to this new site at the end of April, though it meant that he had to add to his other burdens 'the oversight and management of all their affairs'.[123] On 9 May, he baptized a man who had been a sorcerer and a murderer, and fifteen more converts were baptized in June.[124] This meant that he had now baptized seventy-seven people; thirty-eight adults and thirty-nine children: 'and it must be noted', he wrote, 'that I have baptized no adults but such as appeared to have a work of special grace wrought in their hearts.'[125] On 13 July, he administered the Lord's Supper to thirty-one Indians. 'God seemed to be present in this ordinance', he wrote. 'There was scarcely a dry eye among them.'[126]

On 10 August, he baptized three adults and three children, and on 12 August, he set out with six Indians on his last visit to the Susquehannah. He travelled by Charlestown and worked his way up the river to the scene of former visits. There was still much opposition, but he was cheered by some response and on 26 August, he wrote: 'I pressed things with all my might and called out my people to give in their testimony for God.'[127] His work was cut short by illness and he returned feeling 'very weak, and sometimes scarce able to ride'.[128] He reached Cranberry on the evening of 20 September and found them all at prayer. They built a house for him, his fourth home in four years, and he struggled on with his work between bouts of fever and near delirium. On

5 October, he administered the Lord's Supper for the third and last time, although he was so weak that he could hardly make his way home. But his soul was refreshed and he rejoiced in his people. 'One might hear them all the morning before public worship', he wrote, 'and in the evening till near midnight, praying and singing praises to God in one or other of their houses.'[129]

But he was now so ill that he could no longer perform his work and he knew that he had little hope of recovery. He had been told that his only chance of relief would be by 'much riding',[130] and he made up his mind to take a long journey among his friends in New England. On Monday, 3 November, he took his leave amid the tears and sad farewells of those who loved him as shepherd and guide. 'I visited them all in their respective homes', he wrote, 'and . . . I scarcely left one house but some were in tears; and many were not only affected by my being about to leave them, but with the solemn addresses I made them upon divine things.'[131] He rode away in the morning, but did not get any further than Elizabeth Town in New Jersey. He was too ill even to write in his Diary, and for almost three months there was no entry at all. The dawn of the new year found him so low that his friends did not think he would survive from day to day. He had become the prey of coughs and chills; he was subject to fever and asthma; he was bereft of appetite and digestion; his health was in ruins.[132]

Yet in February 1747, he made a surprising recovery, and in March he was well enough to ride back to visit the settlement at Cranberry. On 20 March, he rose early and walked once more among his people like one who had come back from the dead. At ten o'clock he called them to worship; they sang a Psalm, and he engaged in prayer. But it was the last time; they were to see his face and hear his voice no more. An hour later, at eleven o'clock, in a state of extreme weakness, he was compelled to mount his horse and ride away. He could only travel slowly and spent most of April in New Jersey. On his birthday, 20 April, he was confined to bed and could only note in his Diary: 'This day I arrived at the age of twenty-nine years.'[133] The next day brought him to New York, and May found him among his friends at East Haddam. At length, on 28 May, he rode from Long Meadow to Northampton where he was made welcome in the home of Jonathan Edwards.

Jonathan Edwards was born in 1703 and ordained as minister for Northampton in 1727. He was tall, slender, delicate, with comely features, piercing eyes, and a quiet voice capable of great pathos. His great strength was as a theologian, and his works are steeped in creative argument. But he won fame in his own day as a preacher, and his sermons were a noble combination of massive thinking and moral fervour. There were two great revivals while he was at Northampton and he proved a skilful guide for scores who were in search of peace with God. The first took place during 1734–1735 when his congregation was stirred into newness of life by the Spirit of God. The next was part of a wider movement linked with the work of George Whitefield during 1740–1741, and it was then that he preached his famous sermon on 'Sinners in the Hands of an Angry God'. That sermon at Enfield on 8 July 1741 was on the text: 'Their foot shall slide in due time' (*Deut.* 32:35); and its tremendous metaphors shattered the last trace of torpor in his congregation. The sinner was standing at that moment on a single plank over the mouth of hell, and every board in that plank was rotten; he was hanging by a solitary cord over the brink of ruin, and every thread in that cord was breaking. Jonathan Edwards will never be forgotten for that sermon alone.

Edwards first came into contact with Brainerd in 1743 at New Haven where he joined Aaron Burr in interceding on behalf of Brainerd with the authorities at Yale.[134] He had become deeply interested in him and kept himself closely informed about his work through the Society Correspondents.[135] Only the most slender information is now available as to the growth of more intimate relations between the family at Northampton and the orphan missionary. It is clear that Edwards became like a father to the young man, and his help and counsel were a source of special strength and comfort. It was to his home that Brainerd came for the last months of his life, and in that home he was received with a warmth of family affection such as he had scarcely known since childhood. As a result, all his private papers were left in the hands of Edwards, and it was through Edwards that most of his Diary was rescued from destruction.[136]

JOURNAL AND DIARY

Brainerd's Journal, written at the request of the Society Correspondents, covered twelve months from June 1745 to June 1746, and was published late in 1746. His surviving Diary covered five and a half years from April 1742 to October 1747: it was written for his own eye alone, but was published in a somewhat abridged form by Jonathan Edwards in 1749. Edwards left out many details because his only real concern was to provide an account of spiritual progress; but such a loss makes it impossible to fill out our knowledge of his personal history in more mundane matters. Nor was this all, for his edition of the Diary did not include the bulk of the material which had appeared in the Journal. But a uniform edition of the Works of Jonathan Edwards was brought out by Edward Williams and Edward Parsons between 1806 and 1811; the Diary and the Journal were both included, as neither is complete apart from the other. It used to be thought that Edwards must have destroyed all the handwritten manuscripts left by Brainerd, but at least some of the original pages in his clear script have been preserved in the Beineike Rare Book Library at Yale.

Modern readers may feel slightly confused as they turn back and forth from Diary to Journal; they may wish that Edwards had taken the trouble to interweave both documents so as to form one plain consecutive record. But this would not have been true to Brainerd's spirit in the original composition; the Diary and the Journal were each written for a distinct purpose, and each had its separate character. The one is a remarkable record of the interior life of the soul, and its entries still throb with the tremendous earnestness of a man whose heart was aflame for God. The other is an objective history of the missionary work of twelve months, and its details are an astonishing testimony to the grace of God in the lives of men. The one tells the story of his hidden life of prayer and travail, his fasts and vigils, his dreams and aspirations. The other tells the story of long hours on horseback, and the neglect of all proper rest and diet, and the ceaseless effort to win men's souls. Each needs to be studied as the revelation of a Christian character as rare as it was real; the two narratives together make his memory immortal.

Perry Miller says that Edwards edited the Diary and Journals 'with skill and affection, and the volume is a minor masterpiece of psychological confession'.[137] Ola Winslow says that they 'made the name of David Brainerd better known to the average churchgoer of the next generation than the name of Jonathan Edwards'.[138] These two books bring Brainerd before us as a man who was willing to run any risk or accept any hardship as a missionary, and the amount of work which he achieved in such circumstances now seems almost incredible. Jonathan Edwards thought that Brainerd was 'excessive in his labours', and that this was the mark of an imperfect character.[139] Charles Simeon said that he was 'great', but that his greatness had been impaired by 'the extreme impropriety of his exertions'.[140] Simeon and Edwards each had the same ground for criticism: he drove himself 'so much beyond his strength'.[141] Brainerd was well aware of the fact that he was in the grip of a wasting disease, and he simply 'longed to be as a flame of fire' to his dying moment.[142]

His life as a pioneer and an apostle in forest and mountain, by campfire and wig-wam, took a ceaseless toll of his health, though he seldom spoke of the privation and exposure that were involved. He knew what it was to eat coarse food or to go hungry. There were times when he found himself coughing blood or prostrate with high fever. But there is an austerity in his account which leaves the half untold, and he was not wholly to blame. He was constantly told by physicians that the only way to prolong his life was to spend hours in the saddle,[143] and he was spurred on by the love of Christ and his longing for souls. There were moments when his shattered health and lonely heart found vent in some brief remark; but not even in his lowest mood of pain and fatigue was a single word of complaint written down on paper. Edwards noticed that once at least his Diary was not legible because he had used wild berry juice when his ink ran out.[144] That was a small matter, but it suggests much more than it describes. Brainerd knew that his time was short, and in that race with time, he thought it 'sweet to be spent and worn out for God'.[145]

This long battle with ill-health and fatigue helps to explain the strong note of introspection which is everywhere evident. He searched his heart and wrote down his findings in a way and in a language that were common enough in the Puritan tradition, but are almost unknown today. But there is a melancholy in much of this language which needs further understanding. Charles Simeon was emphatic that his spiritual stature had been curtailed by 'the degree of his melancholy'.[146] Andrew Bonar believed that he did not hold such radiant fellowship with the living Saviour as he ought to have done.[147] There is truth in this point of view; but it does not explain the cause of such melancholy. The sorrows of childhood, the struggle with disease, the disappointment in College, had all combined to lend a sombre hue to his native temperament: they were perhaps the main cause of the strange fluctuations in his conscious experience of the life of God in his soul.

Words wrung from the depths on 23 January 1743 show how real at times was his sense of dejection: 'None know but those who feel it what the soul endures that is sensibly shut out from the presence of God. Alas! it is more bitter than death!'[148] It was because he had known this sense of terrible desertion that he kept watch over his life with such unsleeping vigilance. It made him such a disciple of discipline that the searching analysis of his heart came to have all the force of a fire that would either cleanse or consume. Sorrow for sin had an ever-present meaning for him; 'he was a mourner for sin all his days'.[149] But this habit of deep introspection was the servant of true humility as well as of melancholy. On 24 May 1747, he wrote: 'Could not but think that much more of true religion consists in deep humility, brokenness of heart, and an abasing sense of barrenness and want of grace and holiness than most who are called Christians imagine.'[150] As a result, he was so purged from sin and self that his developed character shines through such words as those which he wrote on 22 April 1745: 'The Lord enabled me to cry, I hope, with a childlike temper, with tenderness and brokenness of heart.'[151]

Perhaps the most singular impression which this revealing Diary makes on one's mind is the magnificent ideal of loving surrender and willing sacrifice. Lord Ernle once observed that bare, simple, detached though it may seem, it stands apart from all similar diaries in its absorbing devotion to one supreme object; it has one great virtue, and that consists in its picture of strenuous, concentrated effort to attain true nearness to God.[152] There is conflict, struggle, travail, in its daily entries such as to our later and less earnest age seems almost beyond mortal effort. On 19 October 1742, for example, he wrote: 'My soul seemed so to reach and stretch towards the mark of perfect sanctity that it was ready to break with longings.'[153] And on 7 November 1742: 'It seemed as if such an unholy wretch as I never could arrive at that blessedness, to be holy as God is holy. At noon, I longed for sanctification and conformity to God. Oh, that is THE ALL, THE ALL! The Lord help me to press after God for ever.'[154]

It is very moving to see this blend of deep self-abasement and high aspiration, to see his soul, now hiding wingless in the dust of rebuke, now soaring freely in the light of heaven. Both traits are strewn through the pages of his Diary, and there is a touch of sublime beauty in the contrast between their light and shade. Jonathan Edwards declared that Brainerd not only thought meanly enough of himself in the presence of God, but that he looked upon himself as the least and poorest of his servants.[155] He could never think that he had fully attained, nor could he rest in his current experience. On 2 November 1744, he wrote: 'I have ever found it, when I have thought the battle was over and the conquest gained, and so let down my watch, the enemy has risen up and done me the greatest injury.'[156] And on 17 May 1746: 'Oh, what a death it is to strive and strive; to be always in a hurry and yet do nothing, or at least, nothing for God!'[157] But this kind of lament always had its sequel in a renewed desire to spend himself for God, as he wrote on 18 May 1746: 'Oh that I could be a flame of fire in the service of my God!'[158]

Jonathan Edwards made it clear that in his judgment Brainerd's melancholy found its counter-balance in the strong and unshaken assurance which he enjoyed in a striking degree to the end of his life. 'He had it too in its fulness and in the height of its exercise under repeated trials.'[159] Edwards also made it clear that the goal before his eyes was that of true personal holiness; he strove to live for God and to be brought into perfect conformity to him. 'This was what drew his heart; this was the centre of his soul; this was the ocean to which all the streams of his religious affections tended; this was the object that engaged his eager thirsting desires.'[160] There was nothing merely selfish in such desires; they were all joined with a ceaseless passion for souls. Edwards was at pains to point out that all his ardent desires were not just for joyful discoveries of God's favour; they were for a heart more engaged to walk with God, and a life more resolved to work for souls. 'His longings were for ability to serve God better, to do more for His glory, and to do all that he did with more of a regard . . . to the enlargement and advancement of Christ's kingdom in the earth.'[161] He was neither cold nor tepid in his views on doctrine; he had imbibed the strong Calvinistic teaching of his fathers. But he dealt with men as those who had an eternal destiny at stake, and his eyes were focused on the supreme need to lead them to faith in Christ. He might be racked with fever or fatigue, but he would not let a single hour slip through his fingers. He spent long hours on his knees and turned night into day in order to give himself to prayer. He crawled from his hut and sat on the ground when he was too weak to stand up and preach. And the very last words in his Journal are an articulate declaration of this lifelong desire for the increase of God's kingdom: 'May this blessed work in the power and purity of it prevail among the poor Indians here as well as spread elsewhere till their remotest tribes shall see the salvation of God! Amen.'[162]

Brainerd was well aware that it is a law of heaven that the intercession of saints on earth must 'fill up that which is behind' in the intercession of our great High Priest at God's right hand (*Col.* 1:24). This is clear in what he wrote on 19 April 1742: 'In the afternoon, God was with me of a truth. O it was blessed company indeed! God enabled me so to agonize in prayer, that I was quite wet with perspiration, though in the shade, and in the cool wind.'[163] He was twenty-four years old the next day, and his entry in the evening explains why he counted it a happy birthday: 'I think my soul was never so drawn out in intercession for others as it has been this night . . . and I hardly ever so longed to live to God.'[164] Nor was this an isolated experience, for on 25 April, he wrote again: 'This morning I spent about two hours in secret duties and was enabled more than ordinarily to agonize for immortal souls; though it was early in the morning and the sun scarcely shined at all, yet my body was quite wet with sweat.'[165] On 14 June, he wrote again: 'I set apart this day for secret fasting and prayer, to intreat God to direct and bless me with regard to the great work I have in view, of preaching the Gospel , , , Had little life and power in the forenoon: near the middle of the afternoon, God enabled me to wrestle ardently in intercession for absent friends; but just at night, the Lord visited me marvellously in prayer; I think my soul never was in such an agony before. I felt no restraint, for the treasures of divine grace were opened to me. I wrestled for . . . multitudes of poor souls and for many that I thought were the children of God . . . I was in such an agony from sun half an hour high, till near dark, that I was all over wet with sweat; but . . . my dear Jesus did sweat blood for poor souls. I longed for more compassion.'[166] J. H. Jowett quoted this passage in *The Passion for Souls,* and then went on to add his own keen but slightly inaccurate comment.[167] But he was right when he affirmed that there is a moral kinship between this *cri de cœur* and the cry in Gethsemane. Brainerd was in some sense like him who 'being in an agony . . . prayed more earnestly' (*Luke* 22:44).

Brainerd must be held in honour for one reason *par excellence:* this was his own total dedication as a missionary. He was born in an age when the church as a whole had ceased to care for the world at large, but he never faltered in what he called his own 'proper business as a missionary'.[168] He had told a friend on 31 July 1744: 'I would not change my present mission for any other business in the whole world.'[169] His work grew both in thoroughness and in dignity with the passage of time, and God gave him astonishing success in the final sixteen months of sustained effort. He had baptized two more Indians on his final Sunday at Crossweeksung, bringing up the total to eighty-five people: forty-three were adults; forty-two were children.[170] He had drawn them from a life of vagrant idolatry and had settled them on new lands. He had put their children to school and had formed them into a church. They were never far from his mind in the months that remained, and plans for a continued ministry were soon in full operation.

David's younger brother John had graduated from Yale in 1746 and was licensed by the New York Presbytery in 1747. He was appointed by the Correspondents to take over David's work at Cranberry, and on 14 April 1747, David was able to record: 'This day my brother went to my people.'[171] David's visit to Boston in July led to the choice of two more young men who were sent to start work with the Six Nations.[172] One of the two went to see John Brainerd at Cranberry in January 1748 and declared that it was 'a difficult thing to walk out in the woods in the morning without disturbing persons at their secret devotion'.[173] And Jonathan Edwards wrote in 1749: 'It is now more than three years ago that this work began . . . since which time the number of visible converts has greatly increased and . . . they still generally persevere in diligent religion and strict virtue.'[174] But the settlement at Cranberry did not long survive. The Indians died from the plague; their lands were taken away; and in 1755 John Brainerd relinquished the mission and went to the church at Newark.

Brainerd's life and work were to stir the long dormant sense of duty towards non-Christian peoples in a way that the church had not experienced for centuries. His Diary and Journal were soon to become known in England and to awaken the missionary conscience of the finest men in all the churches. Brainerd's spirit lived on in the lives of William Carey and Henry Martyn who were inspired by his amazing devotion; and no men did

more than they in their turn to inspire a new ideal of true
missionary service.[175] Almost fifty years were to pass after
his death before the great missionary Societies were
brought into being. The Baptist Missionary Society was
founded in 1792; the London Missionary Society in 1795;
the Scottish Missionary Society in 1796; and the Church
Missionary Society in 1799. The Baptist Missionary
Society was the pilot body in this famous decade of fresh
missionary activity, and it drew its inspiration from the
steadfast vision of William Carey. His great sermon before
the ministers at Nottingham in May 1792 had urged them
to attempt great things for God and to expect great things
from God. On 13 June 1793, Carey sailed from England
as the Society's first missionary, and on 19 April 1794,
he wrote in his Diary as the heat of Calcutta began to
oppress his spirit: 'I was much humbled today by reading
Brainerd. O, what a disparity betwixt me and him! He
always constant; I as inconstant as the wind!'[176] Eleven
arduous years passed away; then, on 7 October 1805,
Carey, Ward, and Marshman signed the historic
agreement which laid down the principles of their work
at Serampore. The tenth article of this document is a
remarkable testimony to the persistent influence of one
man's life. 'Let us often look at Brainerd in the woods of
America', so it prescribed, 'pouring out his very soul
before God for the perishing heathen without whose
salvation nothing could make him happy.'[177]

Brainerd was not to know how his Diary and Journal
were to affect readers in a later generation but they will
always hold a place of their own in that class of devotional
literature which forms part of the heritage of Christendom.
One can trace its spiritual impact through letters and
records in England and Scotland alike, and it is still worthwhile to take stock of what those who lived nearer to his

age had to say on this matter. John Newton of Olney voiced his thoughts on 11 January 1769. 'Next to the Word of God', he wrote, 'I like those books best which give an account of the lives and experiences of His people . . . No book of this kind has been more welcome to me than the life of Mr Brainerd of New England.'[178] Then in 1793, Samuel Marsden sat and pored over the life of Brainerd as he sailed on the long voyage to New South Wales; and it was the study of this book that inspired him to make his seven crossings of the Tasman to bring the good news of great joy to the Maori warriors of New Zealand.[179] But Newton and Marsden belonged to the Church of England: what of men who belonged to the Church of Scotland by whose Society Brainerd had been employed? Robert Murray M'Cheyne may be taken as one whose life represented all that was best in the Church of Scotland, and he was moved to the depths of his soul when this book came into his hands. On 27 June 1832, he wrote: 'Life of David Brainerd. Most wonderful man! What conflicts, what depressions, desertions, strength, advancement, victories, within thy torn bosom! I cannot express what I think when I think of thee. Tonight, more set upon missionary enterprise than ever.'[180] That book had a tremendous influence on his spiritual development; it comes to the surface again in a letter which he wrote in 1840: 'Oh to have Brainerd's heart for perfect holiness; to be holy as God is holy; pure as Christ is pure; perfect as our Father in heaven is perfect!'[181]

No one ever felt this impact more than Henry Martyn who found in David Brainerd his missionary ideal. His own Journals make this plain year by year, whether in Cornwall or Cambridge, in Cawnpore or Shiraz. On 13 November 1803, he wrote: 'I longed to draw very near to God, to pray Him that He would give me the Spirit of wisdom and revelation. I thought of David Brainerd, and ardently desired his devotedness to God and holy breathings of soul.'[182] And on 23 September 1804: 'Read David Brainerd today and yesterday, and find as usual my spirit greatly benefited by it; I long to be like him.'[183] A year later, on 11 September 1805, he wrote: 'Past experience encourages me, and David Brainerd's advice. What a quickening example has he often been to me!'[184] On 8 May 1806: 'Read . . . some of Brainerd's letters . . . Blessed be the memory of that holy man!'[185] Four days later, he wrote again: 'My soul was revived today through God's never ceasing compassion, so that I found the refreshing presence of God in secret duties; especially was I most abundantly encouraged by reading David Brainerd's account of the difficulties attending a mission to the heathen. Oh! blessed be the memory of that beloved saint! No uninspired writer ever did me so much good.'[186]

On 17 May 1806, the day after his arrival in Calcutta, he penned the now famous entry: 'Let me burn out for God!'[187] It reads like an echo of the words which he had often read as part of Brainerd's dedication on 23 May 1746: 'I longed to burn out in one continued flame for God.'[188] There are two more entries in which Martyn looked back to his ideal. On 18 February 1810, he wrote: 'My birthday; today I completed my twenty-ninth year; how much had David Brainerd done at this time of life!'[189] And on his next birthday, he wrote: 'This day I finish the thirtieth year of my unprofitable life, an age in which Brainerd had finished his course. He gained about a hundred savages to the Gospel; I can scarcely number the twentieth part.'[190] On 16 October 1812, Henry Martyn died a lonely death at Tokat, and like David Brainerd, passed within the veil to stand before 'the King in His beauty' (*Isa.* 33:17).

The Journals and Letters of Henry Martyn are imbued with romance and pathos in a way that gives them uncommon interest. This is not so in the case of Brainerd; there is scarcely a sign of that inward struggle with the claims of human love and friendship. On 24 July 1744, he had written with self-forgetting dignity: 'God does not suffer me to please or comfort myself with hopes of seeing friends, returning to my dear acquaintance, and enjoying worldly comforts.'[191] There were times when he was conscious of desperate loneliness; such a feeling, he wrote in June 1746, 'made me long for a colleague to be a partner of my cares, hopes, and fears, as well as labours amongst the Indians'.[192] And there is one memorable passage in which he seems to weigh his heart's desires on the scales of heaven. On 22 May 1746, this searching self-analysis took place. 'I never since I began to preach', he wrote, 'could feel any freedom to enter into other men's labours and settle down in the ministry where the Gospel was preached before . . . But God having succeeded my labours and made me instrumental in gathering a church for Him among these Indians, I was ready to think it might be His design to give me a quiet settlement and a stated home of my own.'[193] This is one of the rare entries in which there is a clear wish for something of his own choice. But it was not to be; what things might have been gain to him he had renounced as loss for Christ. 'Now these thoughts seemed to be wholly dashed to pieces, not by necessity, but of choice; for it appeared to me that God's dealings towards me had fitted me for a life of solitariness and hardship.'[194] Therefore he knelt down to yield himself once more without reserve to the will of God. 'And if ever my soul presented itself to God for His service without any reserve of any kind, it did so now.'[195] Dreams of home and 'tender friendship . . .

vanished like the stars before the rising sun'.[196] The whole passage concludes on a note of high self-abnegation. 'I was constrained, and yet chose to say, "Farewell, friends and earthly comforts, the dearest of them all, the very dearest, if the Lord calls for it; adieu, adieu; I will spend my life to my latest moments in caves and dens of the earth if the kingdom of Christ may thereby be advanced."'[197]

There is little doubt that Jerusha Edwards was in his mind as he wrote this passage. It is impossible now to know when David Brainerd first came into contact with the second daughter in Jonathan's large family; they may have met at New Haven as early as 1742, but his missionary calling as well as their disparity in age stood in the way of an early romance. It was twelve months after his words of self-abnegation when he came to her home on 28 May 1747, and a 'tender friendship' soon burst into blossom.[198] It is often assumed that they became engaged, but this is open to doubt. He was twenty-nine, and she was only seventeen: yet her mother had been married at the age of seventeen, and her girlhood was no bar to marriage.[199] But he was a dying missionary, and he could no longer hope for such an event. There had been no reference to her in his Diary; the few details which are known were furnished by her father. There may have been no formal engagement, but there was a deep and most tender attachment. She was Jonathan's favourite daughter, delicate, devoted, and rich beyond her years in true Christian attainment. It was no less a judge than her father who said that she was of 'much the same spirit' as Brainerd.[200]

If ever a missionary stood in need of the love and care of wife and home, it was Brainerd; and the union of two kindred spirits such as theirs would have been one of super-lative fitness. This was impossible; but her companionship was to brighten the last weeks of his life with a sweetness that made him feel as though 'God had granted all his desire'.[201] He told Edwards not long before he died that she was one 'who by the temper of her mind was fitted to deny herself for God and to do good' beyond any woman he knew.[202] She was to him all that had been in his mind when he wrote of 'the very dearest',[203] and he rejoiced to know that their last tryst would be in the everlasting glory of the presence of God.

Brainerd was tall and spare, with sad and lustrous eyes and an eager burning spirit. His health and strength were now in a state of total collapse; the long strain on all the reserves of body and spirit had been beyond his power to bear. The worst symptoms of his disease were now painfully evident, and the family physician told him plainly that there was no hope of recovery. Edwards could not help but observe that this caused no discomposure; he was just as serene in spirit and pleasant in conversation as always.[204] On 7 June, just after this verdict, Brainerd's own thoughts ran in another direction. 'I saw that true grace is exceeding precious indeed', he wrote; 'that it is very rare; and that there is but a very small degree of it; at least I saw this to be in my case.'[205] But his physician recognised that his life of constant physical exercise had become almost a necessity for him, and he advised him to spend as much time as he could on horseback. Brainerd took this advice with a literal precision and was henceforth seated in the saddle as much as his strength would allow.

Contrary to all that would have seemed probable, on 9 June, he set out for Boston and Jerusha rode at his side. He knew that the fires of life were burning out, but he was aflame for God. On 18 June, he was delirious; he could hardly whisper, and the friends round his bed did not think he could long survive. He was panting for

breath, and it seemed as though death must be at hand;
'which they looked for every moment, as I myself also
did'.[206] But he was nursed back from the edge of death,
and the disease seemed to abate. On 30 June, he wrote
to his youngest brother 'from the sides of eternity' with
a moving appeal:[207] 'If you have reason to think you are
graceless, oh, give yourself and the throne of grace no
rest till God arise and save.'[208] And to another acquaintance he wrote: 'How rare are the instances of those who
live and act from day to day as on the verge of eternity!'[209]
On 19 July, he was able to attend the Lord's Supper; and
on 20 July, he left Boston with Jerusha and his brother
to ride at the rate of sixteen miles a day for six days to
reach Northampton.

'I Longed to Be with God ...'

Edwards was to observe him with close and penetrating
insight in the weeks that followed, and came to speak
freely of the great 'strength of his natural genius'.[210]
Brainerd strove to live as he begged his friends to live: to
'live to God in every capacity of life'.[211] This was the real
secret of the high praise of a man like Edwards: 'I never
knew his equal', he declared, among others 'of his age
and standing'.[212] But the journey home from Boston had
drained his scant remnant of strength and he daily became
more frail. Edwards affirmed that 'his calmness, peace,
assurance and joy in God during the long time he looked
death in the face without the least hope of recovery'
continued 'without interruption to the last'.[213] He was
buoyed up with the hope of release, and the approach of
death only served 'to exhilarate his mind'.[214] His heart
was drawn out in constant prayer and longing for the
triumph of the gospel, and he declared 'that he never in

all his life had his mind so led forth in desires and earnest prayers for the flourishing of Christ's kingdom.'[215]

On 20 September, these strong desires found voice in his Diary: 'I longed to be with God, to behold His glory, and to bow in His presence.'[216] On 2 October, his Diary came to an end with words written by the hand of a friend. 'Oh that His kingdom might come in the world . . . and that the blessed Redeemer might see of the travail of His soul and be satisfied! Oh come, Lord Jesus, come quickly! Amen.'[217] Jerusha Edwards devoted herself to him during this long illness and was seldom away from his bedside in the last phase of that losing struggle.[218] She came into his room early on Sunday morning, 4 October; he was looking cheerful; his eyes were bright and his mind was clear as he now began to bid farewell. 'Dear Jerusha,' he said, ' . . . if I thought I should not see you and be happy with you in another world, I could not bear to part with you. But we shall spend a happy eternity together!'[219] He was in great pain for the next five days, and yet also in a kind of holy rapture. At length, in the early morning of 9 October 1747, although not yet thirty years of age, he swept in triumph through the gates of glory.

Jerusha's reflections in that hour of sorrow for the death of one whom she had loved so dearly were not placed on record. It was a mark of her father's superb trust in them both that she had been allowed to travel so freely with him; and this in an age when, to say the least, such freedom was unusual. But so little did they understand the real nature of his illness or its contagious character, that she had nursed him in general ignorance of the risk she incurred. Only four months later, on 14 February 1748, after a few days of illness, Jerusha followed him into the presence of the King, where they shine as the stars for ever. She was only seventeen years old, and in her father's words she was 'generally esteemed the Flower of the Family'.[220] She was buried beside David in the Northampton cemetery, which I visited on 2 May 1981. The stone over Brainerd's grave had fallen down, but the wording was clear. His name was spelt 'Brainard',[221] and both the date of his death and his age were wrongly given.

SACRED TO THE
MEMORY OF THE
REV. DAVID BRAINARD
A FAITHFUL AND LABORIOUS
MISSIONARY TO THE STOCKBRIDGE,
DELAWARE, AND SUSQUEHANNAH
TRIBES OF INDIANS
WHO DIED IN THIS TOWN
OCT. 10, 1747.
Ae. 32.

Jonathan Edwards and his wife were buried at Princeton, but a stone inscribed in memory of Jonathan stands next to the grave of Jerusha at Northampton.

BIBLIOGRAPHY

Certain Brainerd manuscripts, including part of his Diary, are housed in the Beineike Rare Book Library at Yale.

1. *The Works of Jonathan Edwards, with a Memoir by Sereno E. Dwight; revised and corrected by Edward Hickman,* 2 vols. 1834; repr. Edinburgh: Banner of Truth, 1998.

   'The Life and Diary of the Rev. David Brainerd, with Notes and Reflections' vol. 2, p. 313.

   'Mr Brainerd's Journal, in Two Parts' vol. 2, p. 387.

   Three Appendices, vol. II, 416. 'Mr Brainerd's Remains' vol. 2, p. 435.

'*A Sermon Preached in Newark at the Ordination of Mr Brainerd by E. Pemberton, A.M.*', vol. 2, p. 442.

'*Some Reflections and Observations on the Preceding Memoirs, &c*' vol. 2, 447.

'*True Saints, When Absent from the Body, Are Present with the Lord*, A Sermon Preached on the Day of the Funeral of the Rev. David Brainerd', vol. 2, p. 26.

2. 'Memoir of the Life, Experience and Character of the late Rev. Jonathan Edwards, A.M., by the Rev. Samuel Hopkins, D.D.': Jonathan Edwards, *Complete Works* vol. 1 (edited by Edward Williams and Edward Parsons 8 vols.), 1806–1811.
3. J. M. SHERWOOD, *The Life and Character of David Brainerd* (being an Introduction to the Memoirs of David Brainerd), 1884.
4. ALEXANDER SMELLIE, *Introduction to the Diary of David Brainerd* (Books for the Heart Series), 1892.
5. ALLEN JOHNSON and DUMAS MALONE, *The Dictionary of American Biography* (see articles on John Eliot; David Brainerd; Jonathan Edwards), 1931.
6. OLA ELIZABETH WINSLOW, *Jonathan Edwards, 1703–1758*, 1940 (my copy, 1979)
7. PERRY MILLER, *Jonathan Edwards*, 1949 (my copy, 1973).
8. DAVID WYNBEEK, *David Brainerd, Beloved Yankee*, 1961.

NOTES

[1] August 8th 1767: 'Find preachers of David Brainerd's spirit, and nothing can stand before them.' – John Wesley (cf. L. Tyerman, *The Life and Times of John Wesley*, vol. 2, p. 606).
[2] I visited the site of this farm on 2 May 1981; no trace of the farmhouse now remains.
[3] Jonathan Edwards, *Works* (2 vols. 1834; repr. Edinburgh: Banner of Truth, 1974), vol. 2, p. 316.
[4] Ibid. p. 320.   [5] Ibid. p. 318.
[6] Ibid. p. 319.   [7] Ibid. p. 319.

[8] Ibid. p. 319.

[9] Ibid. p. 447.

[10] Ibid. p. 320.

[11] Ibid. p. 320.

[12] L. Tyerman, *The Life of George Whitefield,* vol. 1, p. 496; cf. pp. 429–430.

[13] Ibid. p. 477.

[14] Edwards, *Works,* vol. 2, p. 320.

[15] David Wynbeek, *David Brainerd, Beloved Yankee,* p. 31.

[16] Edwards, *Works,* vol. 2, p. 321.

[17] Ibid. p. 322.

[18] Ibid. p. 324.

[19] Ibid. pp. 325–6.

[20] Ibid. p. 335.

[21] Ibid. p. 337.

[22] Ibid. p. 338.

[23] Ibid. p. 321.

[24] Ibid. p. 322.

[25] Ibid. p. 323.

[26] Ibid. p. 324.

[27] Ibid. p. 324.

[28] *Dictionary of American Biography.*

[29] Edwards, *Works,* vol. 2, p. 325.

[30] Ibid. p. 326.

[31] Ibid. p. 378.

[32] Ibid. p. 328.

[33] Ibid. p. 329.

[34] Ibid. p. 329.

[35] John A. Mackay, *Christianity on the Frontier.*

[36] Thomas Chalmers, *Works,* vol. 4, p. 16.

[37] *Dictionary of American Biography.*

[38] Edwards, *Works,* vol. 2, p. 431.

[39] Ibid. p. 329.

[40] Ibid. p. 322.

[41] Ibid. p. 322.

[42] Ibid. p. 322.

[43] Ibid. p. 327.

[44] Ibid. p. 329.

[45] Ibid. p. 326.

[46] Ibid. p. 331.

[47] Ibid. p. 333.

[48] Ola Elizabeth Winslow, *Jonathan Edwards,* p. 269.

[49] Ibid. p. 269.

[50] I visited Stockbridge and Brainard on 2 June 1982.

[51] Edwards, *Works,* vol. 2, p. 333.

[52] Ibid. p. 335.

[53] Ibid. p. 335.

[54] Ibid. p. 336.

[55] Ibid. p. 336.

[56] Ibid. p 338.

[57] Ibid p. 334.

[58] Ibid. p. 344.

[59] Ibid. p. 344; see fn. p. 345.

[60] Ibid. p. 433.

[61] Ibid. p. 345.

[62] Ibid. p. 181. The Forks of Delaware was a name applied to the whole district north of Easton. The Forks township is on the west bank of the Delaware; Martin's Creek runs into the Delaware a little further north.

[63] Ibid. p. 346.

[64] Wynbeek, ibid. p. 93.

[65] Edwards, *Works,* vol. 2, p. 347.

[66] Ibid. p. 347.

[67] Ibid. p. 348.

[68] Ibid. p. 348.

[69] Ibid. p. 349.

[70] Ibid. p. 349.

[71] Ibid. p. 349.

[72] Ibid. p. 349.

[73] Ibid. p. 349.

[74] Ibid. p. 349.

[75] Ibid. p. 349.

[76] Ibid. p. 433.

[77] Ibid. p. 350.

[78] Ibid. p. 350.

79 Ibid. p. 434.
80 Ibid. pp. 350–351; 401.
81 Ibid. p. 352.
82 Ibid. p. 352.
83 This was seen by me on 4 May 1981.
84 Edwards, *Works,* vol. 2, p. 353.
85 Ibid. p. 357.
86 Ibid. p. 358.
87 Ibid. p. 358.
88 Ibid. p. 32.
89 Ibid. pp. 359; 388. I visited Crosswicks on 4 May 1981, but no trace of Brainerd's presence remains.
90 Ibid. p. 360.
91 Ibid. p. 391.
92 Ibid. p. 391.
93 Ibid. p. 392.
94 Ibid. pp. 416–417.
95 Ibid. p. 392.
96 Ibid. p. 392.
97 Ibid. p. 394.
98 Ibid. p. 394.
99 Ibid. p. 394.
100 Ibid. p. 395.
101 Ibid. p. 395.
102 Ibid. pp. 395–396.
103 Ibid. p. 397.
104 Ibid. p. 398.
105 Ibid. p. 362.
106 Ibid. p. 362.
107 Ibid. p. 399.
108 Ibid. p. 399.
109 Ibid. p. 399.
110 Ibid. p. 398.
111 Ibid. p. 453.
112 Ibid. p. 401.
113 Ibid. p. 401.
114 Ibid. p. 363.
115 Ibid. pp. 401; 421.
116 Ibid. p. 419.
117 Ibid. p. 407.
118 Ibid. p. 409.
119 Ibid. p. 411.
120 Ibid. p. 412.
121 Ibid. p. 410.
122 I visited Cranbury on 4 May 1981. A lake at the entrance to the town is known as Brainerd Lake.
123 Edwards, *Works,* vol. 2, p. 421.
124 Ibid. pp. 413; 414; 415.
125 Ibid. p. 418.
126 Ibid. p. 369.
127 Ibid. p. 371.
128 Ibid. p. 373.
129 Ibid. p. 374.
130 Ibid. p. 375.
131 Ibid. p. 375.
132 Ibid. p. 376.
133 Ibid. p. 377.
134 Ibid. p. 338.
135 Ibid. pp. 377–378.
136 Ibid. p. 315.
137 Perry Miller, *Jonathan Edwards,* p. 246.
138 Ola Elizabeth Winslow, *Jonathan Edwards,* p. 240.
139 Edwards, *Works,* vol. 2, p. 315.
140 William Carus, *Memoirs of Charles Simeon,* p. 436.
141 Ibid.
142 Edwards, *Works,* vol. 2, p. 367.
143 Ibid. p. 378.
144 Ibid. p. 361.
145 Ibid. p. 364.
146 William Carus, ibid. p. 436.
147 Marjory Bonar, *The Diary and Letters of Andrew A. Bonar,* p. 382.
148 Edwards, *Works,* vol. 2, p. 332.
149 Ibid. p. 449.
150 Ibid. p. 377.
151 Ibid. p. 357.
152 R. E. Prothero, *The Psalms in Human Life.* p. 327.

153 Edwards, *Works,* vol. 2, p. 328.   154 Ibid. p. 329.

155 Ibid. p. 449.   156 Ibid. p. 352.

157 Ibid. p. 366.   158 Ibid. p. 367.

159 Ibid. p. 448.   160 Ibid. p. 449.

161 Ibid. p. 450.   162 Ibid. p. 420.

163 Ibid. p. 323.   164 Ibid. p. 323.

165 Ibid. p. 323.   166 Ibid. p. 325.

167 J. H. Jowett, *The Passion for Souls,* pp. 86–88.

168 Edwards, *Works,* vol. 2, p. 401.   169 Ibid. p. 437.

170 Ibid. pp. 418; 370; 374.   171 Ibid. p. 377.

172 Ibid. pp. 379; 457.   173 Ibid. p. 455.

174 Ibid. p. 454.

175 Stephen Neill, *A History of Christian Missions,* p. 226.

176 R. E. Prothero, *The Psalms in Human Life,* p. 329.

177 George Smith, *Twelve Pioneer Missionaries,* p. 54.

178 John Newton, *Works,* vol. 6, p. 211.

179 S. M. Johnstone, *Samuel Marsden.* pp. 13–14.

180 Andrew A. Bonar, *Memoir and Remains of R. M. M'Cheyne,* p. 18.

181 Ibid. p. 289.

182 Henry Martyn, *Journals and Letters,* vol. 1, p. 67.

183 Ibid. p. 162.   184 Ibid. p. 316.

185 Ibid. p. 441.   186 Ibid. p. 444.

187 Ibid. p. 447.   188 Edwards, *Works,* vol. 2, p. 367.

189 Martyn, ibid. p. 283.   190 Ibid. p. 340.

191 Edwards, Works, 2, pp. 349–350.   192 Ibid. p. 428.

193 Ibid. p. 367.   194 Ibid. p. 367.

195 Ibid. p. 367.   196 Ibid. p. 367.

197 Ibid. 367.   198 Ibid. 367.

199 Edwards, *Works,* vol. 1, p. xl.

200 Edwards, *Works,* vol. 2, p. 385, fn.   201 Ibid. pp. 384–385.

202 Ibid. p. 385, fn.   203 Ibid. p. 317.

204 Ibid. p. 378.   205 Ibid. p. 378.

206 Ibid. p. 378.   207 Ibid. p. 438.

208 Ibid. p. 438.   209 Ibid. p. 438.

210 Ibid. p. 33.   211 Ibid. p. 439.

212 Ibid. p. 33.   213 Ibid. p. 34.

214 Ibid. p. 34.   215 Ibid. p. 381.

216 Ibid. p. 383.   217 Ibid. p. 385.

218 Ibid. p. 385, fn.   219 Ibid. p. 385.

220 See Ola Elizabeth Winslow. *Jonathan Edwards,* pp. 236; 363, note 21.

221 Note the spelling: Brainard; not Brainerd.

THE MANSE AT NORTHAMPTON.

Jonathan Edwards's Northampton manse,
where David Brainerd died on 9 October, 1747.

Henry Martyn

A Star in the Orient
1781–1812

*An engraving of Henry Martyn taken
from the portrait belonging to Charles Simeon.*

Up, O ye lovers and away! 'Tis time to leave the world for aye;
Hark, loud and clear from heaven the drum of parting calls –
   let none delay, –
The cameleer hath risen amain, made ready all the camel train,
And quittance now desires to gain: why sleep, ye travellers, I pray?
Behind us and before there swells the din of parting and of bells;
To shoreless space each moment sails a disembodied spirit away.
O heart, towards thy heart's love wend, and, O friend, fly
   toward the Friend!

SELECTED POEMS FROM THE DIVAN-I-SHAMS-I-TABRIZ
(*translated by R. A. Nicholson; quoted by C. E. Padwick*).

H enry Martyn's life and work were crowded into the brief space of thirty-one years, but they made a unique appeal to the Victorians in the nineteenth century. This appeal first became articulate when John Sargent published his *Memoir of the Rev. Henry Martyn* in 1819; it rapidly ran through many editions, of which my own is the sixteenth in 1848. Its value was greatly enhanced when Samuel Wilberforce published *The Journals and Letters of Henry Martyn* in 1837. These two volumes assumed that the reader would have Sargent's *Memoir* in front of him, and they did not repeat quotations already contained in that biography. Then in 1892 George Smith brought out his splendid biography, *Henry Martyn: Saint and Scholar,* setting his life in the widest context of its environment. A very readable and more popular narrative appeared in 1922 when Constance Padwick published her book, *Henry Martyn: Confessor of the Faith*. There were also lesser biographies from time to time, such as *Henry Martyn* by Charles Bell in 1886; *Henry Martyn, 1781–1812* by A. G. Pouncy in 1947; and *My Love Must Wait: The Story of Henry Martyn* by David Bentley-Taylor in 1975. Two small volumes of his sermons were brought out by his friends after his death; viz. *Sermons,* published by the Church Mission Press at Calcutta in 1822, and *Five Sermons,* edited by the Rev. G. T. Fox in 1862. Valuable information was contained in *The Memoirs of the Life of the Rev. Charles Simeon* by William Carus in 1839; *The Life and Times of Mrs Henry Sherwood* by F. J. Harvey Dutton in 1910; and *One Hundred and Seventy-Five Years at the Old or Mission Church Calcutta* by E. T.

Sandys and G. F. Westcott in 1945. In addition, the Manuscript Diary of Lydia Grenfell has been preserved in the Library of the Royal Institution of Cornwall at Truro. It runs to some two thousand pages, but extracts were published by her great-nephew, Henry Martyn Jeffery, in 1890. Other significant material may be found in *Arabia, The Cradle of Islam* by Samuel Zwemer in 1900, and *The Early Cornish Evangelicals, 1735–1760* by G. C. B. Davies in 1951.

CORNWALL AND CAMBRIDGE

Henry Martyn was born in a house which faced a little square in front of the old Coinage Hall of Truro on 18 February 1781. The old Coinage Hall stood opposite to what is now the south wall of the Cathedral; that is, in High Cross Street. The house in which Henry Martyn was born apparently stood on ground on which the south wall of the Cathedral now stands. He was the third of four children in a home which was to be schooled in great trial and sorrow. His mother died little more than a year after his birth, and his father, his half-brother and his sisters were all to die in the course of his own short life. But John Martyn was a prudent father who brought up his motherless family with an unselfish devotion, strengthened no doubt by his lifelong experience of the goodness of God. He had been converted through the ministry of the Curate of St Mary's Church, Samuel Walker, and was never absent from church service or prayer meeting while Walker was alive. Walker's death in 1761 paved the way for open hostility to his converts, and John Martyn had begun to prefer the prayer meeting to church worship. He had become one of Wesley's hearers on his frequent tours of Cornwall and had often stood in the crowd at the preacher's pit at Gwennap, a few miles from Truro. Wesley's Journal records that on 27 August 1776 he stood beneath one of the arches of the Coinage Hall in Truro and preached at noon to the people who filled the square. 'I was enabled', so he wrote, 'to speak exceeding plain on "Ye are saved through faith."'[1] Henry Martyn himself may have seen the trim and erect figure of the little 'human gamecock' during his last visit to Truro in 1789; he was in fact to grow up in a world which had been more than half-moulded by the Wesleys.[2] But the heart of that world in his childhood was the garden that ran down to the bank of the river, or the street that opened on to the square with the cloistered arches of the Coinage Hall just beyond. And so durable were those memories that they would live again in his dreams when he was far away in India.

At the age of seven he began to attend Truro Grammar School, and it soon became clear that he had mental gifts of a high order. He was only fifteen years old when he offered himself as a candidate for a scholarship at Corpus Christi College, Oxford, and he missed it only by a narrow margin and a contested decision. He spent two more years in Truro; then in October 1799 he was enrolled as a member of St John's College, Cambridge. He had to turn aside from his studies in the Classics and start to work on the Tripos in Mathematics. This was the only Tripos until 1824 when the Tripos in Classics was founded; but even then, until 1850, the Tripos in Classics was a postgraduate course of study for men who had gained Honours in Mathematics. Henry Martyn found it almost unbearable at the outset; he could not make sense of even the first problem in the Book of Euclid. He was soon in a state of sheer despair, ready to give up and take the coach for Truro and home. Then the light shone, and he began to work so hard that he soon made up for lost time. It was not long before he felt nettled to the quick if he were second rather than first, and in 1799 he stood at the head of his year. But his growth in spiritual understanding had not kept pace with his academic progress and he passed through a phase of much inward uncertainty. His lack of peace only served to feed the flame of hidden temper; there were moments when it burst out in a blaze of ugly passion. He had always been apt to break into sudden anger when his feelings got out of hand. His worst offence had been to fling a knife at a friend; he was startled to see it stick and quiver in a wooden panel. But God had planned all his steps in perfect wisdom, for the ministry of Charles Simeon had now begun to make its great impact on the life of Cambridge. All that Samuel Walker and John Wesley had been to his father, Charles Simeon was to become for him and in the dawn of another century he came into the full orbit of a new and mighty experience.

He went home for Christmas 1799 and his father seemed to be in splendid fettle; but he had no sooner returned to Cambridge in January 1800 than he received news from his half-brother that their father was dead. He was stunned with sorrow, but could hardly fail to reflect on the strong faith which had been his father's mainstay. He found that his thoughts were turning to that invisible world to which his father had now gone and where he must one day go. He grieved for the 'consummate selfishness' with which he had tried his father's patience, and took up his Bible in an attempt to find comfort.[3] It brought little relief and he turned to other books for escape; but an older friend from Truro Grammar School came to the rescue. This was John Kempthorne, who had been Senior Wrangler in 1796 and then became a Fellow of St John's College until 1802. Kempthorne urged the younger man to treat his bereavement as a time for 'serious reflection'.[4] As a result, Henry Martyn turned back to the Bible. 'I began with The Acts', he told his sister, 'as being the most amusing; and whilst I was entertained with the narrative, I found myself insensibly led to inquire more attentively into the doctrines of the Apostles.'[5] His interest was awakened, for he soon saw how their teaching corresponded with that of his father's Cornish Evangelical contemporaries. The next evening he took his first real step to seek the face of God in prayer. 'I began to pray from a pre-composed form in which I thanked God in general for having sent Christ into the world. But though I prayed for pardon, I had little sense of my own sinfulness.'[6] He was moving gradually towards the truth. 'Soon I began to attend more diligently to the words of our Saviour in the New Testament and to devour them with delight; when the offers of mercy and forgiveness were made so freely, I supplicated to be made partaker of the covenant of grace with eagerness and hope.'[7] The main features of this great change were still clear and distinct as he recalled them in the last year of his life. On 18 January 1812, he told Aga Ali what his experience had been: 'I took my Bible before God in prayer, and prayed for forgiveness through Christ, assurance of it through His Spirit, and grace to obey His commandments.'[8]

Henry Martyn now began to attend the Sunday services at the Church of the Holy Trinity, and soon found his own place in the inner circle of those for whom Simeon's ministry was the pivot for warm Christian fellowship. It was Simeon who made him long to walk with God; it was also Simeon who knew how to whet his sense of purpose as a student. Martyn himself came to believe that he was too immersed in his pursuit of a degree. 'I can only account for my being stationary for so long by the intenseness with which I pursued my studies', so he declared. ' . . . That in which I now see I was lamentably deficient was a humble and contrite spirit, through which I should have perceived more clearly the excellency of Christ.'[9] But John Sargent, who knew all the facts, said that there was no ground save his own humility for such strictures.[10] The time came at length in January 1801 when for three long mornings he sat around a table with his fellow students in the cold Senate House, and again each evening in the room of one or other of the examiners. When the results came out on the fourth day, he was at the head of the list as the Senior Wrangler. He was not yet twenty, but no Wrangler could have been more modest. 'I obtained my highest wishes', he wrote, 'but was surprised to find that I had grasped a shadow.'[11] Two months later he was listed as Smith's Prizeman, and in April 1802 he was chosen as a Fellow of his College. He turned once more to his early studies in the literature of Greece and Rome, and won first prize for a Latin essay which he had to declaim. No doubt it was this long apprenticeship to close study that built up the muscles of character and intellect; such a discipline was to brace his energies for the yet more arduous requirements of the future. Meanwhile he went back to Cornwall at the end of July to stay with his elder sister, while the romantic solitude of the country and the constant reading of the Bible began to lift his mind to new heights of spiritual hope and aspiration.[12]

Martyn had been inclined to reject the idea of the Christian ministry 'chiefly because he could not consent to be poor for Christ's sake',[13] but he returned to Cambridge in October 1802 with his mind made up. He would devote himself to the service of Christ and would read for ordination as Simeon's curate at Holy Trinity. He had begun to keep a brief Journal during 1802, but his published Journals date from January 1803. They open a window into his heart and throw a flood of light on his spiritual progress. It is clear that he was well liked as a Fellow and had a large circle of friends. He was well known for the 'simplicity and ease' of his manners,[14] and the men who climbed the staircase to his set of three rooms in the highest storey of E Block would often stay longer than he wished for conversation or music or mathematics. His relations with Simeon were growing in personal affection. Simeon looked on him as a son, and he looked up to Simeon as a father. But he could not escape the price which such friendship entailed, and his Journal made this clear on April 22nd: 'Was ashamed to confess that I was to be Mr Simeon's curate; a despicable fear of man from which I vainly thought myself free.'[15] He was ordained at Ely on 23 October 1803, and his Journal records his thoughts at the close of the day: 'I could scarcely believe that so sacred an office should be held by one who had such a heart within.'[16] He returned to Cambridge to join his friend Thomas Thomason as a curate with Charles Simeon. He had to read for Simeon at Holy Trinity, but his preaching was mainly at Lolworth, four miles away. He was soon hard at work in the crowded streets of Cambridge as well as in the country lanes at Lolworth, although he felt that he was 'a mere schoolboy' as he faced the sterner realities of life.[17] But the donnish nature of his language could not disguise his deep longing for the spiritual well-being of others. With College Fellows or country yokels, it was always the same: his was a light which could not be concealed.

Meanwhile a brief reference by Charles Simeon to the amount of good which a single missionary had done, opened his eyes to a wider vision. That chance remark had referred to William Carey; it was strengthened by the *Diary and Journals of David Brainerd* which began to exert a great influence on his character.[18] Martyn longed to be like him in his stern discipline of self and his utter devotion to God. 'Ah my soul', he would say, even when his soul was in no evident disorder, 'is this the life of Brainerd?'[19] It was an age when the church had hardly begun to think in terms of its missionary calling, but he offered himself as a missionary to the newly formed Society for Missions to Africa and the East. But early in 1804 he felt obliged to withdraw this offer as a result of the loss of 'all his slender patrimony'[20], for this left his younger sister Sally in need of his support. This led him to accept Charles Grant's invitation to become a Chaplain with the East India Company, knowing that it would open the door to missionary service while it would also provide an adequate salary for family commitments. 'Blessed be God', he exclaimed in September 1804, 'I feel myself to be His minister! This thought which I could hardly describe came in the morning after reading Brainerd. I wish for no service but the service of God: to labour for souls on earth and to do His will in heaven.'[21] On 10 March 1805, less than a month after his twenty-fourth birthday, he was ordained to the priesthood in the Chapel Royal at St James. His great concern was to rule his heart by the will of God, as his Journal on 20 March made clear: 'To keep the heart clean is a hard matter indeed, and what I know very little about; it requires more labour, care and self-denial than my flesh can easily submit to.'[22] He preached his last sermon in Cambridge on 7 April, and the congregation rose as one man to watch him in silence as he walked down the aisle. He had received his degree by mandate as a Bachelor of Divinity and the next three months were spent in London. He made friends with Charles Grant and Wilberforce; he drank tea with Richard Cecil and John Newton. On 8 July he set out to join the Fleet at Portsmouth, and on 16 July he took an affecting leave of Simeon. The next day his ship weighed anchor and the convoy set sail on its long and trying voyage.

Lydia Grenfell

The Senior Wrangler and College Fellow had laid all his academic honours at the feet of the Son of God; but the costliest sacrifice had yet to come, for he had now fallen in love with Lydia Grenfell. She was born in 1775 and grew up at Marazion where her home stood across the street from the chapel-of-ease. This was under the care of the Rev. T. M. Hitchins who lived two miles away 'on a wooded hill-top beside the church at St Hilary'.[23] Henry Martyn had known her all his life, for the Grenfell children had been playmates of his kinsfolk. Emma Grenfell, her elder sister, had married Tom Hitchins, his cousin, and the happiest memories of his boyhood were bound up with their home. He was six years younger than she, and this was a big gap while he was no more than a boy. He was only nineteen when she became engaged to a solicitor named Samuel John from Penzance. She was to find him an impossible suitor, and the marriage never took place. But this shattered romance was to prove in her case very much what Henry Martyn's hopeless love for her was in his. It stood astride her path, and the shadow it cast filled her with morbid scruples. It was in the early part of 1804 that she was made aware of John's plans to marry someone else, although the marriage did not in fact take place until 1810. But all that time she was preoccupied in feeling and conscience with the Penzance affair, and it left her convinced that she was no longer free to marry. Mr H. M. Jeffery summed up her attitude by saying that she felt 'the attachment of a widow with the responsibility of a wife',[24] and yet she was neither. But by 1804 she was a sad woman at the age of twenty-nine who saw in Henry Martyn no more than a younger cousin of her brother-in-law. Nevertheless the Journal which she kept for twenty-five years proves that her heart was at length won by him, though too late for any earthly union. The two Journals, his and hers, at each point where they meet, record the ebb and flow of hope and love with a human pathos that will always invest the story of Henry Martyn with a surpassing interest in the chequered chronicles of earth's hopeless affections.

The first hint as to his feelings was an entry in his Journal on 23 January 1803, when he referred to something which Sargent described as 'a strictly private matter': 'Rose with a dead weight upon my mind, found it very difficult to pray at all, and seemed very little the better for it.'[25] There is nothing more until 12 June 1804, when the prospect of an adequate salary stirred his feelings: It 'filled my heart with concern about earthly happiness, marriage, etc.'[26] Thoughts of marriage were from that time forward often before his mind, and they rose to a peak during his visit to Cornwall in July and August that year. Lydia Grenfell's engagement had fallen through at least six months before, and his love for her broke into the light. On 29 July, he rode to St Hilary for the morning service and was keenly disappointed because she was not there. He called on her after tea and had some conversation about things of spiritual concern. 'All the rest of the evening and at night, I could not keep her out of my mind', he wrote. 'I felt too plainly that I loved her passionately.'[27] But this, he thought, would be fatal to his missionary calling; his mind was in turmoil. How could he ask her to share the hardship of a missionary exile? He gave himself to an hour and a half of prayer. 'But in dreams her image returned, and I awoke in the night with my mind full of her.'[28] He left St Hilary in the morning and rode back to Gwennap. The next day he walked to Redruth and his Journal tells the story: 'On the road I was enabled to triumph at last, and found my heart as pleased with the prospect of a single life in missionary labours as ever.'[29] On 22 August he returned to the Hitchins at St Hilary and was with her four days later, walking by the sea or reading aloud in her home at Marazion. On 27 August the Journal records: 'I continued conversing with her, generally with my heart in heaven, but every now and then resting on her. Parted with Lydia, perhaps for ever in this life, with a sort of uncertain pain which I knew would increase to greater violence afterwards on reflection.'[30] Two days later, on the road to Truro, he tried to fix his mind on a resolve to cleave to God alone: 'Yet', he wrote, 'still I enjoyed every now and then the thought of walking hereafter with her in the realms of glory.'[31]

He left Cornwall without having declared his love, but this did not mean that it was unrecognised. His heart looked through his eyes, and his unspoken devotion was more welcome to her than she cared to admit. She had heard him preach at St Hilary on 26 August and her private comment was one of friendly pleasure: 'Heard H.M. . . . A precious sermon. Lord, bless the preacher and those that heard him.'[32] He met Emma Hitchins again when he passed through Plymouth, and his Journal on 10 September records: 'I learnt from Emma that my attachment to her sister was not altogether unreturned, and the discovery gave me both pleasure and pain; but at night alone, I resigned myself entirely to the will of God.'[33] He returned to Cambridge, telling himself that his dreams were over, and on 18 September he declared: 'My dear Lydia and my duty call me different ways; yet God hath not forsaken me.'[34] But the tension was to increase as the time for sailing approached, and his Journal reveals how it came to haunt him night and day. On 10 January 1805, he referred to what he could only regard as a critical decision: 'I was a long time engaged in writing to Emma, because it was on a subject on which I knew not my own mind; it was about Lydia; after some deliberation I ventured to request a correspondence with her, but my heart felt submissive before God, how He should ordain it.'[35] Two days later he said that he had been in doubt whether he should send this letter: 'However, I did send it, and now may be said to have engaged myself to Lydia.'[36] On 2 May, the love of God seemed to prevail: 'My heart acknowledges no love but that of God; I could not, I would not be happy without being altogether His.'[37] But the fires of human love burst into stronger flame as the time to sail drew near. On 1 June he wrote: 'Tonight I have been thinking much of Lydia. Memory has been at work to unnerve my soul.'[38] And the well-meant advice of his friends in London plunged him into further turmoil. Pratt and Cecil would have none of Simeon's celibate counsel, and told him that he would be mad to go unless he were married. At length he could only exclaim: 'I could attend to nothing else.'[39] What lover could? He was hammered with so many contradictions that he declared that not since he had left Cornwall had he suffered so much pain.

The long conflict, with its fluctuations between love and despair, seemed at last to have been resolved when he summed it all up on 8 June: 'How much have I gone through in the last two or three years to bring my mind to be willing to do the will of God when it should be revealed?'[40] The fleet put out to sea under Captain Byng on 17 July; but the end was not yet. He was too sick to read or take any active part in ship life that day, but he consoled himself in faith: 'I found comfort in fleeing to my only Friend, now all others had left me.'[41] The next day they were off Plymouth and the coast of Cornwall, and his heart was filled with pain. 'The memory of the beloved friends there was very strong and affecting . . . My heart was almost ready to break.'[42] A day later they anchored at Falmouth; he was now so close to Marazion that he marvelled at this unexpected event. It was little wonder that on 20 July he described his feelings with a renewed sense of conflict: 'I have thought with exceeding tenderness of Lydia today; how I long to see her; but if it be the Lord's will, He will open a way. I shall not take any steps to produce a meeting.'[43] The next day he went ashore and his Journal records: 'I . . . have been strongly induced to go to her, but I dare not.'[44] But, 'much deliberation' helped to change his mind, and on 25 July he left Falmouth by the early mail coach: 'I arrived at Marazion in time for breakfast and met my beloved Lydia. In the course of the morning I walked with her, though not uninterruptedly; with much confusion, I declared my affection for her, with the intention of learning whether if I ever saw it right in India to be married, she would come out, but she would not declare her sentiments.'[45] Nevertheless she did confide to her Journal in the evening: 'I felt as if bidding a final adieu to him in this world, and all he said was as the words of one on the borders of eternity . . . May the Lord moderate the sorrow I feel at parting with so valuable and excellent a friend; some pains have attended it, known only to God and myself. Thou, God, that knowest them, canst alone give comfort.'[46] So there were two sad hearts. He returned to Falmouth in the evening, and the only result was that he felt more in love with her than ever. 'The next day I was exceedingly melancholy at what had taken place between Lydia and myself . . . I could not bring myself to believe that God had settled the whole matter.'[47]

Two weeks went by, and the fleet still lay at Falmouth. He had written to Emma on 29 July: 'Another consequence of my journey is that I love Lydia more than ever.'[48] The fleet had been delayed by the needs of the Fleet off Brest and was kept at battle stations. 'Mine', he wrote, 'is with the surgeons in the cockpit.'[49] Then on 7 August, after preaching in a church in Falmouth, he took the road once more to St Hilary. 'The joy of my soul was very great', he declared; '. . . perhaps it might have been joy at the prospect of seeing Lydia.'[50] He arrived that evening and walked down to Gurlyn to call on her in the morning. 'She was not at home when we called, so I walked out to meet her, when I met her coming up the hill, I was almost induced to believe her more interested about me than I had conceived.'[51] But on arrival at St Hilary, he received an express telling him that orders had been issued for an immediate sailing. 'So I returned in the mail to Falmouth in no small disappointment; and yet much pleased and satisfied with the discovery which I thought I had made this morning.'[52] Meanwhile that night, shy and lonely, Lydia knew that she would soon be compelled to come to a decision, and she humbly implored the God of all grace to guide her aright. It was morning before she heard of his sudden recall; then at last she discovered how far her own affections were now engaged. She was greatly distressed to think that she would not see him again, for she felt that she had let him go with too much reserve. But that evening she received a message to say that he would call again in the morning, and she opened her heart in her Journal: 'Oh, I feel less able than ever to conceal my real sentiments, and the necessity of doing it does not so much weigh with me.'[53] Martyn had learnt that the fleet was not to sail on account of the Rochefort Squadron, and had set out for St Hilary on foot. 'Walked to Polkerris in the rain, about eight miles, with my mind very uneasy lest I was not in the way of duty.'[54] He finished the journey on horseback and spent the night at St Hilary. He rose very early the next morning, 10 August, but the rising wind filled him with apprehension lest the fleet should put out to sea. 'Was with Lydia a short time before breakfast', he wrote, 'when a servant came in and said a horse was come for me from St Hilary where a carriage was waiting to convey me to Falmouth.'[55]

All his presentiments were now fulfilled, but he also saw that she was 'painfully affected'.[56] His Journal that evening told the story with bare simplicity. 'She came out that we might be alone at taking leave, and I then told her that if it should appear to be God's will that I should be married, she must not be offended at receiving a letter from me. In the great hurry, she discovered more of her mind than she intended; she made no objection whatever to coming out. Thinking, perhaps, I wished to make an engagement with her, she said we had better go quite free; with this I left her, not knowing yet for what purpose I have been permitted, by an unexpected providence, to enjoy these interviews.'[57] He galloped to St Hilary, caught the chaise to Hildon, took horse again for the final stage to Falmouth, arrived at noon and went on board. 'At nine in the morning', he said, 'I was sitting

at ease with the person dearest to me on earth . . . Four
hours only elapsed, and I was under sail from England.'[58]
That night he wrote with a thankful heart to Emma: 'I
bless God for having sent the fleet into Falmouth; I go
with far greater contentment and peace than when I left
Portsmouth; the Lord will do all things well, and with
Him I cheerfully leave the management of this and every
other affair for time and eternity.'[59] That night Lydia too
felt that her affections were now truly committed and
her Journal confessed: 'Much have I to testify . . . of
what I must consider Divine interference in my favour
and that of my dear friend who is now gone to return no
more.'[60] In the morning, 11 August, the whole fleet was
becalmed at Mount's Bay just below Marazion; it was
Sunday, and his heart was full as he preached on those
who look for a better country. St Michael's Mount was
still in view at five o'clock that afternoon and he knew
that she could see its turrets from her window. It was his
last sight of English soil, and he felt ready to go 'anywhere
so long as the Lord goes with me'.[61] But would Emma
tell him whether Lydia had looked out to sea from
Marazion, and had her eyes lingered on the convoy as it
slowly vanished from sight?

'THE THUD OF CHRISTLESS FEET'

Henry Martyn had left England for one cogent reason:
he would not be 'disobedient to the heavenly vision' (*Acts*
26:19). He felt all the pangs of loneliness and nostalgia
during the first weeks at sea; he was homesick for Cambridge
and Cornwall, and his heart ached with love for Lydia.
But he was the only chaplain in a convoy of one hundred
and fifty sail, and he was no laggard in his Master's
business. All the merchant vessels for the East and West

Indies were there, as well as a squadron of sixty-three
transports with five thousand troops under the command
of Sir David Baird. Martyn was on board the *Union,* and
his cabin was stacked with books, grammars, dictionaries,
and commentaries. He must have been a unique figure
on that crowded transport. Slim, and frail, and careful of
dress, at home in the Classics or with congenial associates,
he was 'a raw academic' among the sea-dogs and soldiers,
wincing at every oath he heard, but talking to every person
he could find, until at last the clear flame of selfless witness
was seen and marked by all.[62] He might have shut himself
up with the cadets and writers in his own mess, young
men who were pleasant enough; 'but he sought his flock
in every corner of their crowded little world'[63] below the
gun-deck among the soldiers; beneath the hatchway
among their wives and children; on the upper deck where
the crew slung their hammocks; in the boatswain's berth
where he could reason with the ship's carpenter. There
was opposition, criticism, ribaldry, blasphemy; but he was
not deterred. His preaching made demands which were
far too direct to be generally acceptable, but two or three
hundred came to the one service he was allowed to hold
on the poop each Sunday when the weather was fine.
Leisure hours were spent in language study, and he sat
down with the Lascar sailors to try out his vocabulary.
He fed his soul on the Word of God as he tried to feed
others, and he poured out his heart with an intensified
ardour in prayer. 'Blessed Jesus', he wrote, on 5 February
1806, 'Thou art all I want, a Forerunner to me in all I ever
shall go through as a Christian, a minister, or a missionary.'[64]

The long voyage was to consume nine months, with
few ports of call and little news from England. Martyn's
presence on the *Union* won it the name of 'a very praying
ship', but he could only wish that it were more true.[65]

The fleet anchored at Cork and then put in at Madeira, where at sunrise on 3 October it parted with the ships for the East and West Indies. They knew nothing of the Battle of Trafalgar on 21 October, but arrived at San Salvador on 11 November. Here he found a retreat on the estate of a Portuguese gentleman who fell under the charm of his manners and his learning. He seized the chance to read the Psalms and pray aloud in the orange orchard, or to study Hindustani roots and devour a Portuguese grammar, or to join in conversation with the Franciscan Fathers who came and went. George Smith said that his was the first voice to proclaim the pure gospel on South American soil since three Huguenot missionaries had been put to death in 1558.[66] On 4 January 1806, the fleet hove to in the bay near Cape Town and Sir David Baird landed his troops with the task of seizing the Dutch settlement of Cape Colony. Martyn followed the troops ashore after the Battle of Blaauwberg on 8 January when a bayonet charge had put the Dutch to flight. He sought out the wounded, knelt by their side to pray, and did what he could for their comfort. At sunrise on 10 January a gun from the Commodore's ship was answered by all the men-of-war, for the British flag was flying from the Dutch fort. It found him on his knees, praying 'that the capture of the Cape might be ordered to the advancement of Christ's Kingdom'.[67] The voyage was resumed after a month spent at Cape Town, but the last stage was the hardest of all. The whole fleet was becalmed under hot skies; men and women were fretful with delay; disease made its inroads on board each ship; rations began to fail. But he had now risen above his early homesickness and he walked in spirit on the sunlit plains of glory. They dropped anchor at Madras on 25 April and sailed up the Hooghly three weeks later. He went on board a yacht to reach Calcutta on 16 May, and his Journal entry one day later still burns with the glow of a soul on fire: 'I feel pressed in spirit to do something for God . . . I have hitherto lived to little purpose . . . now let me burn out for God.'[68]

Henry Martyn had only two predecessors as evangelical chaplains and missionary enthusiasts in Bengal: David Brown who had arrived in Calcutta in June 1786, and Claudius Buchanan who had followed him there in March 1797. David Brown was one of the three Trustees who had taken charge of the Old Mission Church in 1787 and had made it a beacon of light in the heart of the city. Claudius Buchanan had proved himself a scholar and statesman of high order, and his writings brought a tremendous stimulus to the missionary cause in England. David Brown was away at his home at Aldeen where the gardens and lawns sloped down to the river; Claudius Buchanan was on a ship which passed within sight of the *Union* at the Sandheads, on his way to visit the old Syrian Churches of South India. David Brown soon returned to welcome Henry Martyn; but when Claudius Buchanan returned in March 1807, Henry Martyn had gone inland. Five months were to elapse before that move took place; he had to wait until he was assigned to a military station. But not a day was lost in the business of the gospel. He went to live with the Browns at Aldeen, where his quarters were a deserted pagoda at the foot of the lawns, over-looking the broad reach of river towards Barrackpore. Here he wrote the sermons which he preached in the Old Mission Church where he was always welcome; but his occasional sermons in the New Church of St John's which had been consecrated in 1787 caused a ferment in the ruling social circles. It was here, too, that he immersed himself in the study of the vernacular Hindustani and that he welcomed his Cambridge friend, Daniel Corrie, on his arrival in September. Aldeen was only five minutes' walk from Carey, Marshman, and Ward in their Serampore settlement, and he entered into close and frequent consultation with them about their plans for Bible translation. But his call was not to work at Serampore, nor to preach at Calcutta, and at last, on 14 September, he could write to Sargent: 'I am this day appointed to Dinapore in the neighbourhood of Patna.'[69] The Browns and the Serampore families came to farewell him in his pagoda, and found him in a mood of rare exaltation. 'My soul', he wrote, 'never yet had such divine enjoyment. I felt a desire to break from the body and join the high praises of the saints above. May I go in the strength of this many days. Amen.'[70]

On 15 October 1806 he set out on the long river journey to the interior of black Bengal. Six weeks were spent moving slowly upstream on the Ganges while he wrestled with Sanskrit and Hindustani. He went ashore each morning and evening, seeking to make Christ known in the ghats and bazaars. He was deeply stirred as the dense population and the spiritual darkness spread out before his eyes. 'What a wretched life shall I lead', he wrote on 23 November, 'if I do not exert myself from morning till night in a place where through whole territories I seem to be the only light.'[71] Two days later he reached Patna with its suburbs of Dinapore and Bankipore stretching for fourteen miles along the banks of the Ganges. This was to be his home until April 1809, and his work lay in the heart of a vast heathen population. The two Company regiments at Dinapore had seldom been marshalled for a church parade, and they were apathetic; and the British residents at Bankipore had seldom been summoned to a church service, and they were disconcerted. There was no church building; soldiers had to stand while he preached from the drumhead. But he soon planned to move from the barracks to a bungalow in the cantonment and to turn the central room with its verandah into a church. There were daily visits to the sick and dying in the army hospital; there were meetings on two evenings each week for those who were serious. He filled the house with guests or with language teachers, and he carried on a Latin correspondence with the Roman missionaries. He turned the prayers into Hindustani and began a weekly service for the native women who were attached to the barracks. The whole number of women, about 200, attended with great readiness', he wrote in April 1807, 'and have continued to do so.'[72] He was able to start three schools, all at his own expense, for the urchins who swarmed through the streets and bazaars, though not without opposition from those who said that he would turn the children into converts and send them to Europe. He summed up his activities in a single vigorous expression when he wrote of 'the expanding circle of action'.[73]

But the ceaseless thud of Christless feet was always in his hearing, and he lived as no white man should have lived in that climate. The hot winds that scorch the plains had driven him out of the army barracks; the first heavy monsoon rains were to drive him out of his private quarters. He was exposed to the heat and humidity of the summer as he travelled to and fro to marry the living or bury the dead. He was appalled by the dirt and disease in the streets and markets as he went round his schools. Symptoms of the disease which had killed his elder sister Laura during 1807 began to make steady inroads in his own frail body, and the entries in his Journal which spoke of pain grew more frequent. News of Laura's death did not reach him in Patna until 16 August; he was moved to the depths. 'Oh my heart, my heart', he cried, 'is it, can it be true that she has been lying so many months in the cold grave?'[74] There was a more ominous reference in a letter which he wrote on 25 January 1808: 'Last Sunday I felt greatly fatigued with speaking, and for the first time perceived symptoms of injury by pain in my breast.'[75] But he only reproached himself for lassitude and idleness, and then imposed further demands on his weakened constitution. He gave as much time as he could spare to language study, and he agreed to undertake the translation of the New Testament into both Hindustani and Persian. People of all kinds came from all quarters: a Muslim from Patna, a Latin Father from Rome, an Armenian from Jerusalem, a Jew from Babylon. Letters which passed up and down the river allowed him to share his news with Daniel Corrie as a friend and fellow chaplain, or with David Brown whom he had come to revere as a patriarch. But letters from England were few and far between, and they brought him little comfort when they did come. Yet he never faltered; he was more than willing to bear the cross so that he might follow Jesus. His whole heart is revealed by the entry in his Journal on 15 June 1808: 'Oh, it is Thy Spirit that makes me pant for the skies.'[76]

The letters from England came from Sargent and Simeon, from his sister Sally and his cousin Emma, and from Lydia Grenfell, and the latter sometimes lifted his mind to the stars and sometimes dashed his hope to the ground. His love for her pervades his own Journal throughout these years, like a refrain of sad but sweet background music. As he paced the deck on his long voyage out to India, alone with his memories, he had convinced himself that he could now safely dwell with tender feelings on all that lay behind. God was witness that he loved her dearly, but he believed that their farewell had been absolutely final. On 4 December 1805, he wrote in his Journal: 'Dearest Lydia! Never wilt thou cease to be dear to me; still, the glory of God and the salvation of immortal souls is an object for which I can part with thee.'[77] So he wrote while at sea; his self-conquest appeared to be complete. But for all her goodness, she was not cast in the mould of heroic sacrifice; she could not bring herself to let him slip out of her life. She had refused his request for correspondence, but she began to write, and her letters revived all his buried feelings. The first in a series of nine letters was lost at sea;[78] but on 12 July 1806 her next letter was placed in his hand at Calcutta. What true lover would not have been filled with hope when he read that she had him in mind many times each day as she came before the throne of grace in prayer? Was not this the answer which she had failed to give in the hurried moment of parting at Marazion? He read it to David Brown, who certainly understood that he was now free to pursue his suit. He took it as a sign that he should ask again, and a prayer for guidance was drawn from his heart on 29 July. 'May the Lord, in continuance of His loving kindness to her and me, direct her mind that if she comes I may consider it as a special gift from God, and not merely permitted by Him.'[79] Then he took up his pen to ask her to come out and share his life; but there was no vehement effusion of his feelings in that letter. It was marked by the firm restraint of a delicate courtesy which could only commend his cause, but which was all the more remarkable in the case of one whose feelings were so intense.

'You say in your letter', so he wrote, 'that frequently every day you remember my worthless name before the throne of grace. This instance of extraordinary and undeserved kindness draws my heart toward you with a tenderness which I cannot describe. Dearest Lydia, in the sweet and fond expectation of your being given to me by God and of the happiness which I humbly hope you yourself might enjoy here, I find a pleasure in breathing out my assurance of ardent love. I have now long loved you most affectionately, and my attachment is more strong, more pure, more heavenly, because I see in you the image of Jesus Christ. I unwillingly conclude by bidding my beloved Lydia adieu.'[80] He posted a copy of this letter on 1 September with a second letter in which he wrote: 'Now, my dearest Lydia, I cannot say what I feel . . . I could not if you were here; but I pray that you may love me, if it be the will of God, and I pray that God may make you more and more His child, and give me more and more love for all that is Godlike and holy.'[81]

Twelve months were to follow in which his one supreme earthly joy was to think of her and hope for an early union with her. He was cheered by news from her in three more letters which were safely received, but which had been written before she received his invitation. The third in this series of nine was placed in his hand on 24 September and he read a meaning into its lines which it had not perhaps been meant to bear. 'In the evening', he wrote, 'the Lord gave me near and close and sweet communion with Him on this subject and enabled me to commit the affair with comfort into His hands. Why did I ever doubt His love? Does He not love us far better than we love one another?'[82] He was thankful to read that his name was still linked with hers in prayer, it made him feel that she was less aloof than she would have him think.[83] The fourth letter arrived on 21 December, and the sense of her love which it seemed to convey was so grateful to his heart that he was overwhelmed with a flood of affection. 'Yet', he observed, 'the few words my dearest Lydia wrote turned my joy into tender sympathy with her; who knows what her heart has suffered?'[84] The fifth letter came on 3 July 1809 and so quickened his love that he could think of nothing else. He now believed that he had won her heart and hoped that it would soon be his to win her hand as well.[85]

Lydia's diary revealed more of her heart than her letters dared to disclose, for it laid before God her loving concern on his behalf ever since the fleet had sailed from Falmouth. She felt at the time that he had become 'too dear a friend', and that he had more of her heart than she should have allowed.[86] This sprang from the scruples which had fastened on her mind with regard to her erstwhile suitor, she could not feel herself free to become engaged until he had married. This was something which she could not persuade herself to speak of while Henry Martyn was with her in Cornwall; her first letter, written on 16 November 1805, had been meant to explain it all to him. But she was not to know that it never reached him, and he could not know the nature of its contents.[87] They had written to each other since then through a mist of painful uncertainty, but her Journal told its own tale. On 4 August 1806, she observed: 'One year is nearly passed since we parted, but scarcely a waking hour I believe has he been absent from my mind.'[88] It was on 2 March 1807 that she received his first invitation to go out and join him; her mind was thrown into turmoil. But her private scruples were now strengthened by her mother's obvious reluctance at the prospect of her marriage with a 'Methodist' out in India. Therefore she wrote in her mother's name to refuse and sought relief for her feelings through her Journal. 'The pain of writing to him is over', she wrote on 8 March, 'and I feel satisfied I wrote what duty required of me. Now then, return, O my soul, to thy rest!'[89] These facts were all confirmed by Charles Simeon, who paid her a special visit at the end of April. He thought that she ought not to leave England without her mother's full consent; but the situation was not adequately explained in the letter he then wrote to Henry Martyn.[90] The end result was that the old Penzance affair loomed up with fresh force in her mind and she began to feel more than ever that she was not free to marry.[91] Yet on 9 August she wrote again in her Journal: 'Just two years since I parted from a dear friend and brother whose memory will ever be cherished by me.'[92] But her letter reached him at length on 24 October, leaving him to feel as though his heart would burst with grief and disappointment.[93]

But she had not concealed her real feelings and her letter still left some room for hope. He saw the one loophole and he sat down that night to plead his suit once more. 'You say that present circumstances seem to you to forbid my indulging expectations', he wrote. 'As this leaves an opening, I presume to address you again, and till the answer arrives, must undergo another eighteen months of torturing suspense. In the meantime, since I am forbidden to hope for the immediate pleasure of seeing you, my next request is for a mutual engagement . . . The more I write, and the more I think of you, the more my affection warms . . . Farewell, dearest, most beloved Lydia.'[94] Letters from Lydia and Simeon reached him on 25 November, telling him about their conversation at the end of April; but they only filled his heart with fresh grief. 'I cannot bear to part with Lydia', he wrote, 'and she seems more necessary to me than my life; yet her letter was to bid me a last farewell . . . With Thee, O my

God, there is no disappointment: I shall never have to regret that I loved Thee too Well.'[95] He now felt that he ought not to press things further since his plans did not seem to bear the mark of God's favour.[96] Nevertheless, less than a month later he wrote to Emma: 'Of the three in the world who have most love for me; that is, Sally, Lydia and yourself, I believe that notwithstanding all that has happened, the middle one loves most truly.'[97] But in January 1808 he told Simeon that all hope of being joined by Lydia was at an end: 'I cannot doubt any longer what is the divine will, and I bow to it . . . I never loved, nor ever shall love, human creature as I love her.'[98] Her own reply to his second appeal did not arrive until 14 December, and it only renewed his pain. 'Prayer was my only relief', he wrote, 'and I did find peace by casting my care on God.'[99] Three months later, a fresh letter arrived, and he opened his heart to David Brown in a letter written on 28 March 1809: 'I trembled at the handwriting . . . it was only more last words . . . lest the non-arrival of the former might keep me in suspense.'[100] Her ninth letter and last answer came on Christmas Day 1809, and he briefly remarked: 'So now I have done.'[101] This ended the correspondence in which he had poured out all his love with exquisite tenderness; it could not hide the pangs of a deeply wounded spirit.

Cawnpore: Preaching and Translation

Meanwhile there had been an encouraging response to his work at Patna. Thirty soldiers were in regular attendance at a meeting in his house each evening, and their staunchness brought him great joy.[102] But in April 1809 he was ordered to leave Patna for the camp at Cawnpore, three hundred miles further inland. It was almost the worst time of the year for a major journey, but he set out at once in a comfortless palanquin. This proved reasonable until he reached Allahabad; then he was forced to press on for two days and two nights without a halt for rest. The wind was like the blast of a furnace and he arrived in a state of collapse. Fever ensued and brought him to death's door in the suffocating calm which followed in the wake of the winds.[103] Cawnpore was in fact the worst post in the country for a man in his state of health, and this was an ominous beginning. He soon found that there was no church, no tent, not so much as a fly, for his use on parade.[104] Several men and officers were to drop where they stood during his first service beneath the fierce glare of the sun.[105] They could only marvel when they saw how he drove himself in spite of the heat and fatigue, and they were to marvel more still as the ceaseless routine of his daily work at Patna was applied to soldier life at Cawnpore. Outside parades were all cancelled when the rains came, and he had to conduct worship in a riding hall where the atmosphere was 'such as would please only the knights of the turf'.[106] But at length he prevailed on the authorities to reconstruct a bungalow as a camp church, and its bell was rung for the first time to summon people to his farewell service.[107] There were meetings each night in his own house near the Sepoy lines for godly soldiers whose voice in prayer and praise gladdened his heart. There were, as well, evenings with the Sherwoods where music and laughter brought him needed recreation. But his time and strength were more than ever dedicated to new missionary efforts for the untouched heathen population: he had not ceased to feel the stir of that ever-changing human panorama since he had first recoiled from the shock of idolatry in the streets of Madras.[108]

While at Patna, he had started schools for native urchins and had held a weekly service for the native women; but at Cawnpore, he found ways in which to enlarge the whole sphere of his work among all classes of people. Nothing was more remarkable than his attempt to preach every Sunday morning to a motley crowd of beggars in his compound. He had begun to throw the gates open once a week so as to give out small coins or cups of rice to those who came; but he went no further than this until the last month of the year. Then, on 17 December 1809, he took his stand on a platform in his garden and began to address the crowd of more than four hundred. 'I told them', he wrote, 'that I gave with pleasure the alms I could afford, but wished to give them something better.'[109] There were some five hundred in the compound a week later, and no delirious dream could have gone beyond the strange realities of that congregation. There were Hindu yogis and Muslim fakirs who posed as saints and lived as beggars. Some were in rags or near naked; some were plastered with mud and cow-dung; some were covered with sores and diseases. He was often interrupted by the groans and blasphemies of his audience; but when the storm died down, he would resume in the same cool clear voice as if he were impervious to all provocation. 'I still imagine', so Mrs Sherwood recalled, 'that I hear the calm, distinct, and musical tones of Henry Martyn as he stood raised above the people, endeavouring . . . to convince the unbelievers that . . . they needed a Saviour Who was both willing and able to save them.'[110] The last thing he did in Cawnpore was to preach to them once more on 30 September 1810; but he told his friends that 'he was afraid he had not been the means of doing the smallest good' to any of his hearers.[111] But one of them, Sheikh Salih, once a Muslim moonshee, then the keeper

of the King of Oudh's jewels, followed him to Calcutta.
He was entrusted with the task of seeing to the binding
of Henry Martyn's Persian translation. This allowed him
to read it from end to end and he became a convinced
believer. He was baptized with the name of Abdul Masih
by David Brown on Whitsunday 1811.[112]

Meanwhile Henry Martyn had become slowly convinced that 'to translate the Word of God' would prove a
more beneficial work than preaching, which was apt to
leave him in a state of serious exhaustion.[113] He was truly
gifted as a student in the science of grammar and
philology, and he was to apply a rare genius to the task of
translation. His own literary honours had sprung from
the Classics of Greece and Rome, and he found it relatively
easy to dip into French and Italian, Dutch and Portuguese.
He had found his relaxation after a day's work at
Cambridge in the grammar of some oriental language
and he toiled night and day in his plans to master the
great tongues of the East. 'He read grammars as other
men read novels', Canon Edmonds declared, 'and to him
they were more entertaining than novels.'[114] As early as
1804 he was poring over a Bengali grammar and a
Hindustani dictionary, and in 1806 he had become
absorbed in the Sanskrit background from which many
words in Hindi have been derived.[115] In 1808 he attempted
the translation of a passage of Scripture into seven
different languages as an experiment.[116] In 1809 he listed
the grammars and dictionaries of no less than seventeen
languages already in his possession; what he had was just
a whetstone for his desire and made him wish for more.[117]
During his residence near Serampore he had learnt of
Carey's plans for multiple translation of the Scriptures so
that all the sons of the East might have the Word of God
in that language wherein they had been born. He had an

ear for a spoken language and a sense of idiom that were invaluable, and he eagerly responded to David Brown's proposal that he should undertake the translation of the New Testament into Hindustani, Persian, and Arabic.[118] As early as June 1806, he was able to write: 'In Hindustani translations, I begin to feel my ground and can go on much faster than one moonshee can follow.'[119] A small grant helped him to employ the wild Arab Sabat and the sleek pundit Mirza, who came to work with him later that year. On 1 January 1808 he could observe that the translation of the Epistles was complete;[120] on 4 February 1809 he could report that the first draft of the whole New Testament had been accomplished.[121]

Henry Martyn found in Hindustani a great living language, spoken by some sixty million people; but it was a hybrid language which had little recognition among men of letters in east or west alike. It had a strong Persian and Arabic flavour and was in fact the camp language which grew into Urdu.[122] Henry Martyn made its study his own special province, just as Carey had done in the case of Bengali, and he applied himself to the task with an ear that was quick to detect the least change in dialect or idiom as he travelled from village to village on the Ganges. He was indeed the first Western scholar to care for the value of the living tongue and the spoken sound, as compared with the language of grammars and dictionaries. Hindustani was, as yet, the language of life rather than of literature, and he strove to master it with the aid of storytellers and poets from the bazaars, as well as with the help of Mirza and Sabat. There were times when he would have been glad to relinquish the slow grind of translation for the direct work of preaching; but he could not escape the strong sense of duty and he pursued it with unwearied diligence.

His first draft of the New Testament was subjected to rigorous revision before his own critical taste was satisfied; but at last, to his great delight, at the close of the year 1810, it was received and acclaimed by the most competent authorities of the day in Calcutta.[123] It was passing through the press at Serampore when a fire in 1812 destroyed the type, and it was not until 1814 that the first edition of two thousand copies appeared. He had also turned the Book of Common Prayer and the Book of Genesis into Hindustani: the one was printed in 1814 and the other in 1817. But his outstanding achievement was his work on the New Testament, carried out within five years of his arrival in Calcutta and marked by superb scholarship in text and style. Henry Martyn wore the mantle of William Tyndale, and their work had one great trait in common: Henry Martyn's New Testament became the basis of every subsequent translation into Urdu, just as William Tyndale's New Testament had become the basis of every subsequent translation into English.[124]

All that Simeon and Sargent had been to him at Cambridge, David Brown and Corrie were to him in India. Simeon and David Brown were proven veterans on whose counsel he could always rely; Sargent and Corrie were trusted companions in whose friendship he could always rejoice. They looked on from afar, but with anxious eyes, as he dug the spurs of spiritual resolve into his now failing body and pressed on with all his might towards the goal. In March 1810, he received a letter from Simeon with the news that Sally, his youngest and dearest sister, had now succumbed to the smouldering consumption which had proved the scourge of all his family.[125] He could not hide from his friends the fact that it had settled in his own lungs and on 19 April he wrote: 'Study never makes me ill – scarcely ever fatigues me – but my lungs! death is seated there; it is speaking that kills me . . . But the call of Jesus Christ bids me cry aloud and spare not. As His minister, I am a debtor both to the Greek and the Barbarian. How can I be silent when I have both ever before me, and my debt not paid?'[126] On 2 June 1810 Corrie and his sister came to relieve him at Cawnpore. They found him so ill that minimal exertion left him with loss of voice, and a fire in his chest, and a restless fatigue that drove sleep from his mind. Corrie's visit saved him, and his last four months at Cawnpore brought him singular happiness. Corrie shared his household, preached for him, and set him free for incessant translation. Corrie's sister was made welcome by the Sherwoods and, far more than he could have told, Henry Martyn became the real pivot in both households. For a short while it seemed as though his health would be restored.[127] They went driving in his gig each evening, and they even hired a pinnace for a health trip on the river. But he was still failing and they told him that he must go to sea. He was absorbed in his Arabic translation, and the idea slowly took hold on his mind that he should complete it in Arabia itself. At length he was granted leave of absence, and on 1 October he left Cawnpore to float down the Ganges to the home at Aldeen. Corrie's pale face filled him with deep concern lest he should be overworking; he did not know that it was white with the strain of parting.[128]

The Journals

Henry Martyn had planned to burn all his private papers before he left Cawnpore, but was prevailed upon to seal them up and leave them in the hands of Daniel Corrie. News of his death filtered through to Corrie at some point in 1813, and the packet was then sent home to

Charles Simeon and John Thornton as his trustees. 'A life of him will be written by my dear friend, Mr Sargent', so Simeon told Thomason, '. . . and I am collecting all possible materials.'[129] Henry Martyn's packet contained all his Journals from 1803 to 1810, and it arrived safely in England in 1814. The Journals for 1811 and 1812 came into the hands of Isaac Morier in Constantinople, and in due course were sent on by him to Simeon. 'Mr Martyn's papers are all safe', so Simeon told Thomason in a letter dated 19 May 1815; 'we have his Journals till within a few days of his death.'[130] Simeon and Sargent pored over those travel-stained documents in Simeon's college rooms, and they formed the basis for the biography published by Sargent in 1819. It met with an immediate welcome and ran through ten editions before his own death in 1833. But Sargent had suppressed the bulk of the material concerning Lydia Grenfell, as she was still alive; it was only after her death in 1829 that Sargent's son-in-law, Samuel Wilberforce, could bring out a separate edition of *Henry Martyn's Journals and Letters.* This appeared in two volumes in 1837; but it did not include any excerpts used by Sargent and it did not contain any editorial comment or fresh biographical data. It must be read side by side with Sargent's Memoir to fill in the background. But what became of the original Journals used by Sargent and Wilberforce? They were unknown to George Smith in 1892; all his quotations were derived from Sargent and Wilberforce. As a result, all that Henry Martyn wrote in Greek and Latin for eight months in 1809 is lost, as well as those sections in the original whose presence is only indicated by dots. But what has been preserved was described by Stephen Neill as 'one of the most precious treasures of Anglican devotion'.[131]

Entries in the Journal had been made in private and were clearly modelled on what he had found in David Brainerd. They were both cast in the same mould, and the daily record of their inner spiritual life throbs with the hunger that had to feed on Christ or die. Few books, apart from the Psalms of David, reflect more of a man's hidden longing for a perfect conformity to the will and purpose of God. Henry Martyn's Journals were not marked by the same profound melancholy that filled Brainerd's pages, but they reveal the same kind of spiritual travail which in our less earnest age seems almost beyond mortal effort. They were meant for one pair of eyes only, for they told the story of how he strove to walk with God; they were written with a total candour which would have been impossible if they were not written as though he were alone in *His* presence. They were the work of one who was vulnerable at so many points and who was unsparing in self-criticism. This daily and searching analysis of shortcomings and weaknesses helped to sharpen his literary style so that scarcely a page was lacking in some fresh spiritual insight.[132]

But there was a special factor that marked Henry Martyn off from David Brainerd, and lent uncommon interest to his Journals. They were imbued with romance and pathos, as well as with self-analysis and self-criticism. He wrote down in black and white what he had learnt in solitude and suffering, and it was in anguish of soul that he produced notes of unselfconscious beauty. Stephen Neill said that the candid historian has to reckon with the thought that had he married Lydia Grenfell, 'life with so neurotic, demanding and indecisive a woman might have destroyed his mind and spirit more decisively than the pain of separation could do.'[133] It was just this intensely human element, combined with its intensely

spiritual character, that clothed Henry Martyn's name
with exceptional appeal and filled Victorian readers with
an ineffable longing to live for God as he had lived,
burning himself out in a flame of sacrificial zeal for his
glory.

   Nothing perhaps is more remarkable as an illustration
of the impact on the Victorian mind of Sargent's Memoir
or the Journals themselves than the use made of them in
one of George Eliot's early novels. Henry Martyn died
seven years before she was born, and they had very little
in common. But in 1858 *Scenes of Clerical Life* was
published, and one of the stories was called 'Janet's
Repentance'. George Eliot made the spiritual crisis in
Janet's storm-tossed experience turn upon her reading
Sargent's *Memoir of Henry Martyn*. Janet had been driven
out of her home by her husband and the door had been
slammed. It was after midnight, and she stood in the
street in her nightdress while the wind cut through her
ill-clad body. She had to seek shelter, somewhere to hide
herself, and her mother's home was too far away. But she
ventured to knock at Mrs Pettifer's cottage, which was
only five doors away, and when Mrs Pettifer opened her
bedroom window, she cried: 'It is I, Mrs Pettifer, it is
Janet Dempster. Take me in, for pity's sake.'[134] Janet
sobbed her heart out that night and was afraid to leave
when the new day arrived. The new curate at the chapel-
of-ease on Paddiford Common came to see her and tried
to point her from his own experience to the secret of
peace with God; but it was hard to rouse her from the
bleak stupor of trouble and despair into which she had
now fallen. Mrs Pettifer, however, was a subscriber to
the Paddiford Lending Library and had borrowed
Sargent's *Memoir of Henry Martyn*. Janet found it lying
on the table, started to dip into it, and became so

engrossed that she could not leave it alone. It broke the spell of her stupor, gave her a new hold on herself, awoke her dormant energy and moved her to renewed effort. She put on a bonnet and shawl, came down to the kitchen, and told Mrs Pettifer: 'I must go. I feel I must be doing something for someone – not be a mere useless log any longer. I've been reading about that wonderful Henry Martyn . . . wearing himself out for other people, and I sit and think of nothing but myself. I must go.'[135] And off she went, just in time to find and forgive her husband before he died. Janet Dempster was a type of all the thousands through whom Henry Martyn has lived again.

But the rather sombre tone that marks the Journals must be balanced with an account of his manner of life by one who knew him intimately. It is for this reason that *The Life and Times of Mrs Henry Sherwood* is so valuable. Henry Sherwood was a Captain with the 53rd Regiment at Cawnpore and, with his wife, gave Henry Martyn more of the joy of home life than he ever knew in India, except with the Browns at Aldeen. They found that he possessed the strength and charm of a simplicity and sincerity that left their mark on all who knew him. He had once used a diamond to cut the Greek text of one of St Paul's watchwords on the window of his college rooms at Cambridge (*Eph.* 5:14).[136] His own daily response to that summons to awake and arise was self-evident in his total dedication to the gospel. His great accomplishments in Mathematics and Classics were a solid witness to the calibre of his intellect. They light up the nature of a mind that gloried in the revelation of truth through the pages of the Bible. Hints are scattered through his Journals which show how much he was aware of the spell of beauty or the warmth of friendship in all its forms. A rural landscape or sacred music always produced the same effect on his mind: it served to fix his thoughts on the God who reigns in heaven.[137]

It had been with delight that at times he could turn aside to muse and pray in the Fellows' garden in Cambridge, or to watch a sunset from the rugged coastline of Cornwall.[138] On 8 April 1807, while in Patna, he wrote: 'The day I left Cambridge; my thoughts frequently returned with many tender recollections to that beloved seat of my brethren, and again wandered in spirit amongst the trees on the banks of the Cam.'[139] Mrs Sherwood said that 'he had an uncommonly fine voice and fine ear, and could sing many fine chants, and a vast quantity of hymns and psalms.'[140] He taught himself these chants and tunes, with the aid of a flute.[141] All the hidden passion of his Celtic nature sought and found an outlet in an aesthetic hunger and a beauty-loving mind which were all too rare among men of his school, and which bowed in awe and wonder before the God of all glory.

He moved among his friends with the winsome charm and cheerful ease of natural courtesy, and his pleasant laughter filled the house when he could relax. Nothing could be further from truth than to suppose that his social life was dull or morose. Mrs Sherwood said that she had never met a man who was 'more merry amongst his friends'.[142] Sir John Malcolm and the Honourable Mountstuart Elphinstone knew him as a delightful companion who could bubble over with wit and gaiety.[143] He could laugh and play just like a carefree child, if children were there to play and laugh with him, and he was the idol of the children in the home at Aldeen.[144] Mrs Sherwood observed that his kindness to those little ones as the lambs in Christ's flock was always to the fore; he never seemed more at ease than when they were hanging round his neck or riding on his shoulders.[145]

Her own little Lucy always made her way straight to him, knowing that her welcome was sure. She would sit on his huge lexicon which he might need at any moment, or climb on to his knee and clutch the book out of his hand. He would never allow her to be disturbed, nor send her away.[146] He had subdued his own cherished longings for a wife and home and children to one supreme passion. As early as on 10 June 1804 he had written: 'Now would to God I were quite dead to the world. It will be heaven indeed to me when self is entirely lost.'[147] That deep quest for personal holiness would mean nothing less than to discrown and disown both self and sin so that Christ might reign as Lord of all. On 24 September 1807, the same ideal was viewed from a different perspective: 'To live without sin is what I cannot expect in this world, but to desire to live without it may be the experience of every hour.'[148] His character and genius had qualities of excellence which would have been remarkable in all ages and all circumstances. Janet Dempster did not exaggerate when she spoke of 'that wonderful Henry Martyn': all who knew him would voice the same testimony.

PERSIA

Ill health had so told on the frail form of Henry Martyn that a change had become imperative, and he was cheered for a moment by the prospect of a furlough which would allow him to visit England. But once more he chose to sacrifice his own interests for the sake of others and he planned to leave the scorching plains of India for the desert wastes of Persia. He had long been occupied with the translation of the New Testament into Arabic and Persian, and as early as May 1807 he had begun to have some thoughts of a visit to both countries for the sake of this task.[149] What he had done had been hampered by the erratic conduct and pedantic follies of Sabat, and in the end he found that he had been misled in the whole style of his Persian translation. He was forced to prepare a fresh draft of this work, though still with the aid of Sabat; but this revised version was still severely criticized on the ground that it was loaded with Arabic idiom and stilted diction. His gentleness and forbearance never shone more brightly than in his treatment of Sabat, but this further disappointment lent the force of urgent necessity to the idea of a visit to the countries where the language was that of the people.

On 11 June 1810 he wrote of his desire to go with a version as it were in each hand and to revise them with the help of the ablest scholars in Persia and Arabia.[150] On 8 September he declared that there was no reason why the Arabic should not be done in Arabia and the Persian in Persia.[151] The long journey down the Ganges brought him to Aldeen on 26 October and to Calcutta on 3 November. 'Then had the long expected pleasure of meeting dear Thomason.'[152] Thomas Thomason, once his fellow curate under Charles Simeon, had left his home at Shelford to spend the rest of his life in India. Henry Martyn applied to the Governor-General for official permission to spend his convalescent leave in Persia. After that, he would go to Damascus, or Baghdad, or somewhere in the heart of Arabia itself.[153] On 1 January 1811 Lord Minto agreed to this request, and on Sunday evening, 4 January, Henry Martyn preached for the last time in the Old Mission Church on 'the one thing needful'.[154] The next morning, 'without taking leave of [his] too dear friends', David Brown and Thomason, he boarded a vessel which was to take Mountstuart Elphinstone to Bombay.[155] The six weeks at sea with Mountstuart Elphinstone allowed him to converse with a man whose classical attainments were of a high order and whose service at the court of Kabul had placed him in contact with the Muslim world beyond the Indian frontier. They went ashore at Colombo and Goa, and they sat for hours on the poop talking about Francis Xavier, or the Afghans, or this and that. They did not reach Bombay until 18 February. 'This day', he wrote, 'I finish the thirtieth year of my unprofitable life, an age in which Brainerd had finished his course. He gained about a hundred savages to the Gospel; I can scarcely number the twentieth part.'[156] He was forced to spend five weeks in Bombay before he could arrange for a further sailing, and this gave him time to meet and talk with Jews and Arabs and Parsees and Brahmans. Elphinstone introduced him to Sir John Malcolm, the General and diplomat who had twice been sent to promote British trade and prestige in Persia.

Sir John gave him a letter of introduction to the British Ambassador at the court of the Shah, Sir Gore Ouseley, and it contains the last extant pen sketch of the manner of man he was in the eyes of an English contemporary. 'He is altogether a very learned and cheerful man, but a great enthusiast in his holy calling . . . He will give you grace before and after dinner, and admonish such of your party as take the Lord's Name in vain; but his good sense and great learning will delight you, whilst his constant cheerfulness will add to the hilarity of the party.'[157] He secured a passage on a naval vessel which was to cruise in the Persian Gulf against Arab pirates, and he served as chaplain to the European crew and soldiers on board. The ship sailed from Bombay on 25 March but saw no trace of the wily pirates during the next four weeks at sea. Then on Sunday 21 April, there was a brief sentence in his Journal: 'Anchored in Muscat cove; the work and confusion which this occasioned prevented our having divine service.'[158]

The dour mountains on the coast of Oman climb to a height of ten thousand feet and often reach down to the edge of the sea. The twin townships of Muscat and Mutrah are formed by an indentation of the coastline like a huge capital 'W'. Muscat itself has a perfect harbour, with two ancient Portuguese forts which crown the headlands where they jut out into the Gulf. Mountains retreat from each headland in a kind of semi-circle at the foot of which the town lies; but the mountain background is wild, gaunt, bleak, and desolate. The bare rocks soak in the sun's heat by day and throw it off by night, so that in the summer Muscat is one of the hottest places on earth. This is the main port of Oman; it is also the heir of a maritime tradition which is unique in the Arabian Peninsula. Its historic interest and strategic importance were at their peak at the time of Henry Martyn's visit. Aden was not acquired by the British until 1839, and the Suez Canal was not finished by De Lesseps until 1869. Muscat was still the great market in the flow of slaves from Africa through Zanzibar to Arabia. Henry Martyn had written on 1 January: 'I now pass from India to Arabia, not knowing what things shall befall me there.'[159]

He knew that Arabia had become the cradle of Islam in 622 A.D., and that no missionary had yet carried out even a token visit as a witness for the gospel. What he did not know was that 'the history of direct effort to reach the great Arabian peninsula' was to begin when on 22 April he landed at Muscat and walked through the bazaar.[160] That night he wrote to Lydia Grenfell: 'I am now in Arabia Felix; to judge from the aspect of the country, it has little pretensions to the name unless burning barren rocks convey an idea of felicity. But perhaps as there is a promise in reserve for the sons of Joktan, their land may one day be blessed indeed.'[161] He tried to go inland, but was stopped by soldiers because the Imam was thirty miles away, fighting for his kingdom with the merciless Wahabies. Two days later, he went with an Arab as guard and guide to see the pass out of Muscat through the mountains, and a garden in the valley captured his mind in spite of the desolate surroundings: 'There was nothing to see', he wrote, 'only the little bit of green in the wilderness.'[162]

Henry Martyn spent five days at Muscat, and his visit was itself like a 'little bit of green in the wilderness'. On Thursday evening 25 April, an Arab soldier and his slave came on board to bid him farewell. 'They asked to see the Gospel. The instant I gave them a copy in Arabic, the poor boy began to read, and carried it off as a great prize, which I hope he will find it to be.'[163] That night the ship warped out of the stifling harbour: he had not had one night's real rest since they had cast anchor. But the thought of Arabia was still in his mind when he wrote to David Brown two months later on 24 June: 'I believe I told you that the advanced state of the season rendered it necessary to go to Arabia circuitously by way of Persia.'[164] Muscat in fact was to prove the only part of Arabian soil on which he would stand; yet, in more than one sense, he was the pioneer of missionary work in that country. It was Sabat no doubt who to a large extent had turned his thoughts and plans towards Arabia, and the study of its language had as its sole aim the translation of the New Testament. He had written to David Brown from Cawnpore on 9 September 1810: 'Arabia shall hide me till I come forth with an approved New Testament . . . I cannot devote my life to a more important work than that of preparing the Arabic Bible.'[165] Sir John

Malcolm declared that 'his knowledge of Arabic is superior to that of any Englishman in India.'[166] On the voyage from Bombay to Muscat, he wrote tracts in Arabic, spoke with Arab sailors, read the Koran, studied *Niebuhr's Travels,* and planned for the future. But the final version of his Arabic New Testament was in effect what he had done with the aid of Sabat and it lacked the ultimate perfection of his Hindustani and Persian translations. It was printed at Calcutta in 1816 and passed through two more editions. Sabat's defects were least conspicuous in his native language, and this Arabic translation served a useful purpose 'among the learned and fastidious Mohammedans for whom chiefly it was prepared'.[167] It was superseded in 1865 by the beautiful Arabic Bible which was published in Beirut by Dr Eli Smith and Dr Van Dyck after almost thirty years of patient labour.

On 1 May, four weeks after the ship had warped out of Muscat, it berthed at the steaming Persian port of Bushire. 'Landed this morning in good health', he wrote; 'how unceasing are the mercies of the Lord!'[168] On Sunday 26 May he preached to the European community at a morning service, and was present at a service in the Armenian church in the evening.[169] He lodged with an English merchant and his Armenian wife for part of the month, endured the heat of May, and ordered Persian clothes for the long journey inland. He left Bushire on 30 May mounted on a pony, followed by an Armenian servant with his baggage, and travelled by night with an army officer in a caravan of some thirty mules and horses. The first stage lay across ninety miles of flat and almost treeless desert, hardly above sea level; they rode beneath the light of the stars and to the music of bells. Daylight found them on the plain where they pitched a tent beneath a tree; sleep was impossible as the thermometer rose to 126°F (52°C). They rode again at night, and the cool air helped to revive his strength. At dawn, he wrapped himself up in a large wet towel and was able to rest. The third night's ride brought them to the foot of the hills where the track starts to climb by four long steep passes to the mountain plateau seven thousand feet above sea level. 'There was nothing to mark the road but the rocks being a little more worn in one place than another.'[170] He could only give his pony the rein, content to let it choose the way on a trail that seemed to hug the precipitous edge of mountain chasms. He was so tired that he felt like a man drunk with sleep and fatigue; he was so cold that it seemed as though the wind were slashing through him like a knife-blade. On 7 June they were at last on the central plateau where the temperature was like that of spring in England. 'We pitched our tent', he wrote, 'near a crystal stream, on the banks of which we observed the clover and golden cup; the whole valley was one green field in which large herds of cattle were browsing.'[171] A few hours' sleep renewed his strength and he awoke with a light heart. The next night saw the last stage of the march and the morning of 9 June brought him to the plain of Shiraz.

Sir John Malcolm's letters secured him a welcome in the home of Jaffir Ali Khan, a wealthy, well-educated Muslim who became his host during the next twelve months. Jaffir Ali Khan also owned an orange orchard, enclosed by high brick walls, at a little distance from the city proper. Its central feature was a summer house, octagonal in shape, with neither windows nor walls. A fountain beneath the domed ceiling allowed host and guests to move their carpets to the coolest angle away from the sun at any hour of the day. Henry Martyn was now in the heart of the old Persian kingdom, only forty miles from

Persepolis and the graves of Darius and Artaxerxes and Ahasuerus. Shiraz was the modern seat of the old Persian culture and the home of its most classical dialect. He gave himself up to the two compelling interests of translation and discussion, and the story is told mainly in his letters. He no longer had time for the minute analysis of his faults and failings in the spirit which had filled his Journals before. They now became little more than necessary records of his progress with translation or his debates with visitors. His presence in Shiraz caused no small stir in its schools of learning, and men came from cities as far afield as Baghdad and Basra to put their point of view to the grave and gentle stranger. Jewish converts to Islam and harassed Armenians opened their hearts to him in the shelter of that garden with a freedom which they could not feel with others. Shiahs and Sufis thronged the house to ply him with questions; Mullahs and Moulvies called on him to test his learning. Those long hours of leisurely discussion so took their toll of his time that six months soon stretched into a year, and the Muslim doctors were at a loss to know what to admire the more in that pale and solitary missionary: should it be his skill in argument, or his gifts of persuasion? They were aware of his ability when he drove the Mullahs to an impasse; and they sensed his humility when he brought the gospel to the rescue. One young Muslim who came to scoff was led at last to grasp the truth, and he received one of the first copies of the Persian New Testament. Many years later, Rahim confessed his faith to a Christian traveller and showed him this precious volume. On one of the flyleaves, the words could still be read: 'There is joy in heaven over one sinner that repenteth. Henry Martyn.'[172]

The atmosphere of excitement which filled Shiraz as a result of his presence led to a long round of controversy with some of the leading Muslims in the kingdom. The first contest occurred in the house of the Moojtahid on 15 July 1811. He was one of the four authorities among the Sufis in Persia, and his abortive encounter with the Christian Feringhie only served to fan the general excitement. A fresh debate of more decisive character took place on 4 February 1812, and was only terminated when his antagonists refused to ask any further questions. He had been taxed with the faults and foibles of the sacred authors and his answer was a resolute assertion that their human infirmities could not detract from their divine authority. But the supreme confrontation took place on 12 June at a levée held by the Vizier in the court at Teheran. He was challenged to acknowledge that Allah is God, and that Mohammed is his prophet. The moment was fraught with danger, but his reply was immediate and spontaneous. It ranks him with the most intrepid confessors of the Divine Sonship of Christ, and it almost precipitated his death. 'God is God', he said, 'and Jesus is the Son of God.'[173]

Oral contests led to debate in print, and it fell to his lot, without books to consult, without friends to advise, to bear the full brunt of attack. The chief Mullah in the country had drawn up a Muslim apologia which was said to outweigh all its antecedents and was meant to silence him for ever. But he took up his pen and brought out a reply in the form of a tract. He pressed home a skilful argument to its ruthless conclusion, and matched the strength of the argument with the courtesy of his appeal. This tract passed from hand to hand and percolated throughout Persia. It came to the court of the Shah, who was so concerned that he ordered one of the most renowned controversialists to prepare a reply. Henry Martyn was dead before the reply could appear, but the

Muslim community was so ashamed of its weakness that it was soon suppressed.[174] But the controversy had taught Henry Martyn with a vivid sense of reality that the only key to Muslim thought lies in the integrity and authority of Scripture, and the mighty weapon which he longed to forge was the New Testament in their own language.

'HENCEFORTH LET CHRIST LIVE'

Meanwhile, Henry Martyn had to grapple with an illness which smouldered and threatened in turn, and his hold on life was far from secure. Sometimes his cheeks were reddened with a flush like fire; sometimes his face was pallid with the look of death. But all this went on side by side with his love for Lydia Grenfell which burned with a steady flame and was never far from the surface. It must have seemed as though the end had come when he received her letter on Christmas Day in 1809; but the death of Sally led to a fresh correspondence. He had perhaps ceased to cherish any real hope that he would gain her hand, but her image was still in the background of all his dreams. He felt like a man who could not have her with him, yet did not know how to live without her. The strange world of Shiraz, with its carpets and cushions, or its fountains and orchards, was far less real to him than that other dream world where he walked with her in spirit through the fields of glory. Perhaps one main reason why his Journals touch the heart as so few similar manuals do is because they are full of this most human of all personal interests. They provide an unadorned narrative of the hard-won conquest of self for the Lord's sake. This stands out in what he wrote on 17 February 1811: 'As for self, contemptible self, I feel myself saying, let it be forgotten for ever, henceforth let Christ live, let

Christ reign, let Him be glorified for ever.'[175] This was not the easy triumph of some sexless spirit; he had all the virile passion of a man like all men in his ardent longing for the woman of his choice and desire. The whole story has a wistful pathos which did not cease until he ceased to breathe, and it is steeped in his struggle for the perfect purity of a perfect surrender. He loved as all men love, but his love was transformed by the power of sacrificial denial. He was willing to give up all for the kingdom of God, and that meant all hope of wife and home and earthly comfort. But one may ask, Had not God some better thing for him in that life which knows no pain nor loss?

On 23 March 1810, he received Simeon's letter telling him of Sally's death, and his sense of loneliness increased. 'I have not a relation left to whom I feel bound by the ties of Christian fellowship', he wrote, 'and I am resolved to form no new connection of a worldly nature so that I may henceforward hope to live entirely as a man of another world.'[176] This was followed by an unexpected letter from Lydia Grenfell, offering to correspond with him in place of that last dear sister. On 30 March, his letter in reply gratefully accepted this fresh, though still hesitant, overture.[177] It is unfortunate that none of her letters survives, but this was the first of eleven which he wrote during the last phase of his life. They were tempered with an exquisite courtesy in view of the terms which she had imposed, for he knew that he was meant to sink the lover in a brotherly attitude. But she was no less his dearest and his love throbs through the guarded language.

'When I first heard of the loss I was likely to suffer', he wrote, 'and began to reflect on my own friendless situation, you were much in my thoughts, whether you would be silent on this occasion or not . . . When month after month passed away and no letter came from you, I almost abandoned the hope of ever hearing from you again. It only remained to wait the result of my last application through Emma. You have kindly anticipated my request, and I need scarcely add, are more endeared to me than ever.'[178] On 19 April he mentioned his physical condition, and then wrote with infinite tenderness: 'Death, I think, would be a less welcome visitor to me if he came to take me from a wife, and that wife were you.'[179] Before these two letters could reach her in Cornwall, she was informed of the marriage of her former suitor; it was news which rolled a great load from her mind and fanned her love for Henry Martyn.[180] On 8 August he wrote in his Journal: 'My thoughts today very much towards Lydia; I began even to be reconciled to the idea of going to England for her.'[181] His third letter on 14 August shows that he had begun to toy with this thought in earnest; and yet, conscious of his illness, he felt that they were not likely to meet until they met in the realms of glory.[182] On 6 October, as he floated down the Ganges, he touched on a remark in which she had referred to the prospect of his return, and went on to say that she ought to see it as her duty not to let him sail from England again unless she were to sail with him.[183]

His fifth letter was written while at sea off the coast of Malabar on 4 February 1811[184], and his sixth from Muscat on the coast of Arabia on 22 April.[185] Both are filled with details of the voyage and with projects for the gospel. On 23 June he wrote from Shiraz in terms of wistful reminiscence. 'It is true', he said, 'that I cannot look back upon many days, nor even many hours, passed with you; would they had been more; but we have insensibly become more acquainted with each other so that on my part at least, it may be said that separation has brought us nearer to one another. It was a momentary interview,

but the love is lasting, everlasting.'[186] But he was grieved
that in constant journeys and distant outposts he had
not yet had a single reply to the seven letters he had
written since March 1810.[187] On 8 September he wrote
again from Shiraz, and his heart was sore with loneliness
and love.[188] On 21 October his ninth letter was tender
and wistful in its longing to hear from her and to have
some reassurance. 'When I sit and muse', he wrote, 'my
spirit flies away to you and attends you at Gurlyn . . . If
you acknowledge a kindred feeling still, we are not
separated, our spirits have met and blended.'[189] His next
letter was penned in great pain and debility at Tebriz on
8 July 1812: it was to thank her for one of her own letters,
the only one ever to reach his hand, and to tell her that
though he had applied for home leave, there was scant
hope that he would reach England alive. 'Whether I shall
gain strength enough to go on rests on our heavenly
Father in whose hands are all my times. His eternal,
unchanging love in Christ to my soul never appeared more
clear, more sweet, more strong.'[190] 'The final letter on
28 August was also from Tebriz, and it set his earthly
love once more in a heavenly perspective as he spoke of
the hope that they would meet again. 'Do I dream that I
venture to think and write of such an event as that? Is it
possible that we shall ever meet again below?'[191] Did he
dream that he would need pen and ink no more, but
would soon see her face to face? It was a dream; those
were his last words to one he had loved so well. Seven
weeks later, while pressing on his way home, he reached
the end of his earthly pilgrimage and entered into the joy
of that love which knows no measure nor end.

Meanwhile he had been at work in Shiraz on what Mrs
Sherwood described as 'the court language of the East
. . . the softest, most elegant and melodious' of all oriental

tongues and dialects.[192] He had become increasingly
aware of the values of such a work during his residence in
India, and had written on 18 May 1807: 'The Persian
translation has appeared to me of late of incalculable
importance. One may safely say it is of more consequence
than any three of the Indian languages, Sanskrit excepted,
spoken as it is all the way from hence to Damascus.'[193]
He was absorbed in this work when the new year dawned
on 1 January 1812, and he wrote: 'To all outward appearance, the present year will be more perilous than any I
have seen, but if I live to complete the Persian New
Testament, my life after that will be of less importance.
But whether life or death be mine, may Christ be
magnified in me. If He has work for me to do, I cannot
die.'[194] The translation was completed during February,
barely eight months after he had arrived in Shiraz. 'I have
many mercies for which to thank the Lord, and this is
not the least', he wrote when the last sheet had been
finished. 'Now may that Spirit Who gave the word and
called me, I trust, to be an interpreter of it, graciously
and powerfully apply it to the hearts of sinners, even to
the gathering of an elect people from amongst the long
estranged Persians.'[195] Three months more were spent in
Shiraz while copies were being prepared, and in March
he completed a translation of the Hebrew Psalter as well.
He had arranged for two copies of the New Testament
to be prepared in the beautiful lettering of the finest
Persian calligraphy for the Shah and his son, while four
other copies were made and sent direct to the printing
press at Calcutta. It fell to the British Ambassador in due
course to place the presentation copy in the hands of the
Shah. Later still he placed a copy in the hands of Prince
Galitzin, the President of the Russian Bible Society, and
the first edition was printed at Petersburg in September

1815. Another edition was produced at Calcutta in 1816, and three more were printed in London and Edinburgh during the next thirty years.[196] It was the crowning effort of his life; it is perhaps still his highest title to be held in enduring remembrance.

On 11 May 1812 he left Shiraz, joining a caravan which was ready to start at ten o'clock that night. He had to cross the great Persian desert plateau on his way to Tebriz, where he hoped to secure a letter of introduction from the British Ambassador to the court of the Shah. That long summer journey of more than a thousand miles across the arid wastes of central Persia was to cost eight weeks of gruelling travel, broken only by a week at Isfahan and again at Teheran. Want of food, lack of sleep, and the double furnace of the fire in his chest and the sun in the sky were to accelerate all the symptoms of his disease. Even before he left Shiraz, he was often subject to distress in breathing and a hollow sense of pain which was aggravated by frequent debate. Now he shivered in the cold night air or sweltered under the sun at noon, and the marvel was that he kept his seat in the saddle at all in the delirium which marked the last stages of his journey. It was 5 July when at last he reached the gates of Tebriz; he was so ill that he could only ask with a feeble voice for a guide to the home of Sir Gore Ouseley. Four days later, on 9 July, he wrote to ask Charles Grant for leave to go home to England: 'but', he noted, 'I have scarcely the remotest expectation of seeing it, except by looking at the almighty power of God.'[197] The courier for Constantinople was delayed and this allowed him time to write to Lydia and Simeon as well; but the feverish memory of his busy life at Cambridge made him apprehensive lest Simeon should disapprove. 'But you would not', he said, 'were you to see the pitiable condition to which I am reduced.'[198] Then the Tartar horseman galloped away, leaving him in a state close to delirium.[199] His frail spirit seemed to hover on the margin of the unseen; it was perhaps only the hope that he might reach home that buoyed him up and brought him back from the shadows of death. The climate of Tebriz was ideal for convalescence, and he was nursed by Sir Gore and Lady Ouseley with as much care as if he were their son. At last, six weeks later, he could write on 20 August: 'A day very much to be remembered for the remarkable recovery of strength with which it pleased God to favour me. I immediately began to gird up my loins and prepare myself for my journey.'[200]

He could have stayed longer with great personal advantage, but he was in haste to be gone as soon as his strength would permit. Sir Gore Ouseley procured horses for him as far as Erivan and gave him letters for use in Turkey. It was sunset on 2 September when he left the western gate of Tebriz on the long and doubtful venture, while his hosts looked on with anxious eyes and measured his strength against the toll of that journey. It would have been formidable for a strong man in far better circumstances; for him, it was the last long ride in a losing race with the pale horseman of death. It was thirteen hundred miles from Tebriz to Constantinople, and his dauntless spirit drove his wasting body on for forty-five days until he could go no further. He rode his own horses, and was accompanied by a guide and two Armenian servants. The plan was to travel by day and lodge by night at post stations en route. These were often little better than huts with mud walls on three sides; sometimes they were used as stables and were deep in manure. His strength held out while he was still on Persian soil, and he crossed the Araxes and left Ararat on his left on the fifth day of travel.

On 10 September he wrote briefly in his Journal: 'All day at the village, writing down notes on the 15th and 16th Psalm. Moved at midnight and arrived early in the morning at Erivan.'[201] He called on the provincial governor and then rode to Etchmiazin, which was to the Armenians all that Jerusalem was to the Jews. He was still in Persian territory, although this was the heart of ancient Armenia and is now part of Soviet Russia. He spent the day with a young monk of his own age, and when the bell rang for vespers accompanied him to a church which had survived all the vicissitudes of time. The next day he was received by the Patriarch with a courtesy which made him feel as welcome as though he were a brother.[202] He left Etchmiazin on 17 September and Erivan the next morning, equipped by the Armenians with a new train and fresh baggage, and by the provincial governor with a new guide and fresh horses. One day later, on 19 September, he passed from the Persian province of Erivan into the domains of Turkey.

His new escort was the Tartar Hassan, and troubles soon began. A man who flogged his horse until it fell beneath its load had a worse effect on him than the daily alarms from the Kurdish robbers.[203] He reached Erzerum on 25 September, paused for four days, and then set out again only to find himself in the grip of ague and fever. He was warned that plague had broken out in Tokat, and he knew that his life was in some danger. But there was no respite on the mountain trail of some two hundred miles to Tokat. 'Hassan had no mercy' as they travelled by day and night, in spite of cold and rain and ague.[204] There was a halt for three or four hours at dawn on 4 October; then they hurried on and rode till nightfall. At last Martyn got off his horse and said that he neither could, nor would, go further. He found refuge in a stable where he hoped that he would be left alone; but the others crowded in round a fire until he was almost frantic with heat and fever. 'At last', he wrote, 'I pushed my head in among the luggage, and lodged it on the damp ground, and slept.'[205] He was still feeble and shaken when he awoke, but Hassan was ruthless and hurried him away. It was a short ride and he was well lodged, but a shivering bout was followed by a feverish night which made sleep impossible. Morning brought a welcome respite because no horses were available. It was 6 October and he wrote in comparative tranquillity: 'I sat in the orchard and thought with sweet comfort and peace of my God; in solitude my company, my friend and comforter. Oh! When shall time give place to eternity! When shall appear that new heaven and new earth wherein dwelleth righteousness!'[206] This marks the close of his Journal and a veil of silence descends on the ten days which still remained. Did he manage to reach Tokat with the reins still in his own hands? Or was he at the last too weak to keep his seat in the saddle? We do not know; we know only that in Tokat itself on 16 October 1812, like the evening sun which sinks with golden glory beyond the rim of earth or sea, his bright spirit passed in lonely splendour beyond the world of space and time.

Tokat lies at the head of a valley beneath a line of hills about five hundred and fifty miles from Istanbul, as Constantinople is now called. At the end of World War I, it still had sixteen churches, some Orthodox, some Armenian, and its population was more Christian than Muslim. Fifty years later when I travelled to Tokat in September 1968, all the churches had gone, no Greeks were left, and there were less than two hundred Armenians in the city. But in 1812 Henry Martyn was well known as a friend of the Armenians; he was indeed accompanied on his final journey by two Armenian servants. He was buried by the Armenians in the cemetery of their church of Karasoon Manoog, and a limestone slab was set up with an inscription in Latin. 'Men in 1854 when Dr Henry van Lennep made his home in Tokat as a missionary, he found that the grave was covered to a depth of two feet by soil washed down from the mountains. As a result, he arranged to remove the remains which were reinterred in the first grave of the newly opened missionary cemetery, and a grant from the Board of the East India Company provided for the erection of a suitable monument. This was made by local workmen and cut out of native marble. Each face bore the name of Henry Martyn in English or Armenian or Turkish or Persian. The four sides at the base of the obelisk had an inscription in the same four languages and the last two lines were a simple tribute which read in English: 'He will long be remembered in the East where he was known as a man of God.' But in 1968, this grave could no longer be seen, for the cemetery had been resigned as a site for a school. The obelisk itself would have been destroyed but for the interest of the director of a museum which is located in the semi-ruins of a church which stood opposite to the former cemetery. The director took possession of the obelisk and placed it in his museum, where it now stands. The name has been scratched out on all four sides, and the inscription in Armenian, Turkish and Persian has been defaced. But there is no doubt as to the identity of the obelisk, for the inscription in English is intact. The grave of Henry Martyn like that of Moses is now unknown, but he was a burning and a shining light in his own generation. That light went out on earth when he died at Tokat; but it went out only that he might burn and shine with cherubim and seraphim before the throne of God for ever.

ADDITIONAL NOTES

NOTE ONE: FAMILY CONNECTIONS

Henry Martyn's father was John Martyn. He was born in Gwennap, not far from the famous hollow or pit in which Wesley preached seventeen times in twenty-seven years. In due course he came to live in Truro where his house stood opposite the old Coinage Hall. He was married twice, but little is known of his first wife. She had a son who was called John after her husband; he was born in 1766, but she does not seem to have lived much longer. Some time after her death, John Martyn married Elizabeth Fleming from Ilfracombe in Devon. She died in 1782, after the loss of several children in infancy and after the birth of her youngest daughter. John and Elizabeth Martyn had three children who did survive:

1. Laura, 1779–1807, who married the Rev. Mr Curgenven, curate of Kenwyn and Kea.
2. Henry, 1781–1812, who was a curate of Charles Simeon and a chaplain with the East India Company.
3. Sally, 1782–1810, who married the Rev. Mr Pearson, curate of Lamorran and Penkevil.

John Martyn's first cousin was the Rev. Malachy Hitchins, vicar of St Hilary with its Chapel-of-ease at Marazion. St Hilary was one of the oldest churches in Cornwall, standing on a wooded hilltop twenty-five miles from Truro. Marazion, opposite St Michael's Mount, was a mile and a half further down the road to Penzance. Malachy's son was the Rev. Thomas Martyn Hitchins who married Emma Grenfell, Lydia's elder sister, and who had a church in Plymouth. Henry Martyn and Tom Hitchins were second cousins who had played with each other as boys in the vicarage garden at St Hilary. The

Grenfells lived in a plain but substantial home opposite the Chapel-of-ease in the street that climbed up towards Marazion. References in the Journal to Gurlyn are puzzling. In 1982 this was the name of a farm about half a mile down a steep hill from St Hilary on the road to Helston. But what Lydia's connection was with Gurlyn is not now clear. Perhaps it was the name of her home in Marazion.

NOTE TWO: LYDIA GRENFELL

Lydia Grenfell's Diary is highly subjective in character. Introspection is mingled with aspiration as she strove to renounce the claims of self and fix her eyes on heaven. It throws some light on her relationship with Samuel John and the attitude of her family. Here and there it also has some priceless references to her love for Henry Martyn. She heard the news of his death on 14 February 1813 and wrote of it in her Diary six days later: 'I am fearful to retrace the last week on two accounts, lest the infirmity of nature prevail and I give way to sorrow, and lest in recollecting the wondrous kindness and love of God my Saviour I increase my pride and not my gratitude . . . Heard on the 14th of the removal of my most tender, faithful and beloved friend to the joys of heaven. Oh, I could not wish his absence from them prolonged. What I only wished was, and now I am reconciled to that too, I wished to have been honoured of God so far as to have been near him.'[207] Other entries were made at intervals. On 2 March she wrote: 'Some sorrowful thoughts will enter my mind respecting my late dear friend, and call forth some sighs and tears from my heart; yet is that heart resigned to the will of God, and confident of His having done all things well for His beloved servant.'[208] On

21 April she received his letter from Tebriz, written the year before on 28 August: 'O Thou who readest my heart, direct and sanctify every feeling. May the anguish of my soul be moderated and let me endeavour to exercise faith in Thy divine goodness, mercy and power, and to believe it was well with him in all respects.'[209] And on 3 June: 'It is strange that I should now be more in danger of loving too well a creature passed into the skies than when he lived on earth. But so it is; continually my thoughts revert to him.'[210] Year by year she recalled his love for her and hers for him on the date of his death. On 11 January 1823, she had a print of his portrait hung on the wall in her bedroom. 'Felt affected greatly in doing so, and my tears which seldom flow in the presence of anyone, I could not restrain before the person who was fixing it.'[211] She remained unmarried and suffered greatly from some form of cancer in her last years. Emma Hitchins added her own postscript to Lydia's last reference in which she had expressed her heartfelt longing to be united with him in heaven: 'This prayer was answered on September 21st 1829.'[212]

NOTE THREE: THE BATTLE OF BLAAUWBERG

An article in the *Standard Encyclopaedia of Southern Africa*, coupled with an on-the-spot inspection of the tract of country between Melkbosstrand and Cape Town, provides a clear picture of the locale for the Battle of Blaauwberg, as George Smith spelt it, or Blouberg, as it is spelt today. In August 1805, while the French army was waiting at Boulogne for the invasion of England, a British fleet sailed on a secret mission. This was to capture the Cape which was still part of the Batavian Republic, at that time an ally of France. There were sixty-one vessels under the command of Sir Home Popham and 6,654 soldiers under that of Sir David Baird. Advance reports of this project had reached Lt General J. W. Janssens, Governor of the Cape, and he had prepared as well as he could for the expected attack; but he only had a small and motley force which included some four hundred German, Austrian, and Hungarian mercenaries.

On the evening of 4 January 1806, the fleet dropped anchor between Robben Island and Blaauwberg, and Baird proposed to land in the bay where Melkbosstrand is now situated. But the weather in the morning was too stormy and the landing was postponed until 6 January. Several regiments then went ashore. One boat capsized on the rocks in the surf, and out of sixty-three men on board only seven were saved. Only one other life was lost, but six men were wounded in a skirmish with some of the burghers. Henry Martyn's regiment, the 59th, and the rest of the armed forces landed the next morning.[213]

Janssens spent the night of 7 January in the sand-dunes at Rietoli instead of occupying the summit of Blaauwberg, a hill 750 feet high, a little to the north of the beach where the landing took place. The word means 'blue mountain' because of the colour of the hill as seen from ships approaching Table Bay. At 3:00 a.m. Janssens ordered an advance to halt the British, but his troops were driven off the slopes of Blaauwberg. He then lined up his troops at the southern end of the mountain to await the British attack. The Cape burghers with their French and Hottentot allies held out as long as they could, but the German mercenaries beat a retreat. The British casualties were 15 killed, 189 wounded, 8 missing. The Cape losses have been variously estimated as between 337 and 700 killed and wounded. Janssens, himself slightly wounded, ordered a retreat, but the British were so exhausted by their march across the hot sand-dunes without water that they could not keep up the pursuit.

Henry Martyn had watched the landing from his ship. He went ashore a few hours after the battle and saw the dead and wounded lying where they had fallen. 'I . . . marched six miles through the soft burning sand', he wrote, 'trying to minister to those who were mortally wounded.'[214] They cried out for water. He cast his eyes over the plain which had been the scene of so much bloodshed, and he drew fresh inspiration from 'the blue mountains on the east where I conceived the missionaries labouring to spread the Gospel of peace and love.'[215]

Janssens regrouped his force at Rietoli, then withdrew to Hottentot Holland, leaving the German mercenaries to man the Castle in Cape Town under Count C. Von Prophalow. But at sunrise on 10 January, the British flag was seen flying from the Castle ramparts. Terms of capitulation had been signed, and eight days later Janssens laid down his arms.

The Battle of Blaauwberg was a major milestone in the early history of South Africa, and it fired Henry Martyn's spiritual vision. 'I prayed', he wrote, 'that the capture of the Cape might be ordered to the advancement of Christ's kingdom, and that England, while she sent the thunder of her arms to the distant regions of the globe . . . might show herself great indeed by sending forth the ministers of her church to diffuse the Gospel of peace.'[216]

NOTE FOUR: IN HENRY MARTYN'S FOOTSTEPS

Local colour, derived from a visit to the major places through which Henry Martyn had to travel or where he was stationed, has proved very helpful. Many of those places were seen by me during the years between 1958 and 1968; there were others that lay beyond my reach.

The list reads as follows: Blaauwberg, but not San Salvador; Calcutta and Serampore; Patna, but not Cawnpore; Bombay, but not Goa; Muscat and Bushire; Shiraz, but not Tebriz; Tokat, but not Erivan. A few extra details largely gleaned from such visits may be welcome.

Henry Martyn's spiritual home in Calcutta was the Old Mission Church, built by the Swedish missionary John Zachary Kiernander in 1770. It was the only church in Bengal until the New Church of St John was consecrated in 1787, and it was the centre of evangelical life and worship in the heart of the old city. David Brown, friend of Charles Simeon and Fellow of Magdalen College, recovering from a long illness in 1785, had gone out to Calcutta as a newly ordained deacon in 1786. The Old Mission Church passed into the hands of three Trustees, Charles Grant, David Brown, and William Chambers, during 1787, and David Brown served as its minister until his death in 1812. 'In course of time he came to exercise an outstanding influence on the whole of English society in Calcutta.'[217] I had the great pleasure of preaching in the Old Mission Church in 1958 and in 1960.

David Brown's home was at Aldeen, several miles up river from Calcutta and next door to the Serampore settlement of Carey, Ward, and Marshman. Its lawns swept down to the Hooghly opposite Barrackpore, and the deserted pagoda in which Henry Martyn chose to sleep and study was close to the river. No trace of the house or gardens remains today; they have all been reclaimed for the Howrah Water Works. But the pagoda still stands in moderately good condition, with a plaque to indicate that it was once the temporary home of Henry Martyn. I saw it in May 1958, January 1960, and February 1979.

I spent twenty-four hours in Patna in January 1960 and was driven along the banks of the Ganges through the district of Dinapore. There was nothing that could be identified with Henry Martyn except the ever passing parade which also had its quota of beggars and urchins. I could not visit Cawnpore, but the converted bungalow which Henry Martyn set apart for church worship continued to serve as a church for the garrison until it was destroyed in the Mutiny of 1857.

I will never forget spending the last days of 1967 in Muscat and sharing in a morning service in Arabic and an evening service in English on Sunday, 31 December. There I was in Muscat, with its harbour and the mountains in the background, its walls and forts, and the oasis some miles inland with its 'little bit of green in the wilderness'. Muscat dropped out of view from the missionary angle until 1889 when Alexander Mackay in Uganda declared that the slave trade between Africa and Arabia would never be broken until Muscat had been occupied in the name of Christ. This made a strong appeal to the veteran missionary, Thomas Valpy French, who had spent much of his life in India. He had been the last European to enter the Fort at Agra during the Indian Mutiny, toiling along, bag in hand, with a huge Arabic dictionary inside. He had retired as Bishop of Lahore and returned to England in 1887. Mackay's appeal touched a chord in his heart which he could not resist. He was sixty-five years old, but he left England in November 1890 to spend what remained of his life in this lonely outpost. It was eighty years since Henry Martyn's brief visit to Muscat, and Valpy French was the first missionary to make a deliberate attempt to live and work among its people. He arrived on 8 February 1891, made his home in a borrowed house and began to plan a journey inland; but he only survived for ninety-five days. Heat, and age, and severe dysentery were too much for his frail state of health.

He died on 14 May and was buried in a rocky recess on the coastline where the mountains come down to the edge of the sea. The grave is lapped by the water at high tide, but the gravestone is inscribed in Arabic and English: 'The first Bishop of Lahore and the first missionary to Muscat.' I stood by that grave and thought of Henry Martyn who had briefly touched Muscat eighty years before.

Bushire, on the Persian Gulf, was Henry Martyn's point of entry into Persia. It is hot, though not so hot as Muscat. The once prosperous Armenian community has long since been dispersed, and the little church where Martyn worshipped is no longer in use. But it still stands, and on 14 July 1964 I was allowed to hold an English Communion Service in its peaceful sanctuary. There were only three others present, but my mind was full of Henry Martyn. I was driven across the ninety miles of sun-scorched plain to the foot of the mountains, and was fascinated to find that the mule track up which Martyn had to ride to reach the mountain plateau is still easy to trace. It runs fairly close to the road which was built by British soldiers in World War I. John Coleman, a missionary doctor in the C.M.S. Hospital at Shiraz, made my journey possible.

It was a great pleasure to spend some days in the garden city of Shiraz during that July. Nothing was more thrilling than to visit the house and the orchard which once belonged to Jaffir Ali Khan and to picture Henry Martyn sitting near the fountain to explain the gospel or to pursue his New Testament translation. The long journey after leaving Shiraz took me as it took him via Isfahan to Teheran, the city in which he had a perilous encounter with the threatening Vizier. In the home of the Rev. David Gurney I met the Rev. Jollynoos Hakim, an elderly clergyman who had been a convert from Judaism. His grandfather, so he claimed, had been a physician in the court of the Shah at the time when Henry Martyn was in Tebriz. Mr Hakim died in 1971.

I had followed Henry Martyn from Bushire to Teheran, but I could not follow him to Tebriz, still less to Erivan, and least of all to Tokat. But in 1968 I did travel from Ankara to Tokat and was able to locate the obelisk which had been erected over his grave. I was then driven some six miles beyond Tokat to what was said to be the site of the tel where the village of Komana once stood. A huge rock, perhaps twenty feet high, with an inscription in large capital letters in Greek, about half a mile from the tel, was said to mark the site of the chapel where the golden-mouthed orator John Chrysostom died in 407 A.D. Chrysostom had been driven out of Constantinople by the Empress Eudoxia and sent into exile in the heat of summer. His guards were, like Hassan, men who had no mercy. They forced him to travel by foot from place to place by night and day for three grim months until they reached the village of Komana. Frail and fever stricken, Chrysostom could go no further. He was allowed to halt at the chapel of the martyr Basiliscus. There, on 14 September 407, he died after murmuring his favourite doxology: 'Glory be to God for all things.' He died fourteen hundred years before Henry Martyn, but in the same vicinity and much the same circumstances. They trod the same kind of *via dolorosa*, the one travelling east and passing Tokat to reach Komana, and the other travelling west and passing Komana to reach Tokat. Chrysostom was 59; Henry Martyn was 31.

Henry Martyn was the first missionary to the world of Islam since the valiant enterprise of the Spanish knight and aristocrat, Ramon Lull, five hundred years before. Ramon Lull renounced all earthly honour and material comfort in order to obey the will and call of God. Three times he went to the coast of North Africa to preach to the Saracens. On 30 June 1315, during his third visit, he was stoned to death at Tunis. Henry Martyn may never have had Ramon Lull in mind, but they were cast in the same mould. They were so constrained by the love of Christ that all idea of sacrifice had disappeared from their horizon.

NOTE FIVE: HENRY MARTYN'S SERMONS

The Rev. E. T. Sandys and the Rev. G. F. Westcott in their book *One Hundred and Seventy-Five Years at the Old or Mission Church Calcutta* furnish details of the dates when, and the texts on which, Henry Martyn preached during the five months from May to October 1806.

1. May 22:   Thursday; 1 Corinthians 1:1–3, 'to a modestly large congregation'.
2. May 25:   Sunday; 1 Timothy 1:15.
3. June 1:   Sunday; Matthew 28:18–20.
4. June 4:   Wednesday; text not recorded, but he remarked: 'Grieved that I could not speak with plainness and affection to the people.'
5. June 8:   Sunday; 1 Corinthians 1:23–24. This was his first sermon at the New Church of St John's, and it caused no little comment.
6. June 8:   Sunday evening; 2 Corinthians 5:9; at the Old Mission Church.
7. June 29:   Sunday; Daniel 5:23–24.
8. July 6:   Sunday; John 4:4–10.
9. July 13:   Sunday; Ephesians 2:1–3.

10. July 16:   Wednesday; Isaiah 63:1.
11. July 27:   Sunday; Ephesians 2:4–7.
12. August 3:   Sunday; John 1:14.
13. August 6:   Wednesday; text not recorded, but he
                      observed: 'There were few people at
                      church, and those not very attentive.'
14. August 10:   Sunday; John 1:29; under difficulty
                      as a heavy squall came on.
15. August 13:   Wednesday; Matthew 3:21–23.
16. August 21:   Thursday; Isaiah 4:3.
17. September 7:   Sunday; Mark 8:34–35.
18. September 14:   Sunday; 2 Corinthians 4:17–18.
19. September 21:   Sunday; Acts 16:19–21. Sandys and
                      Westcott note the text for this sermon
                      as 'Acts 12. The jailer's question'. But
                      Acts 12 should have read Acts 16.
20. September 21:   Sunday afternoon at three o'clock;
                      Romans 3:21–23 at the New Church.
                      Corrie said that this was 'the most
                      impressive and best composition I
                      have ever heard'.
21. October 1:   Wednesday; Ephesians 2:4.
22. October 8:   Wednesday; Isaiah 52:7.
23. October 12:   Sunday; Acts 20:32. He noted that
                      with these words, 'I took my leave of
                      the saints in Calcutta.'

All but one of these twenty-three sermons were
mentioned in the Journals and Letters. The exception
was: 'August 21: Thursday; at the Old Mission Church;
Isaiah 4:3.' It should also be noted that the dates for the
first two are wrongly given in the Journals; that is, May
21 should read May 22, and May 24 should read May
25. Further, there is a discrepancy as to the text on Sunday,

September 14. The Journals and Letters say that it was 2 Corinthians 6:17–18; Sandys and Westcott say that it was 2 Corinthians 4:17–18. The Journals and Letters also record several sermons which escaped the notice of Sandys and Westcott:

1. June 22:   Sunday; John 10:2; at the Old Church.
2. June 29:   Sunday; Romans 7:18; at the New Church.
3. July 20:   Sunday; 2 Corinthians 5:17; at the New Church.
4. August 10:   Sunday; Acts 3:26; at the New Church.
5. August 24:   Sunday; Matthew 11:28; at the New Church.
6. August 31:   Sunday; Romans 3:19; at the New Church.
7. August 31:   Sunday; Isaiah 4:5; at the Old Church.

This list of thirty sermons includes twenty-two preached on Sundays; six on Wednesdays; and two on Thursdays. Twenty-three were preached in the Old Mission Church, and seven in the New Church of St John's. Eight of them were included in the collection of Sermons by the late Rev. Henry Martyn B.D., published by the Church Mission Press at Calcutta in 1822. These were the sermons on 1 Corinthians 1:1–3; 1 Corinthians 1:23–24; Ephesians 2:1–3; 2 Corinthians 5:17; Ephesians 2:4–7; Acts 3:26; Acts 16:29–31; Matthew 28:18–20. This volume of sermons lacks the warmth of direct contact with the preacher or of living rapport with the congregation. But they afford a clear idea of the faithful exposition of the Scriptures by Simeon's favourite disciple.

Henry Martyn was again in Aldeen and Calcutta from 21 October 1810 to 7 January 1811. The Journals and Letters record twelve sermons during that period, all preached in the Old Mission Church:

1. November 11: Sunday; Colossians 2:6.
2. November 18: Sunday; Acts 14:22.
3. November 25: Sunday; Acts 24:25.
4. December 2: Sunday; Romans 5:20–21.
5. December 9: Sunday; Jeremiah 17:9.
6. December 16: Sunday; Hebrews 9:22.
7. December 23: Sunday; Psalm 9:17.
8. December 25: Christmas; John 3:16.
9. December 30: Sunday; Luke 16:31.
10. December 30: Sunday; Revelation 22:17.
11. January 1:   Tuesday; Galatians 6:10; on behalf of the Bible Society.
12. January 6:   Sunday; Luke 10:42.

The next morning he boarded a pinnace and slipped down the Hooghly. But he had preached on nine successive Sundays in spite of his fragile physical condition. All these sermons, except the last, were printed in the volume produced in 1822, though not in the order in which they were preached. A brief postscript may be added. T. R. Birks in his *Memoir of the Rev. Edward Bickersteth* (1856) noted that 'the Farewell Sermons of Henry Martyn were among the earliest circumstances that kindled [his] missionary spirit.'[218] When the Rev. G. T. Fox, an Association Secretary of the Church Missionary Society, brought out his small book, *Five Sermons by the late Henry Martyn,* in 1862, he stated that Henry Martyn had given 'the most vigorous impulse to missionary enterprise which our Church ever received'.[219]

NOTE SIX: THE SERAMPORE LIBRARY

In February 1979, I found the following works of Henry Martyn housed in the Serampore College Library:

1 1814: *The New Testament of our Lord and Saviour Jesus Christ,* translated into the Hindoostanee language from the original Greek by the Rev. Henry Martyn, and afterwards carefully revised with the assistance of Mirza Fitrit and other learned natives. (Serampore.)

2. 1817: Another edition with the same title except for the spelling Mirza Fitirut, published in Calcutta with the note that it was 'now printed in the Nagree character'.

3. 1819: Another edition, published by the British and Foreign Bible Society in London.

4. 1815: *Novum Testamentun Domini et Salvatoris Nostri Jesu Christi E Graeca in Persicam Linguam a viro reverendo Henrico Martyno translatum in urbe Schiras. Nunc vero cura et sumtibus Societatis Biblicae Ruthenicae typio datwn Petropoli apud Jos. Joannem 1815.*

5. 1824: *Controversial Tracts on Christianity and Mohammedanism* by the Rev. Henry Martyn and some of the Most Eminent Writers of Persia, translated and explained by the Rev. S. Lee. (Martyn's section pp. 80–100). (Cambridge.)

6 1825: *Psalms in Persian.* (Calcutta reprint.)

7. 1837: *The New Testament of Our Lord and Saviour Jesus Christ* translated from the original Greek into Persian by the Rev. Henry Martyn. (Fourth edition, published by the British and Foreign Bible Society in London.)

8. 1851: *The New Testament of Our Lord and Saviour Jesus Christ* translated from the original Greek into Persian at Sheeraz by the Rev. Henry Martyn, with the assistance of Meerza Sueid

Alee of Sheeraz. (Published by the American and Foreign Bible Society, at Calcutta, in 1851.)

NOTE SEVEN: HENRY MARTYN'S PORTRAIT

At Simeon's earnest request, Henry Martyn had his portrait etched in Calcutta in November 1810 before he sailed en route to Persia. It was unpacked at India House in London in early October 1812, and Simeon went down to see it without delay. He was not to know that at that very moment Henry Martyn's life was rapidly drawing to a close. He was not the kind of man to show his feelings in the presence of strangers, but he was moved and shocked by what he saw. It was a true likeness of the worn and wasted features of his friend, and he could not restrain himself as he read its story of pain and illness. 'I was so overpowered by the sight', he wrote on 14 October, 'that I could not bear to look upon it, but turned away, and went to a distance, covering my face, and in spite of every effort to the contrary, crying aloud with anguish.'[220]

The portrait was hung over the fireplace in his dining room, but at first he could not bear to let his eyes rest on it for more than a moment or so. 'The sight of our beloved Martyn's picture is such a reproach to me from day to day', so he wrote on 24 May 1814, 'that I can never keep my eyes fixed upon it for any time.'[221] But time went far to heal the wound and he used to look at it with peculiar affection. 'There!' he would say: 'See that blessed man! What an expression of countenance! No one looks at me as he does – he never takes his eyes off me; and seems always to be saying, "Be serious, Be in earnest, Don't trifle, Don't trifle."' Then he would smile, and bow gently to the portrait, and say: 'And I won't trifle; I won't trifle.'[222] No doubt it was a print of this portrait that Lydia Grenfell arranged to hang in her bedroom in January 1823 and found that she could not refrain from tears.

Note Eight: Henry Martyn Memorials

There are various memorials in honour of Henry Martyn. The walls of the Old Mission Church in Calcutta are lined with plaques which commemorate those who have been closely associated with its history. The names of Charles Grant and Claudius Buchanan, David Brown and Henry Martyn, are all preserved on those tablets. Then in Shiraz a very beautiful church was built by the Rev. Norman Sharpe, a gem of architecture in the traditional style of Persia. It does not bear the name of Henry Martyn; this would have been unwise. But it is, in effect, a true memorial of his devoted ministry while in that city. And in Tokat an obelisk was placed over his grave in 1854. Though the cemetery where the grave lay has now been built over, the monument, albeit largely defaced, still stands in the semi-ruins of a church now used as a museum.

The foundation stone for the Cathedral Church of St Mary in Truro was laid on 20 May 1880, and the Cathedral itself was consecrated on 3 November 1887. In due course three stained glass windows were placed in each bay of the north wall, depicting historic figures in the life of the church from the earliest times down to the nineteenth century. Henry Martyn is the central figure in the last bay, standing between John Keble and F. D. Maurice; but the bottom panel belongs wholly to him, represented as in conversation with the learned scholars of Shiraz.

When the Ridley Hall Chapel was dedicated on 1 February 1892, the stained glass windows depicted a series of historical figures including four small missionary portraits in the quatrefoils; one of these was Henry Martyn. There is also a frescoed figure of Henry Martyn on the southern side near the western end of the ceiling in Sir Giles Gilbert Scott's Chapel in St John's College. But more significant is the Henry Martyn Memorial Hall adjacent to Holy Trinity. The foundation stone was laid on 2 December 1886, and the Hall was opened on 18 October 1887. It was vested in the Trustees for the Church Missionary Union, and made available for a low rent to the Cambridge Inter-Collegiate Christian Union, the Church Society and kindred bodies. It became the home for the Daily Prayer Meeting, and its panelled walls bear the names of Cambridge men who have gone forth as missionaries. The inscription over the door reads as follows: 'To the inspiring memory of Henry Martyn, Scholar, Evangelist, Confessor, and Man of God, a later generation of his own Cambridge dedicates this home of Christian converse and counsel.'

Charles Simeon planned from the first to see that a memorial plaque was placed in Holy Trinity. This was carried out in due course, and the plaque is on the south wall of the chancel with the following inscription:

This tablet
is erected to the Memory of
The Rev. HENRY MARTYN, B.D.,
Fellow of St John's College,
and two years Curate of this Parish.

He gained by his talents the highest Academical honours;
but counting all loss for Christ,
he left his Native Country, and went into the East,

as a Chaplain of the Hon. East India Company.
There, having faithfully done the work of an Evangelist,
in preaching the Gospel of a crucified Redeemer,
in translating the Holy Scriptures into the
Oriental Languages,
and in defending the Christian Faith in the heart of Persia
against the united talents of the most learned Mahometans,
he died at Tokat on the 16th of October, 1812,
in the 31st year of his age.[223]
The chief monuments which he left of his piety and talents
are Translations of the New Testament
Into the Hindoostanee and Persian Languages;
and 'by these he, being dead, yet speaketh.'
'Pray ye the Lord of the harvest, that
He will send forth labourers into His harvest.'

BIBLIOGRAPHY

The manuscript of Lydia Grenfell's Diary has been preserved in the library of the Royal Institution of Cornwall at Truro. It was begun on her twenty-seventh birthday and it extends from 19 October 1801 to 18 June 1826. It runs to some two thousand pages. Extracts were published by a great nephew, Henry Martyn Jeffery, in 1890.

1. 1819 – JOHN SARGENT, *A Memoir of Henry Martyn*
[My copy is the 16th edition, 1848].
2. 1822 – HENRY MARTYN, *Sermons*
[printed by the Church Mission Press, Calcutta].
3. 1837 – HENRY MARTYN, *Journals and Letters*
[edited by Samuel Wilberforce in two volumes].
4. 1844 – HENRY MARTYN, *Letters*
5. 1847 – WILLIAM CARUS, *Memoirs of the Life of the Rev. Charles Simeon.*

6. 1862 – HENRY MARTYN, *Five Sermons*
[edited by the Rev G. T. Fox, M.A.].

7. 1863 – ABNER WILLIAM BROWN, *Recollections of the Conversation Parties of the Rev. Charles Simeon.*

8. 1875 – JAMES STEPHEN, *Essays in Ecclesiastical Biography* [my copy marked as a 'new edition'.]

9. 1886 – CHARLES D. BELL, *Henry Martyn* [sixth thousand]

10. 1892 – GEORGE SMITH, *Henry Martyn, Saint and Scholar.*

11. 1892 – H. C. G. MOULE, *Charles Simeon.*

12. 1900 – S. M. ZWEMER, *Arabia, The Cradle of Islam.*

13. 1910 – F. J. HARVEY DUTTON, *The Life and Times of Mrs Henry Sherwood.*

14. 1922 – CONSTANCE PADWICK, *Henry Martyn, Confessor of the Faith* [I.V.F. edition, 1953, quoted in this book]

15. 1945 – E. T. SANDYS and G. F. WESTCOTT, *One Hundred and Seventy Five Years at the Old Mission Church, Calcutta.*

16. 1947 – A. G. POUNCEY, *Henry Martyn 1781–1812.*

17. 1951 – G. C. B. DAVIES, *The Early Cornish Evangelicals, 1735–1760.*

18. 1969 – ANGUS MACNAUGHTON, *David Corrie, His Family and Friends.*

19. 1975 – DAVID BENTLEY–TAYLOR, *My Love Must Wait: The Story of Henry Martyn.*

NOTES

1 *The Journal of the Rev. John Wesley, AM.*, ed. Nehemiah Curnock, vol. 6, p. 124.

2 Constance Padwick, *Henry Martyn, Confessor of the Faith* (IVF edition, 1953) p. 25.

3 John Sargent, *A Memoir of the Rev. Henry Martyn*, p. 8. An 1862 edition of this title is currently published by the Banner of Truth Trust: *Life and Letters of Henry Martyn*, (Edinburgh: Banner of Truth, 1985), 463 pp. ISBN 0 85151 468 5.

4 Ibid. p. 10.

5 Ibid. p. 10.

6 Ibid. p. 10.

7 Ibid. pp. 12–13.

[8] Ibid. pp. 374–375.

[9] Ibid. p. 14.

[10] Ibid. p. 14.

[11] Ibid. p. 15.

[12] Ibid. p. 24.

[13] Ibid. p. 18.

[14] Padwick, p. 45.

[15] *Journals and Letters,* vol. 1, p. 38.

[16] Ibid. vol. 1, p. 65.

[17] Padwick, p. 54.

[18] Sargent, p. 25.

[19] *Journals and Letters,* vol. 1, p. 245.

[20] Sargent, p. 53.

[21] Ibid. p. 72.

[22] *Journals and Letters,* vol. 1, p. 243.

[23] Padwick, p. 64.

[24] George Smith, *Henry Martyn, Saint and Scholar,* p. 56.

[25] *Journals and Letters,* vol. 1, p. 29.

[26] Ibid. vol. 1, p. 127.

[27] Ibid. vol. 1, p. 145.

[28] Ibid. vol. 1, p. 146.

[29] Ibid. vol. 1, p. 146.

[30] *Journals and Letters,* vol. 1, p. 152.

[31] Ibid. vol. 1, p. 153.

[32] George Smith, pp. 55–56.

[33] *Journals and Letters,* vol. 1, p. 157.

[34] Ibid. vol. 1, p. 159.

[35] Ibid. vol. 1, p. 215.

[36] *Journals and Letters,* vol. 1, p. 216.

[37] Ibid. vol. 1, p. 249.

[38] Ibid. vol. 1, p. 258.

[39] Ibid. vol. 1, p. 263.

[40] Ibid. vol. 1, p. 264.

[41] Ibid. vol. 1, p. 275.

[42] Ibid. vol. 1, p. 275.

[43] *Journals and Letters,* vol. 1, p. 277.

[44] Ibid. vol. 1, p. 279.

[45] Ibid. vol. 1, p. 279.

[46] George Smith, p. 84.

[47] *Journals and Letters,* vol. 1, pp. 279–280.

[48] Ibid. vol. 1, p. 281.

[49] Ibid. vol. 1, p. 283.

[50] *Journals and Letters,* vol. 1. p. 287.

[51] Ibid. vol. 1, p. 287–288.

[52] Ibid. vol. 1, p. 288.

[53] George Smith, p. 92.

[54] *Journals and Letters,* vol. 1, p. 288.

[55] Ibid. vol. 1, p. 289.

[56] Ibid. vol. 1, p. 289.

[57] Ibid. vol. 1, p. 289.

[58] Ibid. vol. 1, p. 289.

[59] Ibid. vol. 1, p. 291.

[60] George Smith, p. 92.

[61] *Journals and Letters,* vol. 1, p. 296.

[62] Padwick, p. 72.

[63] Ibid. p. 74.

[64] Sargent, p. 157.

[65] *Journals and Letters,* vol. 1, p. 382.

[66] George Smith, p. 107.

[67] Sargent, p. 147.

[68] *Journals and Letters,* vol. 1, p. 447.

[69] Ibid. vol. 1, p. 495.

[70] Sargent, p. 177.

[71] Ibid. p. 197.

[72] *Journals and Letters,* vol. 2, p. 45.

[73] Ibid. vol. 2, p. 45.

[74] Ibid. vol. 2, p. 99.

[75] Ibid. vol. 2, p. 150.

[76] Ibid. vol. 2, p. 199.

[77] Ibid. vol. 1, p. 365.

[78] George Smith, p. 99 footnote.

[79] *Journals and Letters,* vol. 1, p. 473.

[80] Ibid. vol. 1, p. 478.

[81] Ibid. vol. 1, p. 491.   [82] Ibid. vol. 1, p. 497.

[83] Ibid. vol. 1, p. 498.   [84] Ibid. vol. 1, p. 524.

[85] Ibid. vol. 2, p. 86.   [86] George Smith, p. 99.

[87] Abner Brown, *Recollections of the Conversation Parties of the Rev. Charles Simeon,* p. 249.

[88] George Smith, p. 188.   [89] Ibid. p. 192.

[90] William Carus, *Memoirs of the Life of the Rev. Charles Simeon,* pp. 226–228.

[91] George Smith, p. 195.   [92] Ibid. p. 196.

[93] *Journals and Letters,* vol. 2, p. 113.   [94] Ibid. vol. 2, pp. 114–117.

[95] Ibid. vol. 2, p. 130.   [96] Ibid. vol. 2, p. 132.

[97] George Smith, pp. 242–243.

[98] H. C. G. Moule, *Charles Simeon,* p. 201.

[99] *Journals and Letters,* vol. 2, p. 230.   [100] Ibid. vol. 2, p. 237.

[101] Ibid. vol. 2, p. 278.   [102] Ibid. vol. 2, p. 239.

[103] Ibid. vol. 2, p. 240. cf. F. J. Harvey Dutton, *The Life and Times of Mrs Henry Sherwood,* p. 333.

[104] Ibid. vol. 2, p. 240.   [105] Ibid. vol. 2. p. 241.

[106] Ibid. vol. 2, p. 242.   [107] Ibid. vol. 2, p. 318.

[108] Sargent, p. 162.   [109] Ibid. p. 286.

[110] *Mrs Sherwood,* p. 380.   [111] Padwick, p. 128.

[112] George Smith, pp. 285–286.

[113] *Journals and Letters,* vol. 2, p. 272.

[114] *The Churchman,* September 1889, p. 635.

[115] *Journals and Letters,* vol. 1, p. 506.   [116] Ibid. vol. 2, p. 205.

[117] Ibid. vol. 2, p. 264.   [118] Ibid. vol. 2, p. 89.

[119] Ibid. vol. 2, p. 76.   [120] Ibid. vol. 2, p. 137.

[121] Ibid. vol. 2, p. 234.   [122] George Smith, p. 432.

[123] *Journals and Letters,* vol. 2, p. 326.

[124] George Smith, pp. 431–434.

[125] *Journals and Letters,* vol. 2, p. 288.   [126] Ibid. vol. 2, pp. 294–295.

[127] Padwick, p. 125.

[128] *Journals and Letters,* vol. 2, p. 319.

[129] Williain Carus, p. 366.   [130] Ibid. p. 407.

[131] Stephen Neill, *A History of Christian Missions,* p. 267.

[132] David Bentley-Taylor, *My Love Must Wait, the Story of Henry Martyn,* p. 18.

[133] *Stephen Neill, A History of Christianity in India 1707–1758, p. 514, note 4.*

[134] George Eliot *Scenes of Clerical Life* (Cabinet edition in two volumes), vol. 2, p. 206.   [135] Ibid. vol. 2, p. 264.

[136] George Smith, p. 56 (εγειρε ο καθευδων και αναστα).

[137] *Journals and Letters,* vol. 1, pp. 87; 158.

[138] Ibid. vol. 1, pp. 245; 292.

[139] Ibid. vol. 2, p. 49.

[140] *Mrs Sherwood*, p. 335.

[141] *Journals and Letters*, vol. 1, p. 320.

[142] *Mrs Sherwood*, p. 384.

[143] George Smith, pp. 327–332.

[144] *Journals and Letters*, vol. 2, pp. 314; 323.

[145] *Mrs Sherwood*. pp. 335; 343.

[146] *Mrs Sherwood*. p. 383.

[147] *Journals and Letters*, vol. 1, p. 126.

[148] Ibid. vol. 2. p. 109.

[149] Ibid. vol. 2, pp. 124–127.

[150] *Journals and Letters*, vol. 2, p. 307.

[151] Ibid. vol. 2, p. 315.

[152] Ibid. vol. 2, p. 323.

[153] George Smith, p. 331.

[154] *Journals and Letters*, vol. 2, p. 328.

[155] Ibid. vol. 2, p. 328.

[156] Ibid, vol. 2, p. 340.

[157] George Smith, pp. 331–332.

[158] *Journals and Letters*, vol. 2, p. 348.

[159] Ibid. vol. 2, p. 326.

[160] Samuel Zwemer, *Arabia, The Cradle of Islam*, p. 316.

[161] *Journals and Letters*, vol. 2, p. 349.

[162] Ibid. vol. 2. p. 352.

[163] Sargent, p. 317.

[164] *Journals and Letters*, vol. 2, p. 367.

[165] Ibid. vol. 2, p. 316.

[166] George Smith, p. 331.

[167] Ibid. p. 435; cf. *Journals and Letters,* vol. 2, p. 356.

[168] *Journals and Letters*, vol. 2, p. 355.

[169] Ibid. vol. 2, p. 356.

[170] Sargent, p. 325.

[171] Ibid. p. 327.

[172] George Smith, p. 526.

[173] Ibid. pp. 466–467.

[174] Ibid. pp. 399–405.

[175] *Journals and Letters*, vol. 2. p. 340.

[176] Ibid. vol. 2, p. 288.

[177] Ibid. vol. 2, p. 289.

[178] Ibid. vol. 2, p. 290.

[179] Ibid. vol. 2, p. 295.

[180] George Smith, p. 300.

[181] *Journals and Letters*, vol. 2, p. 308.

[182] Ibid. vol. 2, p. 312.

[183] Ibid. vol. 2, p. 320.

[184] Ibid. vol. 2, p. 332.

[185] Ibid. vol. 2, p. 349.

[186] Ibid. vol. 2. p. 363.

[187] Ibid. vol. 2, p. 366.

[188] Ibid. vol. 2, p. 372.

[189] Ibid. vol. 2, p. 379.

[190] Ibid. vol. 2, p. 395.

[191] Ibid. vol. 2, pp. 399–400.

[192] *Mrs Sherwood*, p. 376.

[193] *Journals and Letters*, vol. 2, p. 67.

[194] Ibid. vol. 2, p. 384.

[195] Sargent, p. 387.

[196] George Smith, pp. 483–491.

[197] *Journals and Letters*, vol. 2, p. 394.

[198] Ibid. vol. 2, p. 396.

[199] Ibid. vol. 2. p. 398.

[200] Sargent, p. 412.

[201] Sargent, p. 420.

[202] Ibid. p. 424.

[203] Ibid. p. 431.

[204] *Journals and Letters*, vol. 2, p. 405.

[205] *Journals and Letters*, vol. 2, p. 406.

[206] Ibid. vol. 2, pp. 406–407.

[207] George Smith, p. 537.

[208] Ibid. pp. 538–539.

[209] George Smith, p. 540.

[210] Ibid. p. 541.

[211] Ibid. pp. 549–550.

[212] Ibid. p. 551.

[213] *Journals and Letters*, vol. 1, pp. 390–392.

[214] Ibid. vol. 1, p. 395.

[215] Ibid. vol. 1, p. 395.

[216] Sargent, p. 147.

[217] Stephen Neill, *A History of Christianity in India, 1707–1758*, p. 256.

[218] T. R. Birks, *A Memoir of the Rev. Edward Bickersteth*, vol. 2, p. 484.

[219] G. T. Fox, Preface to *Five Sermons by the Rev. Henry Martyn*, p. iii.

[220] William Carus, p. 358.

[221] Ibid. p. 390.

[222] Ibid. p. 391, fn.

[223] This ought to have read 'in the 32nd year of his life'.

*Henry Martyn's Pagoda at
Aldeen, near Serampore, India.*

3

Robert Murray M'Cheyne

An Heir of the Covenant
1813–43

*Robert Murray M'Cheyne, drawn by himself, and
found in a little pocket notebook belonging to the year 1843.*

When I stand before the throne,
Dressed in beauty not my own,
When I see Thee as Thou art:
Love Thee with unsinning heart:
Then, Lord, shall I fully know –
Not till then – how much I owe.

ROBERT MURRAY M'CHEYNE
(Memoir and Remains, p. 637)

Early Days in Edinburgh

Robert Murray M'Cheyne was cradled and nurtured in the historic environs of Auld Reekie, where he was born on 21 May 1813. The frail bairn who then lay in his mother's arms was destined to light a lamp that would shine with lambent beauty before his short life of not quite thirty years had come to an end. His father was a man of means, a Writer to the Signet, one of that inner coterie of Edinburgh solicitors whose sole right it was to prepare all writs for the Supreme Court of Justice. His mother had come of good stock and was a woman of great charm and sweetness, with gifts of mind to match her warmth of heart. They had two sons and two daughters before Robert was born, though he never saw the second daughter who died when nine months old. Robert was the last child, and he grew up as the youngest member of a solid middle-class family. Both father and mother sought to order the steps of their children in the footprints of the divine Shepherd, and it is clear that their spiritual welfare was fostered from childhood. Their first home had been in Dublin Street where Robert was born, but in 1819 they moved to a still more pleasant home in Queen Street; and Queen Street, with its then spacious mansions and its charming vistas towards the Firth of Forth, was all that a child could have wished. Robert was frail in health and build, but that did not impede the swift development of his natural intellect. His life at school began when he was five, and he soon proved himself quick and alert, readily teachable, a natural and attractive boyish figure. Canon Bell of Cheltenham could still remember him in 1889: a tall slender lad, with tartan dress and pleasing features, richly dowered with the charm of generous sympathies, 'bright yet grave, fond of play, and of a blameless life'.[1]

Robert M'Cheyne was enrolled in the University of Edinburgh at the age of fourteen in the winter term of 1827; he took his Arts degree four years later in the spring of 1831. He was a good rather than a brilliant student, and he carried off some prize from each class in turn. The treasure-troves of poetry were always a delight to him, and the classics of Greece and Rome helped to shape his sense of literary values. He was a gay and light-hearted student, and his skill in singing or in recitation made him a favourite on social occasions. His quick ear and true voice were a source of constant pleasure in and beyond his home all the days of his life. He had always cherished the high virtues of a chivalrous character, and his father could say with the sober judgment of his professional background: 'I never found him guilty of a lie or of any mean or unworthy action; and he had a great contempt for such things in others.'[2] But he was a stranger during those years to the penetrative power of true faith, and the great change in his spiritual experience did not take place until he had finished his course in Arts. It was only when the cold, bleak wind of sorrow began to blow that he awoke to his need for spiritual reality. This came as a result of the illness and death of his eldest brother.

David M'Cheyne had been like a sunbeam in the life of that home; he had all the sparkle of a selfless vivacity. He had begun to assist his father as a Writer to the Signet, and he had been Robert's friend and tutor from his school-days. But he had caught a chill on a walking tour in the English Lake District, and it slowly turned into a fatal illness. The end came on 8 July 1831, and his death left a gap in that home which only the Lord could close. But no one could doubt that it was the Lord himself who had come to pilot his soul across the dark waters into the last haven of rest.

Robert M'Cheyne had long looked up to this brother as the ideal of all that a true man should be, and his death touched him more deeply than words could well express. He had become aware of a richer quality in his brother's character as a result of his mature dedication to God, and he was not indifferent to that brother's longing for a decisive conversion in his own case. He was eight years younger than his brother, and was eighteen years old at the time of his death; and he kept that day in devoted remembrance to the end of his life. As each anniversary came round, he would refer to it as the turning point in his own experience. Twelve months later, on 8 July 1832, he wrote in his diary: 'On this morning last year came the first overwhelming blow to my worldliness; how blessed to me, Thou, O God, only knowest who has made it so.'[3] And on 8 July 1842, the last return of that date which he lived to see, he wrote to a member of his congregation: 'This day eleven years ago, I lost my loved and loving brother, and began to seek a Brother who cannot die.'[4] It was indeed from that very day that the grace of God began to shine within his heart, and his friends were quick to observe the change. 'His poetry was pervaded with serious thought', so Andrew Bonar declared, 'and all his pursuits began to be followed out in another spirit; he engaged in the labours of a Sabbath school, and began to seek God in the diligent reading of the Word'.[5] He was himself to say that 'he was led to Christ through deep and ever-abiding . . . convictions'.[6] There was nothing shallow in this new faith in Christ; it was a deep, enduring commitment of his mind and heart

to the Son of God. It was fully described in poems like
Jehovah Tsidkenu,[7] and his feelings may be gleaned from
one of the crisp remarks of his subsequent ministry: 'There
is no rest for the soul like being in the love of God; that
is rest.'[8]

Preparation for the Ministry

Grace now gave a new bent to the course of his life, and
in November 1831 he became a candidate for the ministry
in the Church of Scotland. He took his place in the
Divinity classrooms at a time when Thomas Chalmers
was at the height of his amazing influence; no one since
the days of John Knox had been held in such deep
veneration. Men would never forget his self-defence in
the General Assembly of 1825 after he had been taxed
with a statement which he had made twenty years before
in favour of pluralities. He rose to his feet and frankly
confessed that he was the author of the statement which
had just been quoted. He said that he now stood before
the bar of the Assembly as a penitent, and he gave an
account of the circumstances in which he had made the
statement: it had been his object to prove that an exclusive
devotion to the claims of mathematics was not
inconsistent with a vocation to the ministry. Then he
brought his speech to a close in an air of breathless silence
with the magnificent apology:

> 'Alas, Sir! so I thought in my ignorance and pride. I
> have no reserve in saying that the sentiment was
> wrong, and that in the utterance of it, I penned what
> was most outrageously wrong. Strangely blinded that
> I was! What, Sir, is the object of mathematical
> science? Magnitude, and the proportions of
> magnitude. But then, Sir, I had forgotten two

> magnitudes. I thought not of the littleness of time; I
> recklessly thought not of the greatness of eternity.'[9]

This was the man who had held the Chair of Divinity at
Edinburgh since 1828; he was in the forefront of the
new and stirring movement which had begun to make
itself felt in halls of thought and learning. He cast the
spell of his cosmic thought and solar sweep round all his
students: they could hardly resist the force of his massive
intellect and rugged character and dynamic energy.
Andrew Bonar always spoke of him with unbounded
enthusiasm as one to whom they all owed a debt which
they could never repay.[10]

Robert M'Cheyne could lay no claim to the strength
and splendour of the mental vision of such a guide, but
time was to prove that he was endowed with a double
portion of the grace and ardour of his glowing spirit. His
approach to study was ruled by his supreme desire to learn
of Christ. This was his one touchstone for the value of the
lectures he heard or the books which he read. His own
well-thumbed Bible was a witness to his constant search
for a more profound understanding of truth, and his insight
grew with singular clarity. This was much more than a
student's passion for a text-book: 'It was', as Alexander
Smellie so finely observed, 'the child's craving for the bread
from the father's table'.[11] He made himself familiar with
the finer points of translation, and was as much at home in
the Greek text of the New Testament as he would have
been in Braid Scots[12]. He knew enough Hebrew to be
able to carry on a conversation with the learned Jews of
Europe and Palestine, and he could turn to the Hebrew
text of the Old Testament with more ease than many today
can skim through the Latin Vulgate. He spared no pains
in the effort to master the doctrines of grace and the lessons
of the Reformation, but he had little taste for the vagaries

of speculative philosophy or the dilemmas of mediæval controversy. He thought that church history ought to be seen as a narrative of God's dealings with men: this was why he said that Thomas M'Crie's *Life of Andrew Melville* failed to reflect the true spiritual glory of the man and his age.[13] He was in a totally different category from that of a man like Thomas Chalmers, for he never tried to climb the higher rungs of solid learning. But he knew that the wisdom of all the ages in the Word of God is vastly superior to the most brilliant genius of a passing generation, and his grasp of this fact was so firm that 'he did not readily yield his matured thoughts to be moulded even by men of the highest intellect'.[14]

Truth had begun to shine in the sky of his soul like a star at evening, and its light was to grow increasingly sweet and clear as he moved towards the day. The most striking feature of his career as a Divinity student was the rapid development of grace in his personal character. One may still look through the open window of an intimate diary and watch the growth of his soul in the things of God. It is true that he used to drop into Latin when he wished to conceal the more private entries from the chance gaze of other eyes; it is also true that nothing more than scattered fragments were transcribed and preserved by the hand of a friend after his death. But those fragmentary records have a photographic element, a self-revealing quality, which illuminates the soul and its secrets. Andrew Bonar used those records to compile the Memoir which has all the hallmarks of fine Victorian spiritual biography. Robert M'Cheyne is brought to life before our eyes in his Memoir as David Brainerd and Henry Martyn had been before his eyes in their Journals. He was deeply impressed by each in turn, and they had an enduring influence upon his life. On 12 November

1831, he wrote of Henry Martyn: 'Would I could imitate him, giving up . . . all – for Christ.'[15] And on 27 June 1832, he wrote of David Brainerd: 'Most wonderful man! . . . I cannot express what I think when I think of thee.'[16] M'Cheyne was to reveal the same spirit of unqualified self-surrender as Brainerd, but without his pensive strain of melancholy introspection with regard to inward thought and motive. And he was to reveal the same spirit of other-worldly aspiration as Martyn, but without his painful sense of agonising controversy with regard to human love and despair. M'Cheyne enjoyed certain material blessings to which they were strangers: they were orphans, and he was not; they were missionaries, and he was not. But the roots of his soul were deep in the soil in which they had been nurtured, and the blossom it bore was in some ways even fairer than theirs.

Robert M'Cheyne had a special gift for the firm application of the kind of truth that people do not always relish. 'Your tears will not blot out sin', he declared; 'they do nothing but weep in hell.'[17] But the Memoir makes it clear that the man who was to voice those words knew what it was to shed such tears himself. It lays bare the searchings of a heart which had felt the grave burden of sin, as on 2 February 1832, when he confessed: 'Not a trait worth remembering; and yet these four and twenty hours must be accounted for.'[18] It makes plain the longings of a soul which had glimpsed the true glory of God, as on 9 September that year, when he exclaimed: 'Oh for true, unfeigned humility! I know I have cause to be humble; and yet I do not know one half of that cause. I know I am proud; and yet I do not know the half of that pride.'[19] He drank from the wells of Scripture and he knelt in worship as one who could not do without the peace and strength of things unseen. 'A calm hour with

God', he would say, 'is worth a whole lifetime with man.'[20]
He read the Life of Jonathan Edwards and longed to
follow him even as he had followed Christ. 'How feeble
does my spark of Christianity appear beside such a sun!'
he wrote. 'But even his was a borrowed light, and the
same source is still open to enlighten me.'[21]

In 1834, with Alexander Somerville, he began to visit
the streets and stairs of the Lawnmarket and the Canongate.
'God grant a blessing may go with us', he wrote on 24
March. 'Began in fear, and weakness, and much
trembling. May the power be of God!'[22] He was increasingly assiduous in all that could prepare him for his work
as a preacher of the gospel, and his developed character
was one of rare grace and maturity. He had much of the
charm and few of the faults of Samuel Rutherford in the
poetical imagery of his dreams and aspirations. It is like
an echo from the famous *Letters*[23] written by Rutherford
in Aberdeen to hear him say: 'The world is all winter
time so long as the Saviour is away.'[24]

His work as a Divinity student came to an end in the
spring of 1835, and he applied for a licence to preach.
He passed his trials towards the close of the session, partly
before the Presbytery of Edinburgh, partly before the
Presbytery of Annan. It was through his mother that one
pleasant comment has been preserved. 'We have heard',
so she wrote, 'that Dr Chalmers was highly pleased.'[25]
On 1 July 1835, he was licensed by the Presbytery of
Annan as a preacher of the gospel, and he believed that
this was the highest office to which he could ever aspire.
The brief evening entry in his diary sums up his own
reflections with a disarming estimate of the situation: he
felt all the solemnity that was involved, but was deeply
aware of how inadequate he would always be in himself.[26]
His first sermons were preached the next Sunday at

Ruthwell near Dumfries, and he remarked: 'Found it a more awfully solemn thing than I had imagined to announce Christ authoritatively; yet a glorious privilege.'[27]

From Larbert to Dundee

He preached in various churches until November, when he became assistant minister to John Bonar in the parish of Larbert and Dunipace near Stirling. M'Cheyne liked to remind himself that the famous Robert Bruce had once found in this parish the scene for his prayers and labours; it stirred his soul to ask that God would pour out his Spirit again as in those days of old. There was now a population of six thousand people in some seven hundred families, and the field of labour was as varied as he could wish. Larbert was a noisy, grimy town of miners and iron moulders, while Dunipace was a peaceful and pleasant hamlet of farmers: and each end of this field was tilled with the same care by the minister and his assistant. M'Cheyne's duties were to preach in the two centres on alternate Sundays and to visit in both districts throughout the week. Here the groundwork was laid for his future greatness in the pastoral ministry, for his was the heart of a shepherd who yearned over all who were lost or out of the way.

He soon began to make use of notebooks in which he could record the name and case of each man or woman with whom he dealt. His brief comments are a moving testimony to his diligence as a visitor: he was tireless, patient, shrewd, and systematic. There was nothing cold or dull in the clear methodical entries; they are full of graphic detail, and they disclose his insight and under-standing. Alexander Smellie points out how these entries allow us to follow him from door to door as he worked his way house by house through Red Row. 'John Hunter,

No. 22. He, not at home. She, stout woman with sensible face. Spoke of her four bairns dead; three beside her. Visit, 14th July 1836. "I stand at the door and knock." Altogether a decent woman. Husband to be at meeting.' A week later: 'Widow Hunter, No. 40. Wicked face, but old body has had much trouble. Daughter lame. Visit 21 July. Lost sheep. Spoke plain. She spoke grateful things, but felt them not. Invited me not to pass the door.'[28]

He went to each house in turn as one who knew that there is a tide in the affairs of grace which is fraught with eternal destiny: those who take that tide at the flood will be borne to safety, while those who miss its surge will be washed up in the shallows of a final despair.[29] There were not as many as he would wish who sought to breast that tide, but it was his greatest joy to guide and strengthen the few who did. The chief value of that year for his own spirit was in the way of self-discipline and preparation for the future: the King's arrow still had need of point and polish. But he never forgot his first eager desires for that parish where the gospel was 'free as the air we breathe, fresh as the stream from the everlasting hills'.[30] He came to look upon Larbert and Dunipace as he would on the heath of his childhood. 'It is like the land of my birth', he wrote twelve months later. 'Will the Sun of Righteousness ever rise upon it, making its hills and valleys bright with the light of the knowledge of Jesus?'[31]

In August 1836, Robert M'Cheyne and his two most intimate companions, Alexander Somerville and Andrew Bonar, were asked to preach in St Peter's Church at Dundee. This church had been built to serve a new parish which was carved out of the crowded city, and the congregation was most anxious to call a man who would respond in 'the fullness of the blessing of the gospel of Christ' (*Rom.* 15:29). All three friends were men who would have graced the church with more than usual distinction, and they had been recommended by Chalmers and Candlish and Welsh. Each was more than willing to yield to the others, but the choice fell on M'Cheyne. On 24 November 1836, he was ordained in the presence of his new congregation, and he preached on the next Sunday from the great text: 'The Spirit of the Lord GOD is upon me, because the LORD hath anointed me to preach good tidings . . . ' (*Isa.* 61:1–3). It was the text to which the Lord had turned in the synagogue of Nazareth, and the spirit of that text was to guide all his work in Dundee. That first sermon was the means of spiritual awakening for some of his hearers, and he tried to commemorate the day of his ordination as each new year came round with a sermon on the same words. His prayer at the close of that first Sunday in St Peter's was weighted with longing and with renewed consecration. 'Put thy blessing upon this day', he wrote. 'Felt given over to God, as one bought with a price.'[32] This was the start of that brief but fruitful life of service which has ever since been acclaimed as a model and an inspiration, even in a land so rich in noble ministries as that land of ancient Covenants. His full career as a preacher was to divide into two three-year terms, with his journey to the Holy Land in between. The first three years were the seed-time; the last three years saw the harvest: and the golden glow which those years were to cast over the people of Dundee was long to brood above the grey city on the banks of the Tay.

Robert M'Cheyne soon found that he was in the midst of an impoverished population in the poorest quarter of the city. There were three and a half thousand people in his parish, dwellers in what he called a 'wilderness of chimney tops'.[33] He was convinced that a diligent minister ought to expect success in God's service, but he saw that he could not hope for such success unless he were willing to preach Christ for Christ's sake alone. He learned to pray that he would not seek to attract men to himself, but that he might point them direct to the Saviour. Such was his cry: 'Lord, give me this!'[34] There were signs from the first that his preaching would yield a full reward; on this man or on that, there broke the light of a day which knows no sunset.[35] He built up a congregation of twelve hundred members who came from all parts of town and country and who crowded the aisles of the church or the steps of the pulpit. His thirst for their spiritual welfare was the result of zeal for the glory of God, and a letter which was written in June 1840 serves to express this with pellucid clarity. 'I feel there are two things it is impossible to desire with sufficient ardour', he said; 'personal holiness, and the honour of Christ in the salvation of souls.'[36] He felt that his conscience had to be as clear as crystal if he were to speak in the name of Christ.[37] One word spoken from a heart full of God's Spirit would be worth ten thousand spoken in unbelief and sin.[38] He saw personal holiness as the one great prerequisite for a soul-winning ministry, and this fact must be kept in mind when an attempt is made to weigh up his simple unassuming declaration: 'I think I can say I have never risen a morning without thinking how I could bring more souls to Christ.'[39] His eye was so single and his aim so sincere that men could not mistake his motive, nor yet resist his message. There were some who learned to tremble; there were others who found the way of rest.

The Man

M'Cheyne was blessed with a natural endowment of great gifts and rare charm: his whole life was like a rich and polished gem with many gleaming facets. Country landscape was always a delight to him, though he was drawn to the soft and gentle rather than to what was wild and splendid. He loved to watch the hues of gold in an autumn sunset while he spoke of those whose sun will never go down; his face would shine with a glow of gladness when such a scene before his eyes called up the still fairer vision of faith within his soul. He had the mind and heart of an artist and could use both brush and pencil to paint or sketch any scene or object which he thought uncommon or impressive. He had the gifts of a poet in his nature and could always clothe ideas or ideals in the forms of verse and rhythm. Some of his lines were light and lively, but his deepest feelings also found a voice in words which can be set to music. He had taken more than one prize for an original poem when he was a student, and one or two of his *Songs of Zion* have found a place in most well-known hymnals. He was at home in the world of music, with a wide range of knowledge and a true sense of values, and with some skill in the use of certain musical instruments. His voice had been trained from childhood, and was light and pleasant in its tone and timbre. He had won praise as a schoolboy for his skill in recitation, and he learned to sing with pure and beautiful expression. At times he was a guest in the home of Mary Crawford Brown, who as an Edinburgh girl of nineteen was won for a missionary life in India. Her grand-nephew was to recall M'Cheyne's visits to that home in words of singular interest. 'I have often heard one of my Aunts say', so he wrote, 'that more than once she was awakened in the morning by hearing M'Cheyne's sweet tenor voice singing the morning Psalm with which he always began his private devotions. It was no more disturbing than the song of a thrush or a blackbird in the summer morning.'[40]

M'Cheyne had the love of a child for all that was good and manly, and the soul of a saint for all that was true and holy. He was tall and lithe and slender in build; he was bright and fair and pleasant in face. Full of life and vigour in spite of various handicaps, he was always fond of gymnastic exercise. He was equipped with a clear and discerning intellect, and he had a strong and accurate memory. His mind had been furnished with the finest stores of arts and letters, and he had a remarkable combination of first-class gifts for his work in Dundee. Such a man could never be dry or commonplace in the pulpit, and his congregation soon knew that his preaching was out of the ordinary. 'There was pathos in it; there was winningness; there was fire.'[41] But there was more than this; there was another quality, more luminous, more compelling. It was not the attractive dignity of his finely chiselled features, nor the persuasive utterance of his musically controlled voice which gave him such power: it was the fact that men could not escape from the shining beauty of his personal character. He was, in the highest sense of the term, a saint; one whose face was alight with the vision of things unseen and whose life was fragrant with the presence of God. Andrew Bonar relates how a man from his own parish was so impressed by the very look of M'Cheyne that it spoke to his heart before a word was said.[42] There were others like that man who were so conscious of his nearness to God that they could not resist the grace with which he spoke. His church was filled with what James Hamilton called a 'Bethel-like sacredness' in which men felt the power of a compelling reverence.[43] All the attractive qualities of a sweet and noble nature were merged in the absolute devotion of 'a verray parfit, gentil knyght' who had sworn homage to Christ alone,[44] and whose name was to be woven into the most cherished legends of the North as the Sir Galahad of the Church of Scotland.

M'Cheyne had felt the call of the non-Christian world from the first days of his own new life in Christ, and the hope that he might become one of the King's envoys to the mission field held him to the end. As early as 12 November 1831, he was reading Sargent's *Life of Henry Martyn* and was moved to the depths of his being. 'Would I could imitate him,' he wrote, 'giving up father, mother, country, house, health, life, all – for Christ. And yet, what hinders? Lord, purify me, and give me strength to dedicate myself, my all, to Thee.'[45] On 27 June 1832, he was reading *The Life and Diary of David Brainerd* and found his heart 'more set upon missionary enterprise than ever'.[46] And on 13 April 1836, he heard Alexander Duff at Stirling, speaking on his missionary system, and his thoughts were registered in his diary: 'I am now made willing, if God shall open the way, to go to India. Here am I; send me.'[47] This strong missionary spirit never left him; he was more than willing to go. But the climate of the tropics would have been too severe for his slender powers of physical endurance. He had always had to protect his health, and more than once he was compelled to pause. He had succumbed to a warning illness while at Larbert and spent some weeks away from the parish in order to recuperate. 'I hope and pray', he had written to John Bonar, 'that it may be His will to restore me again to you and your parish, with a heart tutored by sickness, to speak more and more as dying to dying.'[48] He was very fond of Richard Baxter's writings,[49] and the last phrase in this letter was an echo of a famous couplet in Baxter's *Poetical Fragments*. Two years later, while in the midst of his work in Dundee, he was disturbed by the sudden return of grave symptoms. He was attacked by such constant palpitation of heart that he could not even study, much less preach or visit, and as 1838 came to an end, he was once more forced to withdraw from his field of labour in order to regain his health.

He grieved deeply at the enforced silence which he had to endure for much longer than he had feared, but God had much for him to learn which trial alone could teach. The first lesson was that there is nothing like a calm look into the world that lies beyond both sense and time to make one feel both the emptiness of praise and the selfishness of pride.[50] Then he was taught to spread the sails of his spirit in such a way that the winds of adversity would drive him on towards the haven of glory.[51] But this illness was timed in the goodness of God to fit in with other factors: it was to bring him some months of travel which would go far to meet all his missionary longings.

IN THE HOLY LAND

Alexander Keith and Alexander Black had just been chosen by the General Assembly to go abroad in order to explore possible avenues for a Mission to the Jews in Central Europe or in Asia Minor, and it was now agreed, as the result of a hint from Dr Candlish, that Robert M'Cheyne and Andrew Bonar should both join the deputation. It was a cause very dear to M'Cheyne, and he wrote to Bonar on 12 March 1839 to share his thoughts. 'I do hope we shall go forth in the Spirit', he said, 'and though straitened in language, may we not be blessed as Brainerd was through an interpreter?'[52] The full story of their visit to 'those holy fields'[53] was told in a joint volume drawn up on their return by Bonar and M'Cheyne.[54] This book has been deemed by reliable authorities to be one of the best which was for long available on this subject. Thomas Chalmers had the greatest value for it;[55] many others shared his judgment. It is rich in graphic pictures of the country where the Son of Man dwelt and in vivid sidelights on the Scriptures which the Son of Man loved. It is saturated with the spirit of old Hebraic history and steeped in the passion of men who yearned for the return and recovery of Israel.

They sailed from Dover on 12 April 1839; it was not until 6 November that M'Cheyne and Bonar berthed in the Thames on their return. Such a journey in those days was quite an uncommon enterprise. 'We are not aware', they wrote, 'that any clergyman of the Church of Scotland was ever privileged to visit the Holy City before.'[56] A sea voyage from the south of France to Alexandria, and a camel journey through the desert, brought them at length to their goal. Their first Sunday in the ancient home of Israel was 2 June, and they joined in worship with a sense of profound solemnity. M'Cheyne was the first to dismount on 7 June and to hurry forward on foot to catch the first glimpse of Jerusalem.[57] When at last their camels approached its gates and walls, they found themselves inwardly murmuring the words of the Psalmist: 'Our feet shall stand within thy gates, O Jerusalem' (*Psa.* 122:2). Bonar went on alone on 20 June in search of the Well of Sychar, and his Bible dropped out of his pocket to splash into the water far below.[58]

But no place was more like holy ground in their eyes than the garden which still lies at the foot of the Mount of Olives. It was early morning while the sun was still rising when Bonar and M'Cheyne made their way down through the Kidron Valley and crossed the brook to reach the plot of ground which was part of Gethsemane. It was enclosed by a low wall and they sat down among the eight gnarled trees which still survive. They read again each passage of Scripture which describes the anguish in the garden, and thought afresh how it was for them that he had bowed his head in bloody sweat and passion. They gave themselves to prayer, at first alone, and then with each other, seeing their sins in that cup which he had to drink.[59] And in after recollection, each thought of the other and gave a new turn to the old question: 'Did I not see thee in the garden with him?' (*John* 18:26).

M'Cheyne thus found endless delight in his sojourn among the cities of Judah and his rambles upon the mountains of Ephraim. He found that he could watch the great golden sun as it sank westward to the sea while its rays shone clear on the heights of Gibeon; and at the same time, he could see the round silver moon as it climbed upward in the sky while its beams played down on the vale of Aijalon.[60] He took time to sketch the tents of Kedar or the writer's inkhorn. He had music running through his mind as he penned verses for friends at home. One of the most delightful was a poem on the Sea of Galilee whose first and last stanzas reveal its tone:[61]

> *How pleasant to me thy deep blue wave,*
> *O Sea of Galilee!*
> *For the Glorious One Who came to save*
> *Hath often stood by thee.*
>
> *Oh! give me Lord by this sacred wave*
> *Threefold Thy love divine,*
> *That I may feed till I find my grave*
> *Thy flock – both Thine and mine.*

It was at length agreed that the party should divide: Keith and Black would set out for home at once by the Danube, while Bonar and M'Cheyne were to re-visit Galilee and then travel back through Central Europe. The two older men left Beirut for Constantinople on 7 July, while Bonar and M'Cheyne went south again. They were back in Beirut on 20 July, planning to sail for Smyrna a week later. M'Cheyne succumbed to high fever, but they sailed as planned on 28 July in the belief that the cool sea air would prove more beneficial than the sultry heat of Beirut. It was a sad farewell to Palestine and Syria, and they felt it keenly. 'We kept our eye upon the majestic brow of Lebanon', they wrote, 'till it faded from our view in the dim and brief twilight of the evening.'[62]

M'Cheyne was cheered and braced at first by a light breeze, but a sleepless night on deck soon ensued. When they anchored off the coast of Cyprus in the morning, he was in an advanced state of fever. His voice and mind began to fail, and no skilled help could be obtained until the ship berthed at Smyrna on 1 August. He was carried ashore and then travelled on mule-back to the village of Bouja three miles away for the sake of proper care and convalescence. It was only the love and care of an English home that allowed him to regain his strength, but the flowering jasmine and green cypress trees in his hosts' garden gave him as it were a second birthplace. He had sunk to the edge of the grave, and now rose up once more like one from the dead. On 17 August, the two friends were able to board a small ship at Smyrna to resume their journey. They travelled in stages through the Turkish and Balkan States into Austria, and then through the Polish and Prussian realms into Germany. Two-and-a-half months were spent in visits to the major seats of Hebrew life and culture, and it was not until mid-November that they arrived home in Scotland.

Their most cherished hope was that this mission would result in generous exertion on behalf of Israel; and they were not disappointed. It had been their aim to learn all

that the Rabbis could teach as well as to impart all that
they could persuade them to receive. They had amassed
a vast store of information about the state of the Jews in
Central Europe. A Report was prepared for the General
Assembly of 1840, and the result was a unanimous
resolution 'that the cause of Israel should from that time
form one of the great missionary schemes of our church'.[63]
In 1841, Daniel Edward began his work among the Jews
of Poland and Prussia, while John Duncan opened his
mission at Budapest. More than forty years were still to
elapse before a Scottish Mission was established in
Palestine: then stations were opened in Safed and Tiberias,
as Bonar and M'Cheyne had prayed and planned.[64] This
bears out James Stalker's declaration that the result of
their travels was to fasten on the Scottish Church an
altogether new sense of its obligation to the sons of Israel;
and among the first-fruits of the work in Central Europe
were Adolph Saphir and Alfred Edersheim.

   Andrew Bonar was far more to M'Cheyne than a
travelling companion; he had long been his most intimate
friend. He was born three years before M'Cheyne on
29 May 1810, and he came from a long line of godly
forbears. He was the seventh son of a seventh son, and
his grandfather's grandfather had been one of the twelve
Marrow Men in 1721. He became a student at Edinburgh
University in 1825 and took his place in the Divinity
classrooms at the same time as M'Cheyne in 1831. He
was ordained to the cure of souls at Collace in 1838 and
he was to join the great march to Tanfield Hall in 1843.
He was in full middle life, tall and straight and spare, his
head just tinged with grey, when he was called to leave
Collace for a church in Glasgow, and for thirty-six years,
from 1856 until his death in 1892, this great city was his
field of labour. His friendship with M'Cheyne in their

student days at Edinburgh was to ripen with rare unselfishness when they became neighbours north of the Tay. M'Cheyne wrote of Bonar in June 1836 with a radiant affection: 'For learning, experimental knowledge, and all the valuable qualities of a minister, he outstrips all the students I ever knew.'[65]

It was Andrew Bonar who made D. L. Moody so welcome to Glasgow on his Scottish tour in 1873; it was Andrew Bonar of whom Moody said that no one in Great Britain had helped him more.[66] Bonar's insight may be observed in his remark: 'God does not say, Pay what you can, but Pay what you owe.'[67] It is equally evident in his saying: 'God's part is to put forth His power; our part is to put forth faith.'[68] Alexander Smellie said that he was as warmly human as he was truly godly: he was genial; he was brotherly, with a refreshing sense of humour and a lovable charm in manner.[69] When he wrote of himself in his personal diary, it was in the terms of authentic saintliness: 'May 29th 1889: The Lord has enabled me to lean upon Christ day by day for sixty years.[70] 'September 25th 1891: Never was Christ to me more precious than He is now.'[71] He died in his eighty-third year, full of grace and ripe for glory.

WILLIAM C. BURNS AND THE AWAKENING IN DUNDEE

Meanwhile William Burns had been left in charge of the church and parish of St Peter, Dundee, and the bonds of a new friendship were formed between men who were to love each other as each loved his own soul. Burns was born on 1 April 1815, the third son in the manse at Kilsyth, and was dedicated from the cradle to the Lord and to his service. He graduated in Arts at Aberdeen in 1834 and in Divinity at Glasgow in 1839. He was licensed

as a preacher of the gospel on 27 March 1839 and took
up his duties at once as the *locum tenens* in St Peter's
Church, Dundee. It soon became clear that he was a born
evangelist, and he spent the next eight years in ceaseless
activity in the hills and highlands of his native country. 'I
found myself in an agony', so he once wrote, 'to compel
sinners to come to Jesus now, and not even the next hour,
which I felt was not man's but God's.'[72] A ferry once
carried no less than eight hundred people from twenty
miles around to hear him preach before breakfast.[73] His
hearers at Bonskeid hung on his words until the sun went
down and the full moon arose.[74]

He was ordained on 21 April 1847 as a missionary to
China, and he left home on his way to London and the
East the next day at five o'clock in the morning. He lived
with the Chinese as a Chinese, wearing their dress, eating
their food, and speaking their language. He worked both
in and out of the Treaty Ports for twenty-one years,
without ever returning home on furlough, until death
took him on 4 April 1868. He had found his destiny as a
pioneer for the Evangel, first in Scotland, then in China,
and was as much at home in the revival at Pechuia as he
had been in the awakening at Kilsyth. It was Burns who
fired the mind of Robert M'Cheyne in Dundee and
Kilsyth with a passion for souls beyond all he had known
before. It was Burns who warmed the heart of Hudson
Taylor in Shanghai and Swatow with a sense of missionary
purpose beyond all he had felt before.[75] He died in his
fifty-fourth year, consumed with a passion for that spiritual
kingdom which has neither frontiers nor favourites and
can never be moved.

M'Cheyne arrived back in Dundee to find that his
church had become the scene of a remarkable awakening:
it was indeed the seal of God upon his prayers during his

illness and absence from home. It had been his heartfelt desire that the labours of William Burns might prove a thousandfold more effective than all his efforts had been. 'How it will gladden my heart', he wrote on the way home, 'if you can really tell me that it has been so!'[76] And his heart was gladdened beyond his dreams when he returned, for he found that God had opened the flood-gate of blessing in a remarkable manner. This great move-ment had first begun while Burns was at Kilsyth during August, and it had been carried on with growing strength in Dundee as the year wore away. Burns spoke with 'a voice of splendid compass',[77] and he had the accent of a man who had come direct from the presence of God. At the Thursday night prayer meeting two days after his return from Kilsyth, he spoke of what the Lord had wrought and asked those who felt a need for God's work in their lives to remain behind. There were about a hundred who remained, and at the close of his address, the power of God came down. There were many in tears; there were others who felt desperately anxious to find true peace with God. Meetings were held every day for many weeks after that evening, and the whole of Dundee was stirred. It was as though Burns had grasped a rod like that of Moses to strike the seam of unbelief; then he stood back to watch the stream of life which burst from hearts of stone. There were times when he could not bear to let men go until they had felt the awe of standing in the presence of God, and friends who came to help could not escape from the manifest realities of conviction and conversion. Many came to Christ while that flood was at its height; months were to pass before its waters began to recede.[78]

On the very evening of his return in November 1839, M'Cheyne met his people at the Thursday night prayer meeting. He gave out Psalm 64 and was at once aware of a new note in the singing. Then he spoke for more than an hour to a congregation the like of which he had not seen before. 'I never preached to such an audience', so he told his parents in a letter on 26 November; 'so many weeping, so many waiting for the words of eternal life. I never heard such sweet singing anywhere, so tender and affecting, as if the people felt that they were praising a present God.'[79] There may have been a few who felt the pull of that spirit which had split the church at Corinth between those who were of this man and those who were of that man. But no breath of rival feeling ever arose between Burns and M'Cheyne: they were drawn, each to the other, with bands of gold and hoops of steel. M'Cheyne made Burns preach twice the next Sunday and wrote about it all to his parents in words that glow with praise.

The exchange of letters between Burns and M'Cheyne in the days that followed shows how much they rejoiced in each other's success. M'Cheyne knew that as the morning star must fade when the sun appears, so must every preacher vanish from sight when the Lord is in view. 'Let Christ increase, let man decrease', he wrote to Burns at the end of the year; 'this is my constant prayer for myself and you.'[80] Burns left Dundee to spread the light of that fire up and down Scotland during the next three years, and he never ceased to covet M'Cheyne as a fellow worker. The last letter he wrote to M'Cheyne arrived within a few days of his death, and it was in the form of an appeal.[81] Would he not leave Dundee to come and share his work? It is clear that M'Cheyne felt the power of that call; he was rapidly moving to a decision to leave church and parish so that he might devote himself without reserve to the proclamation of the gospel. He did not live to take that step, but his heart was with Burns.

M'Cheyne had now seen how God could use a human sickle to reap the fields with their whitened harvest, and he never lost the spirit of that revival in his ministry. He felt like one who had been taught to look long and calmly into the world to come and had then been sent a second time to preach the Word of life with a more feeling heart and a more faithful spirit.[82] The awakening was sustained for so long that it left its own permanent impression on the life of Dundee. The deep silence of men who hung on the smallest word of comfort was an experience which the city in that generation never forgot. The manse was thronged with scores who came by day in search of salvation; the church was packed with crowds who came at night in need of conversion. He had announced on his return that he would not relax while there was one unreached man or woman in his parish. 'I am resolved', he said, 'if God give me health and strength, that I will not let a man, woman or child among you alone until you have at least heard the testimony of God concerning His Son.'[83] There were altogether some eight hundred men and women who sought counsel and help during those weeks, though he remained very conservative in his estimate of the number of true conversions.[84] He had thought that he could safely reckon on some sixty souls who had passed from death to life before April 1839; but eighteen months later, he could affirm that there were then more than twice that number who had truly chosen Israel's God for their God.[85] There was not a family in his congregation, so he believed, who could not point to some friend or relative who had been born again.[86] It is true that the full force of this flood was to abate in time, but the stream of blessing did not dry up or cease to flow. In December 1841, he refused a call to Kettle in Fifeshire for at least one simple reason. 'I do not think', he said, 'I can speak a month in this parish without winning some souls.'[87]

M'Cheyne's last three years were used to consolidate the work in St Peter's, while at the same time a wider field of service opened out and often summoned him far beyond Dundee. They were years that witnessed spiritual awakenings in Perth and Ancrum and Strathbogie and Aberdeen, such as those at Kilsyth and in Dundee, for the preaching of Burns left a trail of fire in the life of the church which all could follow who had its cause at heart.[88] Burns would labour in some dark field until dawn and daylight appeared; then he buried himself in a new sphere and left others to reap in the splendour of the sunrise. There were many calls on M'Cheyne in such centres, and he never grudged time or strength when such calls came.

His own spirit was tempered and refined during those years, and his preaching was marked by a still more compelling urgency. 'O Thou Hope of Israel, the Saviour thereof in the time of trouble', so he would plead in the words of Jeremiah, 'why shouldest Thou be as a stranger in the land?' (*Jer.* 14:8). He had wept for Dundee as his Master had once wept for Jerusalem, and he yearned in secret for those who had withstood the grace of God.[89] He knew that he had no more skill to convert a soul than he had strength to create a star; but he also knew that the God who is almighty can do the one as well as the other, and he would not despair for the conversion of his people.[90] On 25 July 1840, he described a service in St Peter's when the presence and power of God broke through normal restraints. The tears and cries of those who were under concern offended several members of the congregation. 'But', he said, 'I felt no hesitation as to our duty to declare the simple truth impressively, and leave God to work in their hearts in His own way. If He saves souls in a quiet way, I shall be happy; if in the midst of cries and tears, still I will bless His Name.'[91] He was indeed a prince with God who knew how to wrestle, and knew also how to prevail.

A CIRCLE OF FRIENDS

Robert M'Cheyne was a man who owed much to his friends, but who gave more than he received. The charm of a sunny nature served as a foil to the white heat of his ardent spirit, and he was the central figure in a circle of friends who were all men of great ability. They were all to outlive M'Cheyne, but they never lost the sense of spiritual magnetism which his life had generated. His first close friend was Alexander Somerville, whom he had known from the days of boyhood. They went to the same school, and took their degree at the same time. They passed from death to life in the same year, and became Divinity students in the same term. 'Perhaps we may get a lodging near each other', Somerville once wrote to M'Cheyne, 'in the golden streets of the new Jerusalem.'[92] They were joined by the two Bonars in the Divinity classrooms, and the bond of friendship for two became a bond for four. Horatius Bonar was the elder brother, and one for whom M'Cheyne ever felt the deepest admiration. Poet, preacher, and saint, he looked for the second coming of Christ as the supreme event towards which all history gravitates. His hopes and dreams were all summed up in the words of the text which hung in his bedroom: 'Until the day break, and the shadows flee away' (*Song of Sol.* 2:17; 4:6).[93] Andrew Bonar was a kindred spirit with whom M'Cheyne felt more at home than with any other. Scholar, pastor, and friend, his whole life was summed up in one saying: 'I only yearn to know Him better, and to preach Him more fully.'[94] The four friends would often attend the church where in 1835 Alexander Moody Stuart began to preach, and one luminous quotation still shows what that preaching was like. 'In the law of Moses', he said, 'the sheep died for the shepherd; in the law of Jesus, the shepherd died for the sheep.'[95] He made the four friends so welcome that they arranged to spend an hour with him each week in prayer.

Robert M'Cheyne at Dundee was neighbour to Andrew Bonar at Collace, and they soon found others of like spirit. It was Andrew Bonar who found John Milne of Perth; it was Robert M'Cheyne who found William Burns of Kilsyth. Milne had the faith of a child, and the prayer of his heart shines through his words: 'I long for the purged conscience, the kept heart, the humble mind, the girded loins, the crucified flesh, and the lip and life of truth.'[96] Burns had the strength of a lion, and the fire of his soul bursts through his cry: 'O that I had a martyr's heart, if not a martyr's death and a martyr's crown!'[97] Milne and Burns were among the choice souls of Scotland in that generation, and they were to spend their lives as missionaries of the gospel: the one in Bengal, and the other in China. Then there was James Grierson of Errol in whose manse M'Cheyne had spent the night before his ordination in Dundee;[98] there was Robert Macdonald of Blairgowrie with whom M'Cheyne sometimes went to stay and to whom many of his letters were written;[99] there was James Hamilton of Abernyte who was later called to Regent Square in London and who said of M'Cheyne: 'When I compare myself with him, I see what sinful trifling much of my ministry has been.'[100] There were others as well, less intimate, but like-minded, such as Patrick Miller of Wallacetown, and Cumming of Dumbarney, and Cormick of Kirriemuir. Such was the band of friends for whom M'Cheyne was both first and equal; he loved them as they loved him, for they all shared the same Spirit. They were ever welcome in each other's manse and pulpit; they were always eager for each other's help and counsel. They browsed in the same pastures; they drank from the same waters; they looked for the same fold on the hills of eternity. Bishop Ryle used to say that the ministry of a man like M'Cheyne would have been an ornament for any church:[101] one may well add that his friendship would have been a benediction for any man.

This circle of friendship proves that he was endowed with generous sympathy and sensitive affection: but the record is not complete without further details. The finger of romance touched his heart more than once and stirred him in another direction. Alexander Smellie affirms that for some months at the age of eighteen, he lived in a palace of dreams in which Mary MacGregor reigned as queen.[102] She was some years older than he, and she left her home in Edinburgh while he was still eighteen. His heart was soon changed by the grace of God while hers was not, and he knew that she was not meant for him. He penned an ode for her birthday in 1832 in imitation of Cowper's address to Mary Unwin.[103] The lines mark their separation, but there is a wistful note at the end of every stanza: 'My Mary!' Seven years passed away; then in 1839, he called on her, met her husband, and spent an evening with her in London. 'Mary very little changed,' he observed; 'not seemingly quite happy.'[104] Nothing further is heard of her; but the first place next to his home circle in the list of those for whom he prayed was assigned to the MacGregor family.[105]

But this boyish fancy was not to stand alone, for he was twice engaged to be married during his last five or six years. The full story cannot be told because the facts were not preserved. Andrew Bonar drew a veil of silence over this side of his friend's life, no doubt because he would not hurt those who were most nearly concerned: but this is now the main defect in a superb Memoir because it makes M'Cheyne appear as so other-worldly that he never knew the meaning of true human romance. Alexander Smellie was able to gather up some of the details, enough to show that he did love as all men do when God permits. He did not live to know the joys of an earthly union with a wife and children in a home of his own, but his heart was just as open to all that was true and tender on a human level as it had been to all that was sweet and holy on the level that is divine.

It was during 1837 that he became engaged to the daughter of a Dundee doctor, a Miss Maxwell whom 'none named but to praise'.[106] But her relatives intervened, and the match was discontinued: 'They feared for that frail body of his, and judged it wiser that there should not be any wedding bond.'[107] A year or two elapsed; then a playful comment in a letter from Alexander Somerville in 1839 provides the first hint of a new romance. He wrote of 'a friend of yours', and the word 'friend' was doubly underlined.[108] This was Jessie Thain of Heath Park near Blairgowrie where her father was an elder in Robert Macdonald's congregation. The Thains had at one stage spent some months in Dundee and had become deeply attached to St Peter's and its minister. Mrs Thain wrote to him before he left for the Levant and sent a small pocket Bible for his travels. 'When far away in a land of strangers,' she wrote, 'will you remember my dear children? . . . Poor Jessie has felt your absence all along very much; and now that it has come to this crisis, she is cast down. May she find that Jesus is ever near, though her pastor is far away.'[109] And he wrote in reply on 15 March: 'Tell Jessie to stay herself upon God; Jesus continueth ever.'[110]

Andrew Bonar preserved two other letters to Mrs Thain, one in February 1839 and one in June 1840; and one to each of her two sons, in January and in March 1842.[111] There was something rather pensive in this correspondence; the Thains were a delicate family, 'walking much in the solemn shadows of the other world'.[112] One son died in childhood; the other in early manhood: and it appears that, like them, their sister was by no means robust. It is not clear when he became engaged to her; it was evidently later than his letter in June 1840. There is nothing that would explain why his courtship was so prolonged and was at last deprived of its crown in marriage. Was it that her health, frail as his, would not permit the step? Was the wedding at hand when the end came? There are sanctities in this engagement which no other eye may explore; but the ties which bound him to her and her home were never broken in life or death. There are still two letters from Mrs Thain to M'Cheyne's mother and from Jessie herself to M'Cheyne's sister which overflow with tenderness.[113] God did not grant these twain a home on earth, but it is clear that they were for ever one in spirit.

'A NEW SCHOOL OF PREACHING'

Andrew Bonar and Moody Stuart both remark on the fact that the clan of friends in which M'Cheyne was the central figure brought in a new school of preaching in the Church of Scotland.[114] M'Cheyne himself was a preacher of far greater skill than his short life might suggest, and the secret was his unsparing diligence in preparation and consistent emphasis on the gospel message. He was convinced that a preacher sheds a true light only when he is held as a star in the right hand of the Son of God,[115] and that faithless preachers will be cast out of that right hand into the long night of total darkness.[116] This taught him to prepare for the pulpit with an eye to eternity; he was sure that nothing else would serve but 'beaten oil for the lamps of the sanctuary'.[117]

At first he wrote out each sermon in full, but he learned by degrees to preach from notes: he would meditate with earnest prayer in his study, and then improvise with searching power in the pulpit. 'One thing always fills the cup of my consolation,' he wrote; 'that God may work by the meanest and poorest words as well as by the most polished and ornate, – yea, perhaps more readily, that the glory may be all His own.'[118] There was doctrine in his preaching, but the great issue in all his sermons was to press the invitation of the gospel on his hearers. Andrew Bonar sized it up in one clear picture: 'Is not the true idea of preaching that of one like Ahimaaz, coming with all important tidings, and intent of making these tidings known?'[119] Such a system of preparation and preaching would always reflect the experience of his own soul; he could only give out of the fullness of what he had himself received. It was never enough for him to have bread from heaven for the hungry or the waters of life for the thirsty: it had to be water which he had drawn from the palace wells and bread which he had won from the King's table to meet his own hunger and thirst. He led his flock in the green fields and by the still waters where he himself had found nourishment and rest.

Burns and M'Cheyne might have vied for first place in that group of young men: they were gifted preachers, with a power and success far in advance of their age or

experience. They had both been grounded in the knowledge and culture of the ancient classics; they were alike
in the unction and passion of the Holy Spirit. But there
were great contrasts as well, and the contrasts throw a
broad beam of light on each of them. Burns set out to
study a subject rather than to compose a sermon, and his
preaching cannot be judged by the rough notes which
were taken down and published without his knowledge
or supervision.[120] His voice could travel the round of any
audience; his words would sparkle as clear as any diamond.
He was always direct, and sometimes dramatic; he was
always urgent, and sometimes vehement. Sometimes he
would close the Bible with a look of sadness, as though
afraid that it had been in vain; sometimes he would press
the appeal with a note of patience, as though he could
not let men go.[121] 'He is a very remarkable preacher',
M'Cheyne told his parents. 'The plainness and force of
his statements, I never saw equalled.'[122] 'There is a great
deal of substance in what he preaches', so M'Cheyne told
Bonar, 'and his manner is very powerful – so much so
that he sometimes made me tremble.'[123]

But while grandeur was the hallmark of Burns, the
secret of M'Cheyne was charm. All his talents were called
into action by the art of preaching, and the gifts of nature
were all enhanced by the rich grace of the Holy Spirit.
There was beauty and fancy in each flight of thought;
passion and pathos in each mood of soul. There was music
in his voice and accent; colour in his style and diction.
There was all the fire of poetry in his language; there was
all the force of genius in his insight. M'Cheyne's preaching
had a persuasive quality that drew the heart to God with
a sureness that was not of this world. Yet in the last
analysis, it was the man rather than the preacher who
compelled the people to hear.

The great secret of his success in the pulpit was his combination of faithfulness to the Word of God with tenderness for the souls of men. He went about his work with an air of reverence which made men feel that the majesty of God was in his heart. There were few who could exhort the guilty in more searching or tremendous terms; there were few who could address the troubled in more gentle or persuasive tones. Andrew Bonar once told him how he had chosen for a text the words with regard to the doom of those who forget God and are sent to hell (*Psa.* 9:17). M'Cheyne at once asked him: 'Were you able to preach it with tenderness?'[124] He knew that there is an enormous difference between a voice that scolds and a heart that yearns: the one is mere reproach, while the other may be full of warning. It is not by threats and thunder, but by love and pathos that hearts are made to melt; it is not by words that scorch and condemn, but by a heart that bleeds to bless that souls are won. M'Cheyne himself preached on eternal destiny as one whose heart was wrung with a sense of anguish. He did not spare his hearers a word of truth; still less did he spare his own feelings a stab of pain. There was nothing reckless in such preaching; he knew how to discriminate with the surest intuition. 'Remember,' he would say, 'a moral sinner will lie down in the same hell with the vilest.'[125] J. H. Jowett once said that his severities were terrific simply because they were so tender.[126] He was indeed willing to share in that divine travail by means of which men are born from above in the kingdom of God. Both the motive and the power in all such preaching may be discerned in his sermon on a broken heart and contrite spirit. 'It is not', he said, 'a look into your own heart, or the heart of hell, but into the heart of Christ, that breaks the heart. Oh, pray for this broken heart!'[127]

'It behoves ministers to unite the cherub and the seraph in their ministry', so M'Cheyne once declared; ' – the angel of knowledge and the angel of burning zeal.'[128] These two elements were both present in his ministry, but the two most prominent qualities were his tremendous urgency and his exceeding tenderness. 'Get ripening views of Christ', he would say. 'The corn in harvest sometimes ripens more in one day than in weeks before. So some Christians gain more grace in one day than for months before. Pray that this may be a ripening harvest day in your souls.'[129] His word pictures and the musical quality of his voice both helped to make the truth linger long in the heart. 'There are some among you', he exclaimed, 'that remind me of an aged tree that has been struck with lightning and now stands stript of its leaves . . . I tell you, brethren, if mercies and if judgments do not convert you, God has no other arrows in His quiver.'[130] Preachers who would learn the art of pathos might well take him as guide: his heart was so wistful; his words were so tender. A short phrase would sketch a picture, and the inner throb of yearning could not be hid. 'If God spared not His own Son under the sin of another, how shall He spare thee under the weight and burden of thine own sin? If they do these things in a green tree, what shall be done in the dry?'[131] He had the most telling power of rebuke, but he had an even greater power of appeal. His hearers in Dundee would often recall a saying of his, full of urgent demand: 'When the boat has put off from the shore, you need not run. When should you run? When the bell is ringing.'[132] All his gifts of persuasion were brought to bear in a call for decision which was always hard to resist. 'Brethren,' he would say, 'if I could promise you that the door will stand open for a hundred years, yet it would still be your wisdom to enter in now. But I cannot answer for a year; I cannot answer for a month; I cannot answer for a day; I cannot answer for an hour. All that I can answer for is, it is open now.'[133]

But the final observation must be that not seldom it was his own personal holiness rather than his most persuasive arguments which made the decisive impression. William Milne of Montreux once heard him give an address at a baptismal service. Milne could recall nothing of what was said, except that he referred to the necessity for the new birth. But there was one detail which he could not forget, and that was the light in the eyes of the preacher: 'They seemed to glow with a fire that was not of this world, and that told how God dwelt in him if ever He dwells in man at all.'[134] Many of his converts held that it was not so much what he said as the way in which he said it that won their hearts and drew them to put their trust in Christ.

Burns and M'Cheyne had this power in common; they could not speak even of ordinary things without making men hear the voice of God in the inmost region of their spirit. Burns once paused in the midst of a sermon to point out the fruit trees which were clothed with blossom; then he asked his hearers if they were to come back in the autumn and count the ripe apples, how few they would be in comparison with the blossom which chill winds would nip and scatter.[135] An old Highland woman at Blair Atholl came day after day to sit on the stairs of the pulpit and to wait on every word that fell from his lips: she did not know a word of English, but she understood 'the Holy Ghost's English'.[136]

So it was with M'Cheyne. He stopped one day at a roadside quarry to take shelter from a sudden downpour of rain. There was a fire in the furnace of the engine shed where he was standing with a group of workmen, and he asked them what that fire taught them to think of. That was all; but the way in which the words were spoken made them burn in their hearts. They knew him as a man of God, and one of them was brought to kneel in God's presence with true faith and obedience.[137]

Few who heard him engage in prayer ever forgot the deep solemnity which marked the two words with which he always began: 'Holy Father'. His whole face shone with the unreserved assurance of childlike trust, and he spoke as if he were then looking into the face of God.[138] Eternity alone, he once declared, will be able to teach all that it means to have a son's strong, deep filial interest in God.[139] Perhaps the most telling illustration of this aspect of his life lies in a beautiful incident which took place just two weeks before he died. On 12 March 1843, he preached what was to prove his last sermon; it was away from St Peter's in the little church at Broughty Ferry. 'Arise, shine,' was the text; 'for thy light is come, and the glory of the LORD is risen upon thee' (*Isa.* 60:1). He spoke with great sweetness, and a stranger went home to write to him. 'I heard you preach last Sabbath evening, and it pleased God to bless that sermon to my soul. It was not so much what you said as your manner of speaking that struck me. I saw in you a beauty of holiness that I never saw before.'[140] M'Cheyne was in the last stage of illness when this letter arrived, and it was not opened until after his death.

Forty-five years were to pass by; then on 6 November 1878, the Rev. Hussey Burgh Macartney of St Mary's Caulfield in Victoria, spent an evening at Broughty Ferry with Alexander Somerville. They sat up at the manse until midnight, and their conversation took in the whole company of friends with whom Somerville had been so much at home. At last Macartney went to his room, 'still thinking of M'Cheyne'. His heart was full as he recalled how M'Cheyne's last sermon had been preached at Broughty Ferry and had drawn that letter from a stranger with its spontaneous testimony to the blessing received and its personal reference to the preacher himself. He mused on the facts with exceeding tenderness, and then observed with a flash of insight: 'M'Cheyne was in a fever when this note reached his house. He was spared the pain of the last clause; the pleasure of the first clause he will taste above.'[141]

THE *MEMOIR*

M'Cheyne owes his reputation very largely to the *Memoir* which was prepared by Andrew Bonar soon after his death: it was destined to become a classic in the religious history of the Scottish people. It is true that modern readers may feel disappointed with this biography; they may not like it on the ground that it is too uncritical and too pietistic. It is essentially Victorian in its approach, and the picture it draws is so faultless that it seems to lack in reality. Nevertheless this *Memoir* of M'Cheyne had an enormous influence for a hundred years after its publi-cation, and the reason for this was its revelation of the growth of a soul in the knowledge and love of God. Andrew Bonar did not exaggerate his own feelings in the *Memoir;* he had expressed his own wistful sense of wonder with regard to M'Cheyne as early as 8 November 1838: 'What I wonder at in Robert M'Cheyne more than all else,' so he confided in his diary, 'is his simple feeling of desire to show God's grace, and to feed upon it himself.'[142]

M'Cheyne had come before God as a child, and both his hands were held out as he came. The left hand was

full; it held all that he had and all that he was: this he had
brought that it might be wholly yielded to God. But the
right hand was empty: it had nothing that he could claim
as his own: this he held out that it might be filled with all
the fullness of God.[143] He once said that the peace of
God is the best ground for growth in grace,[144] and this
was the secret of his constant increase in true spiritual
experience. Thus on 1 April 1838, he wrote; 'Much peace
in communion; happy to be one with Christ. I, a vile
worm; He, the Lord my righteousness.'[145] He had long
been content to lay hold on the word 'never' in the
promise: 'I will never leave thee, nor forsake thee' (*Heb.*
13:5). He saw that it would reach beyond all temptation
or affliction, through life and death, beyond the grave,
into eternity.[146] Such were some of the things which made
him what he was, and his friends saw the truth. Some
lives are bright with the beauty of the Rose of Sharon;
his life was sweet with its fragrance as well.

It was this rare combination of fragrance and beauty in
his personal character which gave Bonar's *Memoir* so
strong a hold on the Victorian generation. All that David
Brainerd was to America and Henry Martyn to England,
Robert M'Cheyne soon became to Scotland. He stood
in the authentic line of succession to men whose lives
were marked by an absolute singleness of eye for the glory
of God. He may have been much less austere than David
Brainerd and more buoyant than Henry Martyn; he was
no less absorbed than they in vision and pursuit of things
unseen. Bonar said that M'Cheyne had been led to per-
ceive that it was more humbling to take what grace has
to offer than to lament his own wants and unworth-
iness.[147] On 11 June 1836, he had written: 'It is the
sweetest word in the Bible, "Sin shall not have dominion
over you". Oh, then, that I might lie low in the dust, the

lower the better, that Jesus' righteousness and Jesus' strength alone be admired.'[148] It was in this spirit that he wrote to John Milne five years later: 'I long for love without any coldness, light without dimness, and purity without spot or wrinkle; I long to lie at Jesus' feet and tell Him I am all His, and ever will be.'[149]

Every fibre of his soul wrapped itself round the name of Jesus as Lord of all; and so it was to the end of his life. Andrew Bonar said that in the letters which he wrote in the last few weeks of his life, there were repeated expressions of this supreme desire. 'I often pray,' so he declared, 'Lord, make me as holy as a pardoned sinner can be made.'[150] He longed to stand before the throne where he would see 'the King in His beauty' (*Isa*. 33:17): for then, but not till then, would he know all that grace had wrought.[151] Andrew Bonar never ceased to feel the impact of this heavenly mindedness. It is registered in the words which he wrote in his diary fourteen years after M'Cheyne's death. 'March 27th 1857', so the words run, 'O my Lord, give me a double portion of the Spirit Thou gavest him.'[152]

'The Night Cometh'

'His simple feeling of desire to show God's grace', at which Bonar wondered, taught him to walk in the footprints of Christ and to preserve the edge on his spirit right to the end.[153] His crest or seal was a sunset behind the peak of a mountain, and the motto beneath was the divine watchword: 'The night cometh' (*John* 9:4).[154] His own sun was to set amid skies so dark that they would not clear until the storm of the Disruption had burst upon the Church of Scotland. M'Cheyne had no taste for controversy, and no one could have been less disposed to meddle with the domestic policies of Church and State. But he had sat under Thomas Chalmers and he could not ignore great church issues. In October 1837, he had been at a house party in the home of Mr J. C. Colquhoun at Killermont. 'There was something holy', he wrote, 'about the very atmosphere. Chalmers was sitting opposite to me at this table, writing, his venerable countenance expressing peace and goodwill to men.'[155] This led him to take an active share in the cause of Church Extension, and he even gave his pony this name as it trotted to and fro in the cause. But this meant that he could not stand aside from the Ten Years' Conflict with its challenge to the public conscience, and he was found ready to speak his mind on all the great issues that hung in the balance. A lay patron was as foreign to the Church of Christ as a lord prelate in his judgment, and he was a decided advocate of the principle of Non-Intrusion. The fact was that recent years had produced a number of cases where lay patrons had forced unwanted ministers on churches and congregations. Appeal to the civil courts had upheld the lay patrons at the expense of the Presbyteries. M'Cheyne never had a doubt as to where right lay in this conflict, and he rejoiced to stand behind men like Chalmers in their fight for freedom. He knew that the crown rights of the Sovereign Redeemer in his church were at stake; this meant that the whole cause of the Covenant heritage in the Kirk was on trial.

M'Cheyne followed the long struggle with an unflagging interest, and ranged himself wholeheartedly behind leaders like Chalmers and Candlish. William Milne of Montreux heard him speak at one church meeting on this subject during 1842; he summed up the dispute in one brief sentence which made a tremendous impression. 'They want us to take Christ's crown from His royal brow and place it upon Caesar,' he said; 'but that is what we will not do.'[156] This was the language of the great Covenanters, and the basic struggle was much the same. He took part in preaching tours in country districts where the landlords were trying to destroy the historic ordinance which prescribed the right of a congregation to call a new minister, and those who were present never forgot his prayers in the famous meetings which were convened when the law-courts tried to force their verdict upon the Church. He spoke in the very spirit of the words of Samuel Rutherford: 'There is no sweeter fellowship with Christ than to bring our wounds and our sores to Him.'[157]

He took part in the great Convocation which was held at Roxburgh Chapel in Edinburgh on 17 November 1842: it went on for eight days altogether, and four hundred and sixty-five ministers from all parts of Scotland were there. He had drawn up the plan for prayer which was employed from Dumfries to Caithness, and he kept a record of the speakers and their speeches throughout that week. On Saturday 26 November, he had this to record: 'After an amazing speech from Dr Chalmers which brought tears into many eyes, 427 agreed to the resolutions.'[158] They were resolutions which pledged those who signed them to leave the Church rather than accept State control. M'Cheyne subscribed gladly, and his judgment was as firm as granite when the crucial debate took place in the House of Commons on 7 March 1843. 'Eventful night this in the British Parliament!' he wrote. 'Once more King Jesus stands at an earthly tribunal, and they know Him not.'[159]

He would gladly have thrown in his lot with the men who were to form the Free Church of Scotland had he lived to see the Disruption, but his comment on 7 March was one of the last he would pen. He was the saint of the Disruption, though that was an event he did not live to see. He was one in spirit with that great band of men who rose up and left St Andrew's Church with Thomas Chalmers and who marched through crowded streets to Tanfield Hall in order to found the Free Church of Scotland on 18 May 1843. The trumpets had sounded for him less than two months before and he had been summoned across the dark waters. It was with him as with Samuel Rutherford when he received a summons to Edinburgh to stand his trial on a charge of treason: Samuel Rutherford would have been glad to go, but he could not; he had received a yet higher summons which he had to obey, and he went to stand before God's throne, where few kings and great folk come.

M'Cheyne had often been away from his home and parish after his mission to Israel, and his congregation was not without concern. He travelled to Belfast both in July 1840 and in July 1841.[160] He joined Somerville of Anderston, Bonar of Kelso, Purves of Jedburgh, and Cumming of Dumbarney, to follow a visit by Burns to the north of England in August 1842, and he was in London to help James Hamilton at Regent Square in November 1842.[161] He travelled widely in Scotland itself, preaching at places like Kelso and Ancrum, Huntly and Collace.[162] He had never spared his slender strength in the cause of Christ, but strove so to live that he would make the most of his span of time. He was in such demand that he could not confine himself to his church in Dundee, for all men knew that the secret of the Lord was with him. Robert Candlish said that he had more of the mind of Christ and more likeness to the beloved disciple than any man he ever knew.[163] James Hamilton wrote to M'Cheyne's father after his death and said: 'Since the days of Samuel Rutherford, I question if the Church of Scotland has contained a more seraphic mind, one that was in such a constant flame of love and adoration toward Him that liveth and was dead.'[164]

M'Cheyne had once remarked that those who stand on the edge of the sea sometimes see how a small wave is followed by a large one: even so may God send a small trial first, and thus prepare the heart for the larger trial to follow.[165] He had himself survived more than one trial, and a darker was now at hand; but it held no terror for him, for his ear had caught the footfall of One who came to take him by the hand. In February 1843, he left Dundee at the direction of the Committee of the Convocation to preach throughout Deer and Ellon, and in the next three weeks he spoke in twenty-four centres. 'The oil of the lamp in the temple burnt away in giving light,' he said; 'so should we.'[166] He preached three times in St Peter's on 5 March, and twice the next Sunday. His last sermon was at Broughty Ferry on the evening of that Sunday, and the next day he pledged himself and his congregation to stand with the Free Church when the moment arrived.

On Tuesday 14 March, he was stricken with the typhus which was rife in Dundee, and he knew that the end was near. He had taken no steps to shield himself as he went to and fro, and he quickly succumbed. Tired and worn as he was, he soon took a turn for the worse. It was as though God had come to pluck the flower from its stem while each petal was still fresh and full of colour. First his father, then his mother, came north to watch by his bed as he sank into delirium. His heart still went out for Dundee, though it was with delirious voice that he cried, 'This parish, Lord! This people! This whole place!'[167] He was not quite thirty years old, the age when a priest in Israel would begin his service; but he had long since learned to dwell at the mercy seat as if it were his home.[168] The end came with tranquil beauty on the morning of

25 March 1843. He raised his hands as if to bless, just as the hands of the risen Saviour were raised on the Mount of Olives. Then he sank down, without a sound or sigh, with only a fleeting quiver of the lips to let the watchers know that trailing clouds of glory had received his spirit beyond their sight.

BIBLIOGRAPHY

1. 1844 – Andrew A. Bonar, *The Memoir and Remains of Robert Murray M'Cheyne* (My copy a new edition, 1913. Enlarged edition first published 1892; repr. Edinburgh: Banner of Truth, 2004).
2. *Additional Remains of the Rev. Robert Murray M'Cheyne* (new edition; no date).
3. *A Basket of Fragments, being the Substance of Sermons by the late Rev. R. M. M'Cheyne* (sixth edition; no date).
4. 1868 – Horatius Bonar, *The Life of the Rev. John Milne of Perth* (fourth edition).
5. 1869 – M. F. Barbour, *Notes of Addresses by the Rev. William C. Burns.*
6. 1870 – William Arnot, *The Life of James Hamilton* (third edition).
7. 1871 – Islay Burns, *Memoir of the Rev. William C. Burns* (sixth edition).
8. 1875 – Robert Murray M'Cheyne, *Brief Expositions of the Epistles to the Seven Churches of Asia* (seventh thousand).
9. 1878 – A. A. Bonar and R. M. M'Cheyne, *Narrative of a Visit to the Holy Land and Mission of Inquiry to the Jews* (thirtieth thousand).
10. 1889 – *A Memorial of Horatius Bonar.*
11. 1890 – J. C. Smith, *Robert Murray M'Cheyne.*
12. 1891 – George Smith, *A Modern Apostle: Alexander N. Somerville* (second edition).

13. 1893 – Marjory Bonar, *The Diary and Letters of Andrew A. Bonar.* (repr. Edinburgh: Banner of Truth, 1984).
14. 1895 – Marjory Bonar, *Reminiscences of Andrew A. Bonar.*
15. 1900 – Kenneth Moody Stuart, *Alexander Moody Stuart, A Memoir* (second edition).
16. 1909 – *Memories of Horatius Bonar,* by Relatives and Public Men.
17. 1913 – Alexander Smellie, *Robert Murray M'Cheyne* (third edition).
18. 1913 – William Lamb, *M'Cheyne From The Pew* (second edition).

NOTES

[1] Charles D. Bell, *Reminiscences of a Boyhood in the Early Part of the Century* (1889).

[2] Cf. Alexander Smellie, *Robert Murray M'Cheyne*, p. 32,

[3] Andrew A. Bonar, *Memoir and Remains of Robert Murray M'Cheyne*, p. 10. This title is currently published by the Banner of Truth Trust (London: Banner of Truth, 1966), 648 pp., ISBN 0 85151 084 1. Hereafter, M'Cheyne, *Memoir*.

[4] Ibid. p. 11.   [5] Ibid. p. 10.

[6] Ibid. p. 11.   [7] Ibid. p. 632.

[8] Robert Murray M'Cheyne, *The Seven Churches of Asia*, p. 69.

[9] William Hanna, *The Memoirs of Thomas Chalmers* 2 vols., vol. 1, pp. 64, 66; vol. 2, pp. 61–63.

[10] Marjory Bonar ed. *Diary and Letters of Andrew Bonar*, p. xii. Hereafter, Bonar, *Diary*.

[11] Alexander Smellie, ibid. p. 42.

[12] Braid Scots: older, or dialect forms of the Scottish tongue, a development of old English.

[13] George Smith, *Alexander Somerville*, p. 35.

[14] A. Moody Stuart, *Recollections of John Duncan*, p. 48,

[15] M'Cheyne, *Memoir*, p. 13.   [16] Ibid. p. 18.

[17] Ibid. p. 298.   [18] Ibid. p. 14.

[19] Ibid. p. 19.   [20] Ibid. p. 218.

[21] Ibid. p. 16.   [22] Ibid. p. 25.

[23] *The Letters of Samuel Rutherford, with a Biographical Introduction by Andrew A. Bonar* (Edinburgh: Banner of Truth, repr. 2006).

[24] M'Cheyne, *Memoir*, p. 211.
[25] Alexander Smellie, ibid. p. 45.
[26] M'Cheyne, *Memoir*, p. 33.
[27] Ibid. p. 33.
[28] Alexander Smellie, ibid. p. 54.
[29] Ibid. p. 55.
[30] M'Cheyne, *Memoir*, ibid., p. 492.
[31] Ibid. p. 34.
[32] Ibid. p. 34.
[33] Alexander Smellie, ibid. p.80.
[34] M'Cheyne, *Memoir*, p. 45.
[35] Alexander Smellie, ibid. p. 65.
[36] M'Cheyne, *Memoir*, p. 281.
[37] Ibid. p. 74.
[38] Ibid. p. 93.
[39] Robert Murray M'Cheyne, *A Basket of Fragments*, p. 161. Hereafter, M'Cheyne, *Fragments*.
[40] James Strachan, *Memoir of Mary Crawford Brown*, p. 19.
[41] Alexander Smellie, ibid. p. 66. [42] M'Cheyne, *Memoir*, p. 64.
[43] Alexander Smellie, ibid. p. 66.
[44] Geoffrey Chaucer, *The Prologue to the Canterbury Tales*, line 72.
[45] M'Cheyne, *Memoir*, p. 13. [46] Ibid. p. 18.
[47] Ibid. p. 41. [48] Ibid. p. 37.
[49] Ibid. p. 26. [50] Ibid. p. 85.
[51] Ibid. p. 280. [52] Ibid. p. 87.
[53] William Shakespeare, *King Henry IV,* Part 1, Act 1, Scene 1, line xxiv.
[54] A. A. Bonar and R. M. M'Cheyne, *Narrative of a Visit to the Holy Land*.
[55] Alexander Smellie, ibid. p. 100.
[56] A. A. Bonar and R. M. M'Cheyne, ibid. p. 128.
[57] Ibid. p. 125. [58] Ibid. p. 212.
[59] Ibid. p. 162. [60] Ibid. p. 202.
[61] M'Cheyne, *Memoir*, pp. 640–641.
[62] A. A. Bonar and R. M. M'Cheyne, ibid. p. 320.
[63] Ibid. p. 520. [64] Ibid. p. 284.
[65] Alexander Smellie, ibid. p. 58.
[66] Marjory Bonar, *Reminiscences of Andrew Bonar*, p. xiv.
[67] Ibid. p. 53. [68] Ibid. p. 302.
[69] Alexander Smellie, ibid. p. 62.
[70] Bonar, *Diary and Letters*, p. 375. [71] Ibid. p. 389.
[72] Islay Burns, *Memoir of the Rev. William Burns*, pp. 227 228.
[73] M. F. Barbour, *Notes of Addresses by the Rev. William C. Burns*, p. ix.
[74] Ibid. p. 28.
[75] Dr and Mrs Howard Taylor, *Hudson Taylor in Early Years*, p. 361.
[76] M'Cheyne, *Memoir*, p. 273. [77] Alexander Smellie, ibid. p. 125.
[78] M'Cheyne, *Memoir*, p. 114. [79] Alexander Smellie, ibid. p. 139.
[80] M'Cheyne, *Memoir*, p. 130.
[81] Alexander Smellie, ibid. pp. 185–188. [82] M'Cheyne, *Memoir*, p. 256.
[83] Ibid. p. 116. [84] Ibid. p. 121.
[85] R. M. M'Cheyne, *Additional Remains*, p. 268.

[86] Ibid. p. 268.
[87] Alexander Smellie, ibid. p. 154.
[88] M'Cheyne, *Memoir*, p. 135.
[89] Ibid. p. 239.
[90] R. M. M'Cheyne, *Additional Remains*, p. 435.
[91] M'Cheyne, *Memoir*, p. 134.
[92] Alexander Smellie, ibid. p. 60.
[93] George Wilson, *Memories of Horatius Bonar*, p. 119.
[94] Marjory Bonar, *Reminiscences of Andrew Bonar*, p. xix.
[95] K. Moody Stuart, *Alexander Moody Stuart, A Memoir*, p. 245.
[96] Horatius Bonar, *The Life of John Milne*, p. 421.
[97] Islay Burns, *Memoir of the Rev. William C. Burns*, p. 193.
[98] M'Cheyne, *Memoir*, p. 53.
[99] Ibid. p. 56.
[100] Alexander Smellie, ibid. p. 59.
[101] J. C. Ryle, *Practical Religion*, p. 195; *Principles for Churchmen*, p. 207.
[102] Alexander Smellie, ibid. p. 190.
[103] Ibid. p. 193.
[104] Ibid. p. 194.
[105] Ibid. p. 195.
[106] Ibid. p. 195.
[107] Ibid. p. 195.
[108] Ibid. p. 196.
[109] Ibid. pp. 197–198.
[110] M'Cheyne, *Memoir*, p. 214.
[111] Ibid. pp. 211, 282, 310, 311.
[112] Alexander Smellie, ibid. p. 199.
[113] Ibid. pp. 200–201.
[114] Bonar, *Diary*, p. 67; K. Moody Stuart, ibid. p. 70.
[115] R. M. M'Cheyne, *The Seven Churches of Asia*, p. 6.
[116] M'Cheyne, *Memoir*, p. 130.
[117] Ibid. p. 52.
[118] Ibid. p. 39.
[119] Ibid. p. 46.
[120] M. F. Barbour, *Notes of Addresses by the Rev. William C. Burns*, p. iv.
[121] Ibid. p. 92.
[122] Alexander Smellie, ibid. p. 140.
[123] M'Cheyne, *Memoir*, p. 118.
[124] Ibid. p. 43.
[125] Ibid. p. 406.
[126] J. H. Jowett, *The Passion for Souls*, p. 87.
[127] M'Cheyne, *Memoir*, p. 436.
[128] Ibid. p. 403.
[129] Ibid. p. 417.
[130] R. M. M'Cheyne, *A Basket of Fragments*, p. 86.
[131] M'Cheyne, *Memoir*, p. 204.
[132] Alexander Smellie, ibid. p. 212.
[133] R. M. M'Cheyne. ibid. p. 43.
[134] J. C. Smith, *Robert Murray M'Cheyne*, p. 252.
[135] M. F. Barbour, *Notes of Addresses by the Rev. William C. Burns*, p. ix.
[136] Alexander Smellie, ibid. p. 127.
[137] M'Cheyne, *Memoir*, p. 123.
[138] Ibid. p. 145.
[139] Ibid. p. 377.
[140] Ibid. p. 162.
[141] George Smith, *A Modern Apostle, Alexander Somerville*, pp. 296–297.
[142] Bonar, *Diary*, p. 77.
[143] Alexander Smellie, ibid. p. 40.
[144] M'Cheyne, *Memoir*, p. 512.
[145] Ibid. p. 81.
[146] R. M. M'Cheyne, *A Basket of Fragments*, p. 235.
[147] M'Cheyne, *Memoir*, p. 23.
[148] Ibid. p. 42.
[149] Horatius Bonar, *The Life of John Milne*, p. 68.

[150] M'Cheyne, *Memoir,* p. 159.

[151] Ibid. p. 637.

[152] Bonar, *Diary,* p. 190.

[153] Ibid. p. 77.

[154] William Lamb, *M'Cheyne from the Pew,* p. 95.

[155] Alexander Smellie, ibid. p. 85.

[156] J. C. Smith, *Robert Murray M'Cheyne,* p. 251

[157] A. A. Bonar, *Letters of Samuel Rutherford,* Letter ccxxvii, p. 453.

[158] Alexander Smellie, ibid. p. 174.

[159] M'Cheyne, *Memoir,* p. 147.

[160] Ibid. pp. 134, 138.

[161] Ibid. pp. 144, 145.

[162] Ibid. pp. 135, 136, 141.

[163] Alexander Smellie, ibid. p. 221.

[164] Ibid. p. 222.

[165] R. M. M'Cheyne, *The Seven Churches of Asia,* p. 22.

[166] M'Cheyne, *Memoir,* p. 160.

[167] Ibid. p. 163.

[168] Ibid. p. 166.

St Peter's Church, Dundee. The memorial erected
in M'Cheyne's memory can still be seen to this day.
Its inscription reads:
Erected by his sorrowing flock, in memory of
the Reverend Robert Murray M'Cheyne,
their Minister of St Peter's Church, Dundee,
who died on the twenty-fifth day of March, MDCCCXLIII,
in the thirtieth year of his age, and seventh of his ministry.
Walking closely with God, an example of the believers,
in word, in conversation, in charity, in spirit, in faith, in purity,
he ceased not day and night to labour and watch for souls;
and was honoured by his Lord to bring many wanderers out of darkness,
into the path of life.
'Them also which sleep in Jesus will God bring with him.'

4

The Hon. Ion Grant Neville Keith-Falconer

A Friend of the Bedouin
1856–87

But there –
Beyond the golden veil,
West of the sunset shining trail,
What joys are his –
What solving of all mysteries,
What mighty glories of release,
What wonders of the soul's increase,
What ecstasies of untold bliss,
Through all eternity are his!

CANON HENRY CODY
(in W. C. White, *Canon Cody of*
St Paul's Toronto)

'The Angel' of Keith Hall

The Hon. Ion Grant Neville Keith-Falconer, the third son of the eighth Earl of Kintore, was born in Edinburgh on 5 July 1856. He could trace his descent from 'the gallant Keith'[1] who had fought the Danes with Malcolm II in 1010 and whose valour on the field of battle had led to his appointment as Hereditary Great Marischal of Scotland. Three hundred years later, in 1314, Sir Robert Keith led the Scottish cavalry at Bannockburn, and his attack on the English archers had a decisive influence on the battle. Sir William Keith built Dunnottar Castle near Stonehaven in Kincardineshire about the year 1380, and his grandson was created Earl Marischal by James II in 1455.[2] Dunnottar was a fortress of exceptional strength, standing on a rocky bluff which juts out between a deep ravine and the waters of the North Sea. The two eldest sons of the House fell at Flodden in 1513, and the fourth Earl Marischal took part in the battle of Pinkie in 1547. The fifth Earl Marischal was educated abroad and spent some time as a pupil in the home of Theodore Beza at Geneva. He was always a warm friend of learning, and he founded Marischal College at Aberdeen in 1593. Sir John Keith, the third son of the sixth Earl Marischal,[3] acquired the old Castle of Caskieben in 1663, converted it into Keith Hall, and became the first Earl of Kintore and Lord Inverurie in 1677. His grand-daughter married Lord Falconer of Halkerton, and on the death of the last Earl Marischal in 1778, her grandson became the fifth Earl of Kintore. The great grandson of this Earl succeeded to the title at the age of sixteen in 1844, and brought his bride home to Keith Hall in 1851. Ion was the third of four sons and three daughters who were to fill that home with the joys of childhood. He grew up in a House which was justly famous in the annals of his country; the heroic exploits of Marischals and the historic glories of Dunnottar were a magnificent inheritance. But the blood of noble men which flowed in his veins was not so great a gift as that of a home which was ruled by the love 'which passeth knowledge' (*Eph.* 3:19).

Keith Hall is a massive square-built mansion close to the small town of Inverurie, and Inverurie is situated within the fork made by the Don and the Urie about twenty miles from the mouth of the Don, just north of Aberdeen. The stern whiteness of this seventeenth-century building lacks the warmth and colour of an English house of the same period, but it is the earliest example of Renaissance domestic architecture in the north east of Scotland. The picturesque frontispiece of armorial escutcheons over the front door on the south is a striking feature. The lintel is inscribed with a brief prayer: 'May truth and grace rest here in peace'; and on top of the coat of arms is an original carving of the Scottish Royal Crown, Sceptre and Sword of State as a tribute to the part which Sir John Keith had played in preventing the Scottish Regalia from falling into Cromwell's hands. The view from the porch and garden looks to the line of hills where the Grampian crest of Ben-na-chie stands out; and a few miles above Keith Hall, the wee burn of Gadie flows into the river Urie. There is haunting beauty in the wistful lines of the song:[4]

> *I wish I were whar Gadie rins,*
> *'Mang fragrant heath and yellow whins,*
> *Or brawling doun the boskie lins,*
> *   At the back of Ben-na-chie!*

Ance mair to hear the wild birds' sang,
To wander birks and braes amang,
Wi' frien's an' fav'rites left sae lang
At the back of Ben-na-chie.

Keith Hall was the home and playground in which Ion and his brothers spent their childhood, varied from time to time by long visits to the south of England. His life as an adult was to have its centre in Cambridge or Aden, but his occasional visits to this home at Inverurie were a source of endless pleasure. He could not be insensitive to the splendid history of his forbears or the sweeping majesty of the Highlands, and he was in spirit a true son of Keith Hall all the days of his life.

Francis Alexander, the eighth Earl of Kintore, was an elder in the Free Church of Scotland and a member of the General Assembly. He was called the 'preaching Earl' in the north,[5] and he took a very active share in church work throughout his life. He had married his first cousin, Louisa Madeleine Hawkins, in 1851, a woman of quite outstanding devotion. There was spiritual charm and beauty in the atmosphere which they created, and this had a singular power of attraction for their children. They had their full share of sorrow as well as joy, for the angel of death cast a shadow more than once on their home. Dudley, who was two and a half years older than Ion, and Arthur, who was seven years younger, lacked the robust health which thrives in the vigorous atmosphere of a public school, and had to receive their education through tutors at home. But in November 1873, Dudley's bright young life reached its close, and in December 1877, Arthur's short day came to an end. The two brothers were boys who from childhood had shone with the love of Christ as though it were part of their very nature: sweet and gentle in spirit, true and winsome in conduct, they were early ripe for glory. Ion had been devoted to Dudley; they were seldom apart from each other. Dudley could not hide the joy that was set before him when he was dying, and the radiant memory of this was to pour its strength and comfort into Ion's heart in his own final illness.

Ion himself was a child in whom the grace of God seemed to dwell from the cradle: it was as though the flame of love divine had been kindled within when he was born. His pure childhood love for the Lord Jesus was like that of Nicholas Count von Zinzendorf, and it found an outlet in ways that won the hearts of all. He was indeed so much loved at Keith Hall that he was always known as 'the angel', and his old nurse was quite sure that he would one day be a missionary. Perhaps it was chiefly to his mother that he owed this bright and sunny spirit of love, and it never seemed to fail in freshness or to lack in simplicity as life went on.[6]

SCHOOL DAYS AT CHEAM AND HARROW

Ion was nine years old when his formal education began with a tutor, and for two years he was taught by this means, partly at Keith Hall, partly at Brighton, and at length in Vico, close to Naples. The two strongest features of his boyhood were a truthful spirit and a thoughtful manner: they were the stem of that chivalry and self-sacrifice which were to form the crown of his manhood. He did not need to be amused like so many children; he was always quick and apt in natural resources. Dudley was the leader in each boyish enterprise and their games were full of playful innocence. He was passionately fond of reading and soon turned this to good account. He was only five when he began to read the Bible aloud to the other children on Sunday afternoons, and when he was seven, he began to visit people in their cottage homes in order to read to them. This was wholly his own idea, and his parents had no knowledge of it until they heard from the cottage people themselves. The cottagers were astonished at his knowledge of the Bible and his ability to explain the meaning of what he read.

He was the soul of all that is generous, and his unfailing interest in the needs of others was as rare as it was unselfish. He could not meet men in rags and thin from hunger without turning out his pockets for them. Such a childhood may seem almost too ideal or remote from the rough and tumble which have marked the following century, but all available information points to the fact that the picture was true to life and by no means over-painted. This child in the Highlands was in training for his work as a friend of the poor in the East End of London, and those early years were to mould him in strength of character and in ways of charity. He could never recall a time when he did not love the Saviour, and he had become a true and wholehearted disciple while still in the morning of life. There was exceptional charm in such a childhood, for the story of those years was one of singular piety.

At the age of eleven, he left home in order to start his school life at Cheam in Surrey. Two years later, at Easter in 1869, he sat for a Classical Scholarship which would admit him to Harrow. Arthur Watson, a House Master, was at once drawn to this 'bright, fair, intelligent-looking boy' of thirteen,[7] and said that he would keep a place for him in the event of his success. The best taught boys were all candidates for this scholarship, and the competition was strong; but he headed the list and went up to Harrow in September 1869 as a scholar. G. W. E. Russell met him for the first time at a Christmas party at the end of the year. 'He was tall for his age', so he recalled, 'and looked older than his years; long-limbed, loosely built; with a great crop of fair, almost flaxen, hair; rosy cheeks; and blue, dreamy, distant-looking eyes.'[8] The Head Master, Dr Montagu Butler, was to recall how 'he rapidly passed up the Forms on that Side (the Classical) till he reached my own, the Upper Sixth. I was struck at once by his intelligence and steady work, and was surprised when I learned that he wished to be transferred to our Modern Side with a view to a fuller training in Mathematics, French and German'.[9] The transfer was carried out at the end of the summer term in 1872 and he rose to be at the head of that Side before he left Harrow. Russell entered Watson's House in 1871 and was Keith-Falconer's closest friend in his last two years at school. Russell was later to describe how 'he worked at odd and out-of-the-way subjects . . . not for the sake of prizes or promotion at school, but either simply to improve his own mind or with a view to future usefulness'.[10] Nevertheless he won the Ebrington Prize for German and the Flower Prize for German Prose at the end of the summer term in 1873. Mr E. E. Bowen who was master in charge of the Modern Side was to sum up his work at Harrow in a splendid tribute. 'It would be difficult to find a pleasanter boy to deal with', he wrote; 'he was always interested, always cheerful, with an eye for the picturesque side of things, and a delightful way of running off the rails in any direction that happened to suit his fancy.'[11]

Ion did not excel at games, but he was as blithe and merry as a boy could be, always full of fun and activity. Russell was to write of those years with more than a little nostalgia: 'At lessons, at games, at meals, in daily and hourly walks to school and back again, in preparation of work, in country rambles, at the Scientific Society, at the

Debating Society . . . we were incessantly in one another's company.'[12] His work at school was the herald of his subsequent interests in a variety of ways. He taught himself shorthand and took down the sermons in Chapel for practice. Sometimes he spent hours in writing out these notes in longhand with the result that he would lose his place in the class lists. But he was not perturbed; what he did learn, he made his own. Thus, as Robert Sinker was to assert, in his case if ever, the boy was father to the man: 'The lines of reading, the bent for languages, the keen interest in the study of Scripture, the simple, restful, yet thoughtful faith, the eager desire to be of service to others, the deep warm affection he gave to those whom he called friend – all these characterised Ion Keith-Falconer alike as schoolboy, undergraduate, and to the last.'[13]

The close links which he kept up with masters after he had left school are an indication of the part which Harrow could claim in thus making the man. Bowen's tribute after his death states the case with lucid insight. 'I never knew any one so clear-headed, I had almost said so candid,' he wrote, 'about what he knew. The way in which he could state an unsolved difficulty seemed almost as good as a solution of it . . . I think this clear-headedness in matters of intellect was after all only a reflection of the moral simplicity which was his highest and most beautiful gift. I have often known young men who were candid, many who were devout, and many who were pleasant; but I can hardly remember any who united the three qualities so fully. He approached the world of ideas as great observers approach the world of nature, with wonder, with reverence, and with humility.'[14]

Masters and boys all bore the same testimony to his character as a Christian while still at school. Arthur Watson said that he 'would not flinch for a moment from saying or doing what he believed to be right at the risk of incurring unpopularity or being charged with eccentricity'.[15] There was nothing of the prig or Pharisee in his attitude; far from it; but 'his heart and life were, as far as human eye could see, of unsullied purity'.[16] 'He was not like other boys', so G. W. E. Russell was to recall; 'he was essentially the reverse of commonplace. In every action and quality – in look and voice and manner and bearing – he was individual.'[17] Russell had no doubt as to the only valid explanation. 'When I first came to know him', he wrote, 'he was not merely a Christian, but if such a word is permissible in such a context, an accomplished Christian. He had in full perfection a child's confidence in his Father's love and goodness, and the intuitive peace of an unclouded faith. But he had much more than this. He had a reason for the hope that was in him.'[18]

He might have joined his friends at school who were being prepared for the rite of Confirmation; but he declared that he was a convinced member of the Free Church of Scotland, and he combined a boy's zeal and light-heartedness with the reasoned faith of a man. In May 1873, he wrote to his future sister-in-law, Lady Sydney Montagu,[19] with the self-revealing candour of a boy of seventeen: 'Do you know the hymn beginning, "The sands of time are sinking, the dawn of heaven breaks"? It is my favourite.' He wrote out in full the stanza about 'the deep sweet well of love', and wished that he could drink of that stream more deeply than as yet he knew how. Then he added: 'I have very nearly decided to become a Free Church minister. If so, you will have to look over my Hebrew exercises and hear me The Shorter Catechism.'[20] He would grow in large-hearted sympathy as he became a man, but he never lost the playful freedom of his boyhood. Arthur Watson said with perfect simplicity: 'With me the pleasant memories of his bright and God-fearing boyhood will linger as long as I live.'[21] And Dr Montagu Butler declared that 'his image will remain fresh in the hearts of many as of a man exceptionally noble and exceptionally winning.'[22]

A YEAR AT HITCHIN

He left Harrow when the summer term in 1873 came to an end. This was sooner than was customary, and Dr Montagu Butler handed him his last prize with words of real regret. But his object was to devote twelve months to a closer study of mathematics under the supervision of a tutor before he went up to Cambridge. He had arranged to live with the Rev. Lewis Hensley, the Vicar of Hitchin, who had been the Senior Wrangler in 1846 and a Fellow of Trinity College. Hitchin itself was a little parish half-way between London and Cambridge, and the Vicarage was ideal as a residence for men engaged in hard study. Ion was one of four young men who were there at the time, and they worked for six hours a day under the keen eye of Lewis Hensley. One short sentence in a letter to his sister-in-law provides a clear picture of what this meant. 'I do mathematics exclusively,' he wrote; 'trigonometry and analytical cones at present.'[23]

But while he worked with an unflagging industry, he had no more heart for mathematics at Hitchin than for classics at Harrow. He had yet to discover that area of study which would command his full intellectual enthusiasm. Lewis Hensley observed that 'he was full of all sorts of by-occupations and hobbies, and it was in following these that his eager character expended itself.'[24] He pursued his shorthand with great verve; he became an enthusiast for cycling; he took singing lessons; he led open-air meetings with Sankey's hymns on the outskirts of the parish. He would visit the sick and the infirm during the week, and would sing or pray at their bedside. He was in high spirits and full of fun, always absorbed in such matters and overflowing in conversation about them with others. But his brother Dudley's death on 27 November 1873 made him more than ever resolved to serve the Lord with all his heart, and a letter to his sister-in-law on 25 June 1876 shows the bent of his mind. 'I feel the time has come for me either to go in for the world out and out', he wrote, 'or else to take up with God's people and . . . try to win souls . . . Not that I intend henceforward to spend my time in buttonholing people about their souls in the streets, or in hurling texts at every one I meet, or such like, though I believe that it is the mission of some to do so; but nevertheless I wish to expend my time and energies generally in advancing Christ's kingdom on earth.'[25]

A Scholar at Cambridge

In October 1874, he went up to Cambridge as a member of Trinity College and took rooms at 21 Market Hill, facing the Guild Hall. Here he was to reside throughout the next ten years except in vacations, and Cambridge was henceforth his true *Alma Mater*. His first year was spent in reading for the mathematics Tripos, and in June 1875 he was placed in the first class and received a prize in the College examinations. A letter to Lady Sydney Montagu which bears no date clearly belongs to this time, and was written from Trinity College. 'As I got my first class', he said, 'I was allowed to come up here for the long. It is just a little dull, but it is great fun . . . Today is the first fine day for ever so long. I am going to ride to Hitchin this afternoon and train back, or *vice versa* . . . I have a class in the Choir School on Sunday mornings which is more interesting than Chapel. I am in College now. We are not allowed to be in lodgings in the long. I am in B. New Ct.'[26]

But the time had now come to turn away from mathematics as he had from classics, and he transferred his studies to the Tripos in theology. He was fascinated with his work in Hebrew from the outset, and it was clear that he had found the field wherein his real strength lay. 'In a comparatively short space of time', Sinker declared, 'he was able to compose with accuracy and elegance in that language . . . writing letters in it as a means of communication'.[27] In December 1876, he won one of the two prizes founded by Dean Jeremie of Lincoln for proficiency in the Greek text of the Septuagint, and he was a College Prizeman both in 1876 and in 1877. He sat for the Tripos in January 1878, and was one of six placed in the first class, while he also carried off the prize for Hebrew. He soon began to work for the Tyrwhitt University Hebrew Scholarship which had been founded in 1818, and also for the Tripos in Semitic languages, a course in Hebrew, Syriac, and Arabic which had just come into being. He was awarded the Tyrwhitt Scholarship in May 1879 and was placed in the first class in the Tripos examinations in February 1880. His work was judged to be 'distinctly brilliant and of decided promise'.[28] Robert Sinker, his close friend and tutor, summed it all up very aptly: 'The true scholar's instinct was strong within him, to seek ever for the truth and that alone. Thus . . . the sterner, severer form of study associated with Cambridge with its traditional loyalty to mathematical science and pure scholarship . . . attracted him.'[29]

Thus the virtues of a Highland home were combined with the training of a Cambridge Tripos to mould and shape a career of exceptional promise. But sound training and true learning do not tell the entire story; he was so versatile in interest and unselfish in character that he could not fail to attract others. G. W. E. Russell said that 'what he was in boyhood, that he was in manhood',[30] and his tall and well-shaped figure would have marked him out in any group of young men. He was six feet three inches in height, and his chest and limbs had developed in due proportion. He had shaken off the look of fragile beauty which had clung to him in boyhood, though he still had a child's delicate complexion with its rapid change of colour. Physical exercise and athletic achievement were to prove that his was strength beyond what is given to most. George Smith said that 'he seemed capable of any amount of physical endurance, and he rejoiced in his youth with pure joy.'[31] There was a rare kindness in his voice and a warmth in his smile which soon set people at ease. He could always adopt the burr of his Scottish forbears in fun or in whimsical reverie, and he had an infectious cheerfulness with a wealth of humour. G. W. E. Russell said that 'laughter was a sort of intoxication to him . . . a word or a nudge was enough to set him off.'[32] But this sense of fun was never marred by what was crude or unkind. No undertone of prejudice, no veiled attempt to disparage the character of those who were absent, ever found place in his conversation. He was very fond of certain forms of music, and this gave him great joy in a devotional context; but he had no special knowledge of its higher reaches, and it never appealed to him as a science. He was already proficient in Pitman's system of shorthand when he first went up to Cambridge, and he used it with great advantage as he combed through books or copied out notes in the library. And there was at least one other facet of his early manhood which was quite out of the ordinary: he was a great cyclist, and his feats both in speed and in distance were to train on him a limelight which was remarkable.

CHAMPION CYCLIST

Cycling was a novelty in the 1870s, and bicycles were only just coming into fashion when he first went up to Cambridge. But he was an enthusiast, and had begun cycling while at Harrow; and when he left school, the boys always thought him a sight to see when dressed in his riding costume, and sitting astride his huge machine. It was the old style of bicycle, on which he rode like a giant and was to defeat all the leading professionals of the decade. It was not until 1885 that the first bicycle with both wheels of equal diameter was made, nor until 1888 that pneumatic tyres were employed. Better roads and better machines have brought about revolutionary changes since the days of Keith-Falconer, and speed beyond the dreams of the early cyclist is now quite the normal experience. His time records have been broken, and his distance exploits have been surpassed. But he was a pioneer, and for two years at least, he was the best cyclist in all England: 'and', said Mr Bowen, 'his delight in success only showed in more than common relief the charming modesty with which he carried his honours.'[33]

He was always ready to give encouragement, and he was on terms of pleasant friendship with the professionals against whom he had to compete. He loved cycling for its own sake as a form of exercise and a means of adventure, and a cycling tour of Scotland with a friend of like mind gave him boundless pleasure. But he was an ardent competitor in the cycle races which were becoming popular, and he revelled in the discipline as well as the excitement which hard training and keen riding imposed. There were several occasions when he had no time for special training, and some of his greatest races were won after weeks of gruelling study. But, as Mr Bowen observed, 'he had a real delight in feats of strength and endurance for their own sake.'[34] He had a wonderful staying-power and was at his greatest at the finish; he would often cover the last hundred yards at a pace and with a verve which left other competitors at a comparative stand-still. One might compare him with Eric Liddell some fifty years later – an Edinburgh student, an Olympic athlete, who was to lay down his life as a missionary in China: both men were singularly modest in athletic achievement and noble in Christian character.[35]

Keith-Falconer was elected Vice-President of the Cambridge University Bicycling Club in June 1874 before he had even gone up. On 10 November, he won a ten-mile race in the record time of thirty-four minutes. 'I was not at all exhausted', he wrote; 'the road was splendid, and a strong wind blowing from behind.'[36] He won the Lent Term race in 1875 over a distance of forty-two miles from Hatfield to Cambridge, and he won a fifty-mile race from St Albans to Oxford in a contest between Oxford and Cambridge in May. In April 1876, he won the Amateur Championship Four-Miles Race at Lillie Bridge in the fastest time then on record, and in May he won the Cambridge fifty-mile race at Fenners. In May 1877, he became President of the London Bicycle Club, an office which he was to hold for nearly ten years. In the Cambridge races that month, he won the two, ten, and twenty-five-mile events, and in the Inter-University races held at Oxford, he made record times to win the two and ten-mile events. In May 1878, he won the title of Short Distance Champion in the two-mile race held by the National Cyclists' Union at Stamford Bridge.

Perhaps his greatest race was one which took place in the ensuing October, a five-mile race between professionals and amateurs. It proved to be a duel between Keith-Falconer and John Keen, who was the professional champion; Keith-Falconer won by five yards. 'The time was by far the fastest on record', he wrote. ' . . . the last lap (440 yards) we did in 39 seconds . . . The excitement was something indescribable. Such a neck and neck race was never heard of. The pace for the last mile was terrific, as the time shows (two minutes 52 2/5th seconds); and when it was over, I felt as fit and comfortable as ever I felt in my life . . . I did not perspire or blow from beginning to end.'[37] In May 1879, he met Keen at Cambridge in a two-mile event and won by three inches in record time. Three days later, he made a fresh record to win a twenty-mile event. He was absorbed in hard study all the morning and quite forgot the race. Other competitors were on the course ready to start when he rushed into the dressing room. He rode several miles before he recovered his breath. Then one by one all the competitors dropped out except Keith-Falconer and one other. He was content to ride behind until two hundred yards from home; then 'with a spurt which the Cantabs were expecting but which simply astonished all others, he came right away and won as he liked.'[38] His last major race was the fifty-mile Bicycle Union Amateurs Championship at the Crystal Palace on 29 July 1882. He won the race in a fraction of a second less than two hours, forty-four minutes, and broke the record by nearly seven minutes.

Witness for Christ in Cambridge and London

Keith-Falconer's years at Cambridge saw the formation of the Cambridge Inter-Collegiate Christian Union (C.I.C.C.U.) as a local product of the evangelical upsurge in the Victorian era. The great campaign of Moody and Sankey in Great Britain from 1873 to 1875 formed the background. There were also visits to Cambridge on the part of Sir Arthur Blackwood in 1873 and the Robert Pearsall Smiths in 1874; these in turn had led to the well-known meetings which took place at Broadlands in the heart of Hampshire. Broadlands was the home of William Cowper-Temple, stepson and heir of Lord Palmerston, himself soon to become Lord Mount-Temple. Pearsall Smith had mentioned to him the need to help Cambridge men by drawing them into the country for a few days of quiet and prayer. Thus the first house party to be held at Broadlands was in July 1874, and all kinds of people came in response to the invitation. But the origin of this idea was related to Cambridge, and when a new academic year began in October, its value had become plain and infectious. This was just when Keith-Falconer came up with a faith which shone in every corner of life and activity.

Two years later, in November 1876, the Rev. Sholto Douglas, who was to become better known as Lord Blythswood, addressed a large meeting in the Guild Hall. This paved the way for a return visit in March 1877 when he took part in a meeting at which about 250 men were present and which saw the birth of the C.I.C.C.U. 'We determined,' Sir Algernon Coote recalled, 'that every College in Cambridge where an out-and-out Christian man could be found should be represented in the Union ... and we found such men in sixteen out of the seventeen Colleges in Cambridge.'[39] Keith-Falconer was one such man; one whose faith was so cloudless and steadfast that it could not fail to attract those who knew him. All the early plans in the formation of the C.I.C.C.U. were thought and prayed about in the peaceful setting of Broadlands during those summers in the mid-1870s. Keith-Falconer was at Broadlands at least once in August 1878: he took down each address in shorthand and wrote an introduction for the published account. This was only a slight piece of service, but it revealed a depth of thought and a freedom of style which were sure marks of his spiritual maturity.

Keith-Falconer also found a vent for Christian devotion in the Barnwell Mission. The district of Barnwell was large and poor, a growing and squalid part of Cambridge, in the parish of St Andrew-the-less, and close to the river Cam at its northern boundary. In 1801, the population of the parish was 252 out of a total population in Cambridge of 10,087; in 1881, it was 21,078 out of a total of 35,363. The men were rough, the houses were over-crowded, and there was as much vice as in any slum in Bethnal Green. In 1874, William Rutley Mowll[40] of Corpus Christi College began to hold services for the Barnwell men and women, and in 1875 he hired the Theatre Royal in preparation for the Moody Mission which was to have taken place in Cambridge. Moody could not come in the end, but Mowll used the theatre throughout the month of May to reach people who had never been seen in church. So great was the response that the mission meetings were kept up once a week in a ragged school in New Street. Keith-Falconer took part in the special meetings during that month of May, and then became a firm friend of the whole Mission.

In July 1878, the Theatre Royal which stood in the High Road was put up for auction. Mowll and his friends resolved to buy it if they could, and to bid up to £1,200;

a bold enough figure. Keith-Falconer was able to persuade them to lift their limit to £1,650, and at once set out to raise the money. The theatre fell to a bid of £1,875 by Robert Sayle, but when he heard of the hopes of Mowll and his friends, he let them have it at their own figure. It was Keith-Falconer who closed with the offer, paid the money from his account, called in the promised subscriptions, obtained substantial donations from his father and his future father-in-law, and gave generously himself. The theatre was re-opened in November 1878. Mowll was in the chair, and William Hay Aitken, Frederick Charrington and Keith-Falconer took part. Keith-Falconer gave a very apt and telling address; life was likened to a drama, 'a play once acted and only once', and he urged them to see that the next act in that play was a life renewed by faith in Christ.[41] The theatre was never closed for a single Sunday in the years that followed, and by the mid1880s, it had won a secure niche in the life both of Barnwell and of the C.I.C.C.U. Keith-Falconer was often present though he seldom spoke, and his interest was unabated to the end of his life.

Keith-Falconer's closest friend was Frederick Charrington, six years senior in age but one with him in love for Christ. He was the son of a partner in the brewery firm of Charrington and Head, and a business career with a major fortune was his for the asking. But in 1869, while in the south of France, he was thoroughly converted as he read the story of Nicodemus to please a friend. On his return to London, he began to visit a little mission hall each evening, and the way led him past a beer shop called 'The Rising Sun'. One night as he passed by, he saw a poor woman with her children dragging at her skirts push open the door, and beg her husband 'for some money because the children were crying for bread. That man's only reply was to knock her down and leave her in the gutter. At that moment Charrington glanced up and saw his own name staring him in the face. 'Charrington, Head & Co's Entire' was written in large letters on the sign-board. It flashed through his mind that this was one house out of hundreds which his father's firm owned, and that the case of the woman at this house was perhaps only one of thousands for which they were responsible. 'In knocking down his wife', he was to write, 'the man knocked me out of the liquor trade.'[42]

It was the great turning point in his life; it led him to renounce an income of £20,000 a year and a fortune of £250,000 in order to devote himself to work for Christ in the slums of London. He began with a night-school in a hay-loft; soon a schoolroom was opened; then a boys' home was started. In 1871, he was on a walking tour in Scotland, and Lord Kintore invited him to visit Keith Hall. It was then that he met Ion and the closest friendship was forged. In 1872, he opened the East End Conference Hall in Carlton Square, which could seat six hundred people; this was the origin of the Tower Hamlets Mission. Then he moved to a large piece of land in Mile End Road, where he conducted services in a large tent every night for two full summers. In May 1876, a still better site was obtained and a large tent was set up at the broadest part of Mile End Road. This was replaced in April 1877 by the first great Assembly Hall, which was large enough to hold some two thousand people and which remained open every night all the year round for nearly nine years. Hundreds were turned away for want of room on the Sundays, and there was an average attendance of six hundred on the week nights. Music halls were also hired for mission meetings: the Foresters Music Hall which seated two thousand was used for three winters, and the

Lusby Music Hall which seated three thousand for two winters. It soon became clear that the Assembly Hall would have to be replaced by a larger and more permanent building.

Keith-Falconer was an active friend and ally and a generous supporter of the Tower Hamlets Mission from the beginning. He was full of ideas, always ready to give, to help, to serve. He was the pioneer in what he liked to describe as 'preaching the Gospel from the walls of the city'.[43] This was carried out by means of placards with texts, direct appeals, and short pointed stories. Direct approach to men outside public houses sometimes met with angry opposition. One night Charrington was placed under arrest outside Lusby's Music Hall and falsely charged with creating a disturbance. Mr E. H. Kerwin recalled the scene at the police station. 'In the dark, I could see one tall man standing in the centre, head and shoulders above every one else and perfectly white; this was Keith-Falconer who had been covered with flour.'[44] He scratched his name from the University Champion Bicycle Race so as to be free to give evidence on behalf of Charrington. 'The race is safe with Dodds', so his telegram ran. 'I have made up my mind not to run, having started in the race spoken of in Hebrews 12:1–2.'[45]

He would often come down to spend a week at the Mission; sometimes he would stay a little longer. He did not often speak at the evening meetings, but would sometimes give an address on the Sunday mornings. He liked most to deal with individuals; distress always found in him a generous, albeit discerning, helper. He was ever at hand with shrewd advice, and he entered into every detail with great prudence. In 1880, he became Honorary Secretary for the Tower Hamlets Mission and set out to raise £24,000 for a new hall. He wrote and published a pamphlet which set out what had been done and made a direct appeal for help. 'We have got the site and we have got the people,' he wrote; 'may we not have a hall to accommodate them? The willingness to hear is very remarkable, and it is distressing to see hundreds and thousands turned away for mere want of room.'[46] It was a model appeal for funds: it told clearly all that had to be told, giving reasons and defining principles on which the work would be founded. He gave liberally from his own purse, £2,000 in all, and he secured generous subscribers. At last, in February 1886, a hall capable of seating five thousand was opened, and though a large sum of money was still owing, more than £25,000 had been received. Keith-Falconer was in Aden at the time, but he went to see the hall on his return in the summer. He sat beside Charrington, and each man's face sparkled with quiet joy and earnest resolve. 'Not while any of the present generation of workers survive', wrote Sinker in 1888, 'will the name of Ion Keith-Falconer fade out of loving remembrance in Mile End Road.'[47]

MASTERING HEBREW, SYRIAC, AND ARABIC

After the Tripos examinations in February 1880, Ion Keith-Falconer settled down to pursue the study of Arabic. Oriental language study had a remarkable fascination for him, and he was to become successively an expert in Hebrew, Syriac, and Arabic. In June 1880, he went to Royat in the Auvergne for the summer, but news of his father's sudden death in July brought him back to England in great sorrow. The eighth Earl of Kintore was a devoted Christian, all whose personal sympathies were bound up with the Free Church of Scotland. This fact had left its mark upon Ion in a way that years at Cambridge could not efface, and he never ceased to adhere to the Church of which his father had been such an honoured member. Many of his closest friends were members of the Church of England, and he felt a boundless admiration for Joseph Barber Lightfoot and Brook Foss Westcott.[48] But he did not feel at ease in the use of the formularies of the Church of England; his heart remained firmly entrenched in the Free Church north of the Tweed.

In October 1880, he travelled to Leipzig for five months of concentrated study and made friends with Dr Delitzsch. 'He is by far the greatest theologian here',[49] so he declared. He spent Christmas at Cannes and made his way back by Genoa, Milan, Vienna, and Munich. 'I hope to spend the summer term in dear old Cambridge', he wrote in February 1881. 'A great friend of mine, J. E. K. Studd, has secured the lower rooms, which is pleasant for me.'[50] A genial and light-hearted tone runs through his correspondence, but he was an alert and hard-working student, shrewdly marking all that went on. His own views with regard to the value of true academic work are clearly expressed in one of his letters. 'As to the wisdom so often deprecated in the New Testament,' he wrote, 'it seems to me that Greek philosophies and Rabbinical follies are aimed at. But scholarship in our sense of the word did not exist when the New Testament was written. Scholarship is a laborious and to a great extent mechanical way of getting at the original text. Scholarship assumes no doctrine, and denies none. It is colourless. Scholarship can hardly be called wisdom any more than I can be called wise because I know English . . . The more of a scholar one becomes, the more one fathoms the depths of one's ignorance and estimates the measure of one's dependence on God's Spirit. To take the immense trouble of learning ancient languages in order to ferret out correct readings is a silent but most emphatic protest against the claims of a priori reasoning or philosophy.'[51]

Keith-Falconer had long felt drawn to a life of dedicated service for Christ, though the field was as yet unknown. As early as July 1873, he had told Lady Sydney Montagu: 'I like Charrington because he is quite devoted to Him, and has really given up all for His glory. I must go and do the same soon; how I don't know.'[52] In 1877, while Keith-Falconer was staying with Charrington, E. H. Kerwin happened to pick up Ion's Bible and found himself reading the prayer written on the fly-leaf with his own hand: 'Henceforth Lord Jesus I wish to be wholly given up to Thee that in walk and in life I may glorify Thee every day.'[53] Then in April 1881, he met one of the most remarkable Victorians of that decade, and was greatly impressed. This was 'Chinese' Gordon, who gave him a copy of Clarke's *Scripture Promises* and encouraged him to seek a field of labour where his talents would all be used for God's glory. 'I wish I could put you into something that would give you the work you need', wrote Gordon, 'viz. secular and religious work running side by side. This is the proper work for man, and I think you could find it.'[54] He went on to invite Keith-Falconer to join him at the Hermitage in Syria. Keith-Falconer did not accept this warm invitation, but he never ceased to follow Gordon's life and movements with the closest personal interest. He was deeply moved when news came of his long and lonely watch in Khartoum and his death at the hands of the Mahdi in October 1884. Twelve months later, in November 1885, he wrote from Aden: 'I never cease to regret that I did not spend some time with him in Palestine as he himself proposed.'[55] Again, in January 1886, he told his sister: 'Moffat's *Life* is exceedingly interesting. I bitterly regret not having known him.

I might have, easily. And I cannot understand why we never heard of old Mr Paton before he was on the point of leaving. And Gordon too! I might have lived with him in Syria. What things I have missed!'[56] In Aden, he became a close friend of Gordon's nephew Louis, a young Lieutenant. 'His room contains three pictures of his uncle', so Keith-Falconer wrote, 'and he looks on his Journals etc. as a kind of Bible.'[57] Meanwhile, his own eyes kept turning, if not to Syria, yet to the Orient: he was conscious of need, and call, though not yet clear in what ultimate direction. On 12 June 1881, he wrote: 'It is overwhelming to think of the vastness of the harvest field when compared with the indolence, indifference and unwillingness on the part of most so-called Christians to become even in a moderate degree labourers in the same. I take the rebuke to Myself.'[58]

Keith-Falconer was now anxious to acquire a direct colloquial knowledge of Arabic and determined to spend some months on the Nile at Assiout with this object in mind. Assiout was two hundred miles south of Cairo; it marked the terminus of the railway. Dr Hogg, a Scottish missionary and an accomplished Arabist, had made Assiout the headquarters of his work in Egypt and was more than willing to be of help. Keith-Falconer left England at the end of October 1881 to travel by Calais to Marseilles and from Naples to Alexandria. He arrived in Cairo on 9 November and in Assiout eleven days later. He engaged a teacher for two hours each day and settled down to language study. It was his first direct contact with the East and letters home preserve his initial reactions. On 30 November, he wrote: 'I am disappointed with Egypt, both as to scenery and climate.' But he went on to add: 'The colouring at sunrise and sunset is beautiful – like apricots and peaches.'[59] But the beauty of those desert skies was in strong contrast with the squalor of his slum-like environment. 'The town is truly and unspeakably disgusting', he wrote. 'The streets are all filthy alleys, very crooked and winding, and not lighted at night.' It made him say: 'I shall be very glad to get back to civilization.'[60]

In January 1882, he formulated plans to ride by donkey to Luxor and by camel to Kossair, and he made a journey back to Cairo in order to purchase essential equipment. But a severe bout of fever compelled him to give up these plans and travel back to Europe sooner than he had expected. He reached Cannes in early February 1882 and spent the next three months in the south of Europe. He stayed for some time in Genoa and in Siena; then he passed through Milan to reach the Lake country. He enjoyed its beauty and improved his Italian, and it was not until early in May that he travelled on to England. He had escaped the long northern winter and had come home in good health and cheerful spirits. But more than that; he had seen the desert, and his heart had gone out more than ever to the Arab world still in the chains of Islam.

Keith-Falconer was now eager to fulfil a desire which he had long cherished: this was to ride from Land's End to John O'Groats. It was a novel adventure which had been suggested to him by Mr Bowen of Harrow, and the boys at Harrow were to mark his daily progress on a large map prepared for the purpose. On 1 June 1882, he went down to Penzance to await a favourable spell of weather; four days later, he left Land's End on the long ride. He had a 58-inch bicycle, and he had to traverse roads which were in the most primitive condition. There were few signposts and none of the modern aids for travel. Sometimes he had to ride against strong winds over rough roads in vile weather; sometimes he could pedal away with a light heart through pleasant country. His notes on the towns and country through which he passed reflect his own natural interests. When he rode through Edinburgh on the ninth day, he could not help writing: 'Our city on a beautiful summer's evening presents a spectacle not equalled anywhere else.'[61]

He reached Tain on a fine morning, but rain compelled him to stop at Dunbeath where he had tea and bathed his feet. He reached Wick at midnight and spent an hour and a half at the Station Hotel. Then 'to the blank astonishment of landlord, boots, and waiters,'[62] he set out on the last stretch. 'The utter solitude, stillness and dreariness of the remaining 19 miles made a most remarkable impression on me', he wrote. 'Not one tree, bush, or hedge did I see the whole way – only dark brown moor and a road straight as a rule. At twenty minutes past three, I stood stiff, sore, hungry, and happy before John O'Groats House Hotel. I had ridden 994 miles in 13 days less 45 minutes. This gives an average of 76 to 77 miles a day. I had no difficulty in rousing the landlord, and was soon asleep.'[63] He wrote a fresh and racy account of this journey; it was published both in Aberdeen and in the London Bicycle Club Gazette. The ride from Land's End to John O'Groats has often since then been done in much less time than he required; but he was a pioneer, and the conditions then were totally different.

Keith-Falconer spent most of his time from October 1882 until 1885, apart from vacations, at Cambridge. In the spring of 1883, he was made an examiner for the Tyrwhitt Hebrew Scholarship, and he prepared himself for this duty with as keen an eye for detail as if he were an examinee. In September, he was present at the Congress of Orientalists held at Leyden, but he was not impressed. In October, he began to lecture in Hebrew at Clare, and he was to carry out this duty for two academic years with conspicuous success. He was a born teacher, with a gift for getting right down to the bottom of things so that students could not fail to grasp their basic meaning. He became an examiner in the theological Tripos in January 1884 and in the Semitic Languages Tripos in February 1886, and his ability in each branch of work for which he was made responsible shows how well he could have settled down to the life of a scholar.

But while he was absorbed in a variety of work, Syriac and Arabic had taken the main hold on his time and thought. He was engaged in the translation of a Syriac manuscript called the *Kalilah and Dimnah,* or the *Fables of Bidpai*. This work was a well-known piece of Buddhist literature which had found its way in Sanscrit from India to Persia. An Arabic translation had become the parent of translations into other languages, one of which was Syriac; but the Syriac translation had only survived in one manuscript. This had been found by Dr Wright, but the text was very corrupt; it was published in 1884 with emendations by Dr Wright, Professor Nöldeke, and Ion Keith-Falconer. It was first-class material for keen critical acumen, and he was now working on it with an infinitude of pain and care. At length, early in 1885, he was able to publish a translation from Wright's edition of the Syriac text with an Introduction and Notes. 'The Introduction . . . extending over 85 large octavo pages, dwells on the literary history of the document, and on the history and bibliography of the versions.'[64] It was a piece of work which would have brought credit to a senior scholar; it had all the merit of true learning, lucid thought and mature insight. Professor Nöldeke, himself in the very van of Oriental scholars, declared that it was the work of a new master.[65]

Mission, Marriage, and Moody

Keith-Falconer was still active in the Barnwell Mission and as Honorary Secretary of the Mile End Mission. These were in fact the years in which he was employed in the task of raising money for the erection of a new Assembly Hall. He had become engaged to Gwendolen, the charming daughter of a well-known banker, Robert Cooper Lee Bevan, of Trent Park, New Barnet. They were married on 4 March 1884 at Trinity Church in Cannes, and by mid-April, they had settled down in Cambridge. The Bevans were a highly literate, very talented, rather close-knit and eccentric family,[66] but Gwendolen was to prove a devoted and true-hearted wife.[67] It was at this time that as a memorial for his father, he founded the Kintore Prizes at Harrow: the one was for open competition in the whole school, while the other was confined to junior classes. They were designed to encourage the intelligent reading of Scripture, and he himself acted as an examiner when the awards were made for the first time in the summer of 1885.

There was yet one other piece of work to which he applied himself during those years, and it illustrates both his versatile genius and his remarkable capacity for work. This was the preparation of an article on shorthand for the new edition of the *Encyclopaedia Britannica*. This task involved a great deal of patient research and drew largely on his stock of time; but no effort was spared to make it as complete and thorough as possible. The article ran to some thirteen columns in the large quarto of the Encyclopaedia, and gave a sketch of the progress of shorthand in England since the sixteenth century. He had gone to endless trouble to read all the worthwhile literature that was available on the subject, and he made a special visit to the Bodleian Library at Oxford to inspect unique copies of books on the early systems of shorthand in England. Pitman's system, which had first been given to the world in 1840, was the one which he judged to be the best. He concluded the article with a concise bibliography and an account of the shorthand methods on the European mainland. This was perhaps the last detailed literary work which he did, and its lucid style and thorough treatment were the marks of his own essential character.

Two of Ion's special friends at Cambridge were J. E. Kynaston Studd and his younger brother, C. T. Studd. Early in 1882, Jack Studd, Captain of the Eleven and President of the C.I.C.C.U., proposed to invite the American evangelists D. L. Moody and I. D. Sankey to conduct a mission for Cambridge in the Michaelmas Term. The Rev. H. C. G. Moule, who was asked to lend his name to the invitation, could not persuade himself that it was wise. But Studd knew that some three hundred students had tried to get Moody to Cambridge in 1875; he knew as well that it was through Moody's preaching that his father had turned his back on a life of selfish extravagance to yield himself in his middle fifties to Christ's control. Therefore he went ahead with the invitation, and on 5 November, Moody held his first meeting in the Corn Exchange. Seventeen hundred men in cap and gown were counted as they came in, laughing, talking, rushing for seats. Rowdy songs and crackers shook the hall before the platform party arrived, and the meeting itself was disturbed by laughter, loud talking, mock applause, and pert questions.

On 6 November, the next day, Keith-Falconer wrote: 'Moody has commenced. I was at the first meeting which took place yesterday in the Corn Exchange. It began at 8:00 a.m. sharp. There were more than 1,000 people present, chiefly townsfolk. At 8:30 p.m. there was a meeting for University men only. There came fully 1,600 men, nearly all of them undergraduates. I am afraid many of them could not hear, and that was some excuse for the occasional bad behaviour which marred the meeting. Fancy applauding a prayer! A large number remained to the after-meeting. Moody said that he was quite satisfied. Meetings go on all this week. Moody spoke on Daniel. Towards the end, I thought he was very impressive.'[68] The tide turned when Thursday night came. He spoke in the Gymnasium on the Marriage Supper. As the address came to a close, he asked any who hoped to be present at that marriage supper to rise and go into the gallery; a terrible test. The gallery could only be reached by a steep iron staircase from the centre of the Gymnasium. To reach it a man would have to face his friends in the congregation and the clatter on the iron steps would be enough to open scores of closed eyes. There was utter stillness; then a young Trinity man rose and went up the stairs. In a moment, others were on their feet; fifty-two in all made their way to the gallery.[69] The last meeting was on Sunday November 12th in the Corn Exchange, and there was not the hint of an interruption. Those who had received blessing during the week were asked to stand, and Moule, kneeling beside Moody on the platform, heard him murmur as he looked up and saw some two hundred men on their feet: 'My God, this is enough to live for.'[70]

The moral effect of Moody's mission at Cambridge was beyond question, and the C.I.C.C.U. had been imbued with a sense of purpose which was to re-orientate the whole of life for scores of men. This was most apparent in the great impetus which the cause of foreign missions received. There were many offers to the Church Missionary Society (C.M.S.) during the next two years.

Then, in the autumn of 1884, came the formation of the Cambridge Seven. There was tremendous excitement in the undergraduate world at Cambridge when it became known that C. T. Studd and Stanley Smith, D. E. Hoste and William Cassels, Montagu Beauchamp and the Polhill-Turners, were to become missionaries with the China Inland Mission (C.I.M.). Studd and Stanley Smith brought Hudson Taylor up to Cambridge for some special meetings. On Wednesday 12 November, two years to the day since Moody's final meeting in the Corn Exchange, they went to the Alexandra Hall and told why they were going out to China. Moule was in the chair. 'Most remarkable missionary meeting', he wrote in his diary that night. 'Lord, bless it. Deeply moving testimonies.'[71] Five more meetings were held and the interest continued to grow. It was not that Studd and his friends were willing to renounce material prospects, but that they were doing it with so much enthusiasm, that made Cambridge ring with their names. Then, in February 1885, there were farewell meetings in which the whole Seven took part. The Guild Hall was crowded on 2 February for their farewell in Cambridge itself, and there was a deep hush as one by one they told town and gown why they were going. The last meeting of all was on 4 February in the Exeter Hall in London when Lord Cairns was in the chair. He spoke to them as 'a band of young Englishmen, high bred, high spirited, highly cultivated-men who had before them at home everything that social position and personal capability could ensure'.[72] Stanley Smith touched a chord that would vibrate all round the Hall when he declared that 'a greater than Gordon cries from Khartoum – the voice of Christ from the Cross of Calvary.'[73] The next morning, while all London was agog with rumour that Khartoum had fallen, they left Victoria Station on the first stage of their journey out to China.

Ion Keith-Falconer was a close friend of C. T. Studd and was greatly stirred by his offer to the China Inland Mission. He knew that Studd had an ample income, and a life of ease and pleasure might have beckoned him to stay in England; he was Captain of the Cambridge Eleven and had played for England in Test Matches against Australia. There was little to choose between the two in wealth, and the academic honours of the one were more or less matched by the cricket renown of the other. It was not in Keith-Falconer to be indifferent when Studd had this to say: 'How could I spend the best hours of my life in working for myself and for the honours and pleasures of this world while thousands and thousands of souls are perishing every day without having heard of the Lord Jesus Christ?'[74] Keith-Falconer was at all the farewell meetings for the Cambridge Seven in Oxford and Cambridge, and Studd always held a special place in his heart. On 31 December 1886, he wrote: 'Charlie Studd has written me a delightful letter . . . He thinks the Chinese language was invented by the devil to prevent the Chinese from ever hearing the Gospel properly.'[75] One of his last actions was to pack a box of carefully selected books and despatch them to Studd when he heard of his isolation from friends and all normal amenities. Among them was a book which had greatly impressed him when he first went out to Aden: *The Personal Life of David Livingstone*, by William Gordon Blaikie.[76]

ADEN – THE DOOR TO ARABIA

Meanwhile Keith-Falconer's own eyes were turning more and more towards Arabia: 'Why, he himself knew not, except that he loved the language'.[77] He met John G. Paton, the veteran from the New Hebrides, during his last visit to Britain in 1884, and spent a day with him at his mother's home in London.[78] This meeting filled Paton with an imperishable enthusiasm and he paid a remarkable tribute to Keith-Falconer after his death: 'His soul', he wrote, 'was full of his projected Mission to the Arabs, being himself one of the most distinguished Orientalists of the day: and as we talked together and exchanged experiences, I felt that never before had I visibly marked the fire of God, the holy passion to seek and to save the lost, burning more steadily or brightly on the altar of any human heart.'[79]

The first missionary to the Muslim world was Ramon Lull, who made three journeys to proclaim the gospel to the Saracens of North Africa. 'Many knights do I see who go to the Holy Land', so he had written, 'thinking to conquer it by force of arms. But when I look at the end thereof, all of them are spent without attaining that which they desire. Wherefore it appears to me, O Lord, that the conquest of that Sacred Land will not be achieved . . . save by love and prayer, and the shedding of tears as well as blood.'[80] Ramon Lull was stoned to death at Tunis on 30 June 1315, and five hundred years were to pass before fresh interest was awakened. It was Henry Martyn who took up the torch of Ramon Lull when he set out to visit both Persia and Arabia in order to perfect his work on New Testament translation. He went ashore at Muscat in 1811 and spent twelve months among the Muslims of Shiraz before he died at Tokat in 1812. Sargent's *Memoir of Henry Martyn* was published in 1819, and this captured the heart of John Wilson in 1829. Wilson's life and work was in Bombay, but he sent a number of colporteurs up the Persian Gulf and into Aden. He tried to persuade the

Church of Scotland to start work among the Jews of Aden, Basra, and Bombay: a missionary was ready in the person of William Burns, but their plans were arrested by the Disruption.[81]

George Smith published his *Life of John Wilson* in 1878, and Keith-Falconer read it at once. He was deeply impressed and wrote to a friend the same year: 'Mind to get hold of Dr George Smith's *Life of John Wilson, D. D., F. R. S.,* the great Scotch missionary of India. He was a Free Church man; every Indian missionary must sit at his feet.'[82] The *Life of John Wilson* was one of the pivots of his career; it had turned his mind to missionary service. Then in 1881, Gordon urged him to look to the East for a field where he could serve both God and man, and he went to Egypt in order to become better equipped in his knowledge of language and people. Then the Moody Mission and the Cambridge Seven each in turn were used to strengthen his first half-formed resolves, and Charrington's example of self-renunciation was reinforced by that of Studd. He was conscious of a steady spur to missionary service in the winter months of 1884, and in February 1885, the month during which the Cambridge Seven sailed for China, one field of work made an imperative claim on his mind. This was Aden.

There are few more gaunt and sun-scorched sites than Aden, at least in the eyes of those who look for natural attractions. It is just a barren peninsula of black volcanic rock at the south-eastern tip of Arabia, jutting out at the point where the waters of the Red Sea meet and merge with those of the Indian Ocean. The bridge to the mainland is a long, low sandy isthmus, and its summit is a desolate crag some seventeen hundred feet in altitude.[83] The very low rainfall results in an almost total lack of vegetation, and the burning sun beats down with almost uniform intensity all the year round. Steamer Point is situated at the western tip of Aden, and it provides a good harbour for the shipping of east and west alike. This is also where the British population, both civil and military, used to cluster on the hillside. Perhaps the most fascinating part of Aden is the Crater City which on land is accessible only by a long winding pass and a tunnel cut through the rock. It is enclosed by what Robert Sinker described as 'frowning and cinder-like' crags, except where the sea breaks on the lonely coastline.[84] The dense population in this extinct crater was, and is, mainly Arab and Muslim. Some miles away, at the far end of the peninsula, lies the village of Sheikh Othman, where the presence of wells forms an oasis and where the climate is not quite so severe.

But if Aden be desolate from the point of view of nature, it occupies a position of great strategic importance. It is nearly equidistant from Suez and Bombay, and this fact made it a major fuelling station for the ships which plied their trade in the East. It is one of the keys to the Red Sea and the territories which lie along its coasts, and it was held by Great Britain from 1839 to 1967 as a special military outpost. It was the port to which the long camel trains made their way from the interior, and it was the depot for a thriving trade with many countries.[85] It was the home and the meeting place of men from many races, and in 1885, it was virgin soil for the seed of the gospel.

Aden first came before Keith-Falconer's notice through an article which had been written by Major-General T. F. Haig, strongly urging the need to start missionary work in Arabia. Haig had enjoyed a long career in the army and had never lost an opportunity for seeking the spread of the gospel. In 1860, while a captain in the Royal Engineers, he had begun a prayer meeting for the people in the Godavari District in Central India. The conversion and baptism of a Hindu Rajput soon led to the establishment of the C.M.S. mission at Dummagudem. In 1871, when he held the rank of Colonel, he had been actively interested in the work of Robert Bruce in Persia. In 1881, having retired from the army, he went back to Dummagudem and was in charge of the mission for a year and a half while the missionaries were on furlough. But his vision was not confined to India or Persia, and in December 1882 the Church Missionary Society published his papers on Arabia in the *Intelligencer*. Nothing seemed to happen as a result just then; but in February 1885, a short summary of his articles made its appearance in *The Christian*. This short reprint caught the eye of Keith-Falconer, and spoke straight to his heart. The call of God came to him as it had come a few months before to such men as C. T. Studd and Douglas Hooper. He at once wrote to Haig and asked for a personal interview to discuss Aden and Arabia. This took place in London on 21 February 1885, only sixteen days after the Cambridge Seven had sailed. Keith-Falconer does not seem to have left any record of that important occasion, but Haig afterwards summed up his own reaction. 'My impression of that conversation', he wrote, 'is that he came not only to get information, but to say that his mind was already made up to go out for six months and see what the place and prospects of work were like.'[86] Then the retired soldier and the youthful scholar knelt side by side and joined in prayer that he might be rightly guided in all his thoughts and plans for the future.

Armed thus with the knowledge that a qualified candidate was now available, Haig at once took action. On 9 March 1885, he made a strong appeal to the General Committee of C.M.S. for the establishment of an Arabian

Mission with its base at Aden. He argued that Aden was the door to the whole of South Arabia and was constantly visited by Arabs from every part of that great country; he argued still further that it was opposite the key Muslim country of British Somaliland, and that it was itself British territory. Aden had a chaplain who served the two churches in the army camp and at Steamer Point, but he did not touch the Arab population at all. There was also a Roman Catholic Mission with chapels at Steamer Point and in the Crater, but it had failed to lead any Muslim to a living faith in the Son of God.[87] It was a true virgin field for missionary effort, of great strategic importance in the heart of Islam and with special facilities as a centre for a well-planned spiritual operation.

The C.M.S. General Committee agreed to accept Haig's challenge and to begin a new work in Aden. One of the C.M.S. secretaries at once went up to see Keith-Falconer in his rooms at Cambridge and found that his only hesitation was his fear lest his health would not stand up to the heat and climate of the Red Sea. But he had made up his mind to visit Aden and to reside there long enough to be able to assess the matter. He planned to go out at his own expense, but he did not want to be a free-lance missionary. He knew how much Haig was hoping that he would go out with the Church Missionary Society, but his Free Church affinities were still too strong. He asked the Rev. P. W. Minto to bring the whole question before the Foreign Missions Committee of the Free Church of Scotland.[88] Colonel Young and Dr George Smith were more than sympathetic, and on 14 September he went north for the sake of a personal interview. He described the nature of the work in which he hoped to engage and asked for some formal recognition. His request was warmly received. 'And', he wrote, 'they passed a minute stating that I had made the request and that they recognise me as representing the Free Church.'[89] They all joined in prayer to commend him to the great Head of the Church, and he rejoiced in the knowledge of their goodwill.

A Journey of Exploration

On 7 October 1885, Keith-Falconer and his wife left England to make trial of their health in the sun-baked hills of Aden. They found a house on the hillside, close to the point where the tunnel opens out into the crater, and the whole town lay spread before their eyes. Keith-Falconer was eager to grapple with the colloquial aspects of the language and a steady routine was soon in full operation. 'I begin the day by giving my wife an Arabic lesson', he wrote. 'She is nearly through Socin's little grammar. Then I read Arabic all the morning. About 4, I go to the town and converse with natives, coming home to dinner at 7:30. I always carry an Arabic Gospel, and make a point of reading it with the natives.'[90] It soon became known that he was fluent in literary Arabic; people in the street used to look at him and comment on his knowledge with surprise. He made contact with individuals who were willing to hear a more detailed explanation of the gospel: sometimes in the garden near the great stone reservoir known as Solomon's tanks, sometimes in his own house, he found that he could talk freely. And he also took an active interest in the British garrison: there were soon a dozen or more soldiers who were glad to come to his house for tea and a devotional meeting.

There is a glimpse of his unfailing interest in home affairs as he followed the ups and downs of the Huxley controversy. He read Henry Drummond's analogy between George Macdonald's exquisite little poem called 'Baby's Catechism' and the Genesis narrative: Drummond argued that the latter like the former is only the presentation of one or two elementary truths to 'the childhood of the world'.[91] Keith-Falconer's comment was this: 'I think Drummond must have done himself harm by his contribution to the controversy. Fancy reducing Genesis to the level of George Macdonald's poetry! But Drummond's whole article is vague and intangible to the last degree.'[92] His own views of Scripture were those which he had learned in childhood; he saw no reason to change them. This was not through lack of knowledge; it was his own mature belief in the light of manuscript evidence. He had a firm grasp of the Greek New Testament and was at home with the names and details of the leading manuscript authorities. But it was Hebrew with the cognate Semitic dialects which held for him nothing less than fascination: 'he pored over a Hebrew or an Arabic grammar with the delight that others find in a great poem.'[93]

He soon formed clear ideas about his work in the future, and he wrote to Sinker within a few weeks of his arrival: 'There is a town 10 miles off, within British limits, and with a mixed population of about 7,000, where I hope to settle. Here there is water and vegetation, and the climate is perceptibly cooler than in Aden. My notion is to start an industrial refuge, day-school, and surgery there. There are two principal doors to Arabia, the children who can be trained up in the faith of Christ and the medical aid. Arabs often come from a long distance to Aden to be treated, and these would stop short at our mission house . . . I am sure there is a great opening for a missionary, especially if accompanied by a surgeon.'[94] On 1 December, he wrote to his mother: 'I want to get a qualified surgeon to come out with me next year, and an artisan. My idea is to start an industrial orphanage.'[95] And on 16 December, he wrote to Haig: 'I have made up my mind that the right place for me to settle at is Sheikh Othman, not Aden. This will leave Aden and Steamer Point open to the Church Missionary Society.'[96] His plan for an industrial refuge was to provide a home for waifs who could be trained for skilled manual work; and his great hope was that some would become evangelists or teachers among their own people.

But no one who reads his letters can fail to see that all his plans had the interior in view; he was looking beyond Aden and Sheikh Othman to Lahej and Sana. He knew that more than a quarter of a million camels with their drivers would pass through Sheikh Othman in the course of a year, bringing produce from all parts of Yemen. Therefore he made informal inquiries about a plot of land at Sheikh Othman and was told that he could have it at a nominal rent as soon as he was ready to build. Then on 24 February 1886, he was informed that the site was being reserved for him till the end of the year. 'The plot measures nearly 510 feet by 510 feet,' he wrote, 'and lies exactly between the old village of Sheikh Othman and the new settlement. A better situation could not be desired.'[97] And one more thing; during that month he went with a Scottish army doctor on a journey by camel across the desert to El Hautah, the capital of Lahej. He had been warned to act with the utmost caution because of the fanatical spirit of the local Arabs, but he distributed Gospels without the least interference. 'They were received with the utmost willingness,' he wrote, 'and several came to the bungalow to get them.'[98] He recognized one man to whom he had given a Gospel in Aden, and who now asked for a complete Bible.

Thus, with generous self-devotion and strong practical sagacity, his plans were laid. On 6 March 1886, he and his wife sailed from Aden with their minds made up to return in the autumn, and on 11 April, they arrived in England, full of buoyant expectation for the future. It was his great desire on his return home to receive formal recognition from the General Assembly of the Free Church of Scotland. It was singularly appropriate that the Moderator in 1886 was Alexander Somerville, who for fifty years had been in the forefront of every spiritual movement. Only ten years before, in December 1876, at the age of 64 and as a result of Moody's Glasgow mission, he had offered himself to the Evangelistic Association in that city for a world-wide missionary crusade. 'There he stood before us', wrote Thomas Somerville of Blackfriars Church, 'the man that had a history before some of us were born, the early friend of M'Cheyne, Burns, and the Bonars, advanced in years and yet young in enthusiasm, his eye not dim nor his natural strength abated, the white hair falling upon his shoulders and the bright sparkle in that wonderful eye, strong in the bone and warm in his feeling like all his race, proposing to go forth to the nations in the service of his Master.'[99] And for ten years he had made the world his parish, with a stirring appeal for old and young alike: it was indeed no slight challenge simply to see the old and the young so perfectly united in himself. On 20 May 1886, David Brown as retiring Moderator had proposed his election with a striking tribute to his ministry overseas: 'He has a name as a preacher of Christ more widely known, I suppose, than any minister of this Church.'[100] Somerville was installed in the Moderator's chair and at once delivered his address on the theme of World Evangelisation. 'The privilege and opportunity granted to us today,' he said, '. . . if neglected, shall return never, never, never! The nations of the world seem standing with outstretched arms and with wistful looks, calling to us, Come over and help us! Could we only see them and hear their plaintive cries, our hearts would be profoundly moved. For my own part, these soft voices of the nations, though in one sense unspeakably sad, have an intonation sweet and powerful as a choir of angels, for in them I hear the voice of Jesus Himself.'[101]

Popular interest in this General Assembly reached its zenith on the evening which was reserved for the cause of foreign missions, and on Wednesday 26 May, the hall was packed for this historic occasion. Four young missionaries, destined for Bombay and Madras, the New Hebrides and North Kafraria, received in turn a charge from the Moderator. But the General Assembly could not conceal the fact that its primary interest was concentrated on Keith-Falconer, who had been placed in the seat so long and faithfully occupied by his father. He was introduced to the Assembly by the Moderator as 'perhaps the most distinguished British Oriental scholar alive.'[102] Somerville went on to say that he had consecrated himself, his means and his talents, with his brilliant command of Syriac and Arabic, to the task of winning Islam for Christ. In his reply, Keith-Falconer told the Assembly how he planned to establish a school, to promote the distribution of the Scriptures, and to start a medical mission with a qualified surgeon. He was ready to meet the full expense for the erection of hospital and bungalow, and to provide for the stipend of the surgeon at the rate of £300 a year, for a seven-year period. This offer was formally accepted with the unanimous goodwill of the General Assembly, and he was commissioned as a missionary of the Free Church of Scotland.

Dr George Smith, who was secretary of the Foreign Missions Committee, urged him for his health's sake to start work in Bombay: but he longed to be with Arabs in their own land, speaking their own language, making himself master of their literature and of every other means by which he might lead them to faith in the Son of God.[103] In August, he met Dr Stewart Cowen of the Glasgow Western Infirmary, and he knew at once that he had found a colleague with whom he could work with absolute confidence. In September, while he was at Darn Hall, Eddlestone, with his family, he spent many hours with Dr George Smith, roaming over the Tweed country near St Mary's Loch and Peebles. Dr George Smith was to recall those days with a certain nostalgic tenderness that would not die: 'Ever his talk was of the Arabs . . . to whose utter neglect by the Church of Christ he had not long before awoken.'[104]

It was in the early summer of this year that he reached the crown of his academic career: it came in a way and at a time when it was least expected. He was offered the post of Lord Almoner's Professor of Arabic in the University of Cambridge. This position had become vacant through the resignation of Professor Robertson Smith, and the appointment was in the gift of Lord Alwyne Compton, the Bishop of Ely, who was then Lord Almoner. Keith-Falconer must have been well aware that the duties of this office were real, but slight, for the patent only required him to give one lecture each year. He soon resolved to accept the office as an added source of prestige for his work in Aden. His many and varied interests could not dull his love for Arabia, and he revelled alike in its language and its literature. This had always held an enormous attraction for him and he found an ever growing delight in its richness. But his acceptance of this appointment was now second to his calling as a missionary, and he made up his mind to give his first lectures before his return to Aden. He chose as his subject *The Pilgrimage to Mecca,* and the necessary preparation went on side by side with all his other current activities. He read widely both in European and in Oriental literature, using short-hand to make brief notes in the margins of the books which he read and more ample notes in a book which was always at hand for that purpose. He taught himself Dutch in order to read a book in that language, and at length he read it 'with comparative ease'.[105] He was able to complete the preparation of these lectures during September and the early part of October while he was still at Darn Hall near Peebles. On Tuesday 9 November, he returned to Cambridge for the last time, and on the Thursday, Friday and Saturday afternoons, he gave his three lectures. They were delivered in the Divinity Schools from a manuscript which had only been prepared in shorthand. The three lectures were marked by their clear and ample treatment of the subject and by the skill with which details of a technical character found point and thrust. Cambridge was his *alma mater*, and this was his farewell.

There were other claims on his time during those months at home, for he never lost sight of old causes. In August, he fulfilled the role of judge at the races of the Cycling Club of the Young Men's Christian Association at Cambridge, and in October, he took the chair at the annual dinner of the London Bicycle Club which he had served for so long as President. In a toast to the Press, he said: 'I have always a fellow feeling with gentlemen of the Press, especially those who are experienced in the art of shorthand. This is an art to which I have been a devotee for many years, and I always think of it as the literary bicycle; it clears the ground so quickly. I think, you know, that cycling and shorthand somehow go together.'[106] He still had the closest links with the work at Mile End and Barnwell. He now established a lending library in connection with the Barnwell Mission and chose the first books for it just before he left England. He was also responsible for the idea of a Barnwell Missionary, and promised a contribution of £50 a year for two years to start the fund off.

Early in November, he was back in Scotland to bid farewell to his mother at Darn Hall and to make his last public appeal. On the evenings of Sunday and Monday 7–8 November, he spoke in Glasgow and Edinburgh. His last address left an enduring impression: it was 'so unmistakably spoken from the depth of his heart, so touching in the way self [was] set aside, so strong and emphatic in its statement of the needs of the case and the means of meeting them.'[107] 'As the Law to the Jews', he declared, 'so Islam to the Arabs is a schoolmaster to bring them to Christ.'[108] And he ended with a moving peroration: 'While vast continents are shrouded in almost utter darkness and hundreds of millions suffer the horrors of heathenism or of Islam, the burden of proof lies upon you to show that the circumstances in which God has placed you were meant by Him to keep you out of the foreign mission field.'[109] The next day he travelled down to Cambridge to give his three lectures on *The Pilgrimage to Mecca*. His last lecture ended at 3:00 p.m. on the Saturday afternoon, and he caught an evening train for London. He was very bright and cheerful; there was no excitement and no hurry in last minute preparation. He was as much at ease as if he were merely going away for a few days. He joined his wife at Cannes and they sailed from Marseilles on 18 November 1886.

Ion Keith-Falconer was a tall and well-built figure, handsome and well-proportioned in appearance. He was very fond of singing, and his voice had a fine musical quality. His clear merry laugh was always enjoyed by those who shared in his hours of relaxation. He was endowed with great athletic stamina and his bicycling achievements were proof positive of his powers of endurance. His track performance had placed him in the front rank of cyclists at a time when general conditions were much harder than they are now. He had a sheer delight in the physical exercise which was required, and each event filled him with a boyish glee which was quite spontaneous. His powers for hard, grinding application to work were just as great and he won his academic honours by his unwearied diligence. His great ability in the cause of language study shone with equal lustre in each field to which he applied himself: there is mention of French and Dutch and Greek, German, Italian, Hebrew, Syriac, Arabic, Bedawi and Somali and Hindustani. His love for Arabic made him seek a firsthand knowledge of the vernacular such as he could not hope to find in text books at Cambridge. In March 1887, he was to say: 'I expect to peg away at the Dictionary till my last day.'[110]

He was always blithe and buoyant at the end of a hard morning's study, and his academic pursuits never robbed him of the joys of human companionship. He loved to talk of old friends and teachers; his loyalty and affection for them was always a wholesome tonic. But cycling and study did not absorb all his energies, nor did friends and teachers command all his sympathies. He told the Rev. P. W. Minto how he would not miss the daily prayer meeting when he was an undergraduate,[111] and he poured out his time and strength at Mile End and for the Barnwell Mission as though they were his main concern in life. He was in fact constrained by the love that has no equal, and he could not withhold himself. Christ had been the centre of his childhood, and that was the supreme factor in all that he ever was or achieved. It gave his life the ring of that authentic chivalry which those who knew him loved so well, for they also knew that the springs of unselfishness in his inmost being never ran dry. There was decided character, and strong common sense, in all his kindness of heart and hand; he was indeed in the full flower of a noble manhood when he sailed for Aden in the service of God and the gospel.

To Aden Once More

Keith-Falconer spent six days in Cairo, where his wife was to stay with friends until he had settled down in Aden. His ship moored at Jedda on the Arabian coastline in the Red Sea: this was the main port for pilgrims on their way to Mecca. He longed to go ashore just as Henry Martyn had longed to go inland while at Muscat. This was impossible, but his feelings were clear: 'I gazed long at the hills which hid Mecca from us.'[112] Dr Cowen berthed at Aden on 7 December 1886; Keith-Falconer arrived one day later. Meanwhile, as a result of Haig's appeal to C.M.S., Dr F. J. Harpur had left England some weeks before with a view to work in Arabia, and Haig himself had set out on a great journey which took him to each coast of the Red Sea. He reached Aden within a few days of Keith-Falconer and took Dr Harpur with him to establish a base at Hodeidah; but a severe illness compelled Harpur to leave some weeks later and he returned to England in February 1887. No one occupied Hodeidah after his brief attempt, but Haig's return from his Yemen journey gave him a few days with Keith-Falconer before he went on to Muscat, and Baghdad, and across the desert to Damascus.

Keith-Falconer was a guest of the Resident on his arrival, and was joined by his wife on 28 December. He was

disappointed in an attempt to rent a stone bungalow at
Sheikh Othman, and was obliged to take a small hut of
forty feet square. 'It is a roof on four pillars, with walls of
iron lattice', he wrote; but three wooden partitions helped
to create two bedrooms, a study, and a veranda.[113] It stood
in a garden walled off from the desert and it belonged to a
Parsee merchant. A few alterations made it habitable, and
a simple hut, fifteen feet by twelve, with mud walls and
planked roof and a veranda of mats, was built against the
wall of the garden for out-patients. He moved into these
new quarters after the first week of January 1887, and his
wife joined him a few days later. Arrangements were at
once made for the erection of a permanent bungalow in
stone, though it would be some months before it could
be ready for occupation. Keith-Falconer was as content in
his makeshift quarters as man could be, and there was no
ugly omen during the first six weeks. On 23 January, he
wrote to his mother: 'We have at last got our temporary
abode in order. The rooms are really very comfortable,
and no one need pity us in the least. We hope in another
ten days to have completed the arrangements for building
the bungalow.'[114] He had taken what seemed adequate
precautions to guard health and vitality; perhaps no one
could have foreseen that such a home was no place for
continuous fever such as would soon shatter his strength.

During the first six weeks, some three hundred patients
came for treatment, and the initial reluctance on the part
of local Arabs soon began to dissolve. On 23 January, he
wrote to his mother: 'My own part of the work at present
consists in interpreting for Cowen, and telling the people
why we have come.'[115] On 24 January, they rode out on
camels to Bir-Achmad and made friendly overtures to
the local Bedouin with the aid of medical treatment and
the distribution of the Gospels. All his letters at this time

were animated by a bright and hopeful spirit. His kindness of manner won its way to the hearts of the Arabs, and he was always welcome as 'the English Sahib who spoke Arabic like a book'.[116] But his skill in classical Arabic was not enough, and he was now rapidly acquiring a good working knowledge of the vernacular. This led him to mention as a minor piece of news the fact that he was learning Bedawi while still working hard at Arabic; at the same time, he was also trying to learn something of Somali and Hindustani, since both were in common use in Aden.

Haig returned to Aden with Harpur early in February after his memorable journey to Yemen, and Keith-Falconer was deeply interested in the details of his mission. It filled him with a strong desire to travel into the interior on his own account when time would permit. He saw Haig on several occasions, and Haig later wrote a simple account of their final meeting. 'I saw him last on February 7th,' Haig said, 'when I drove out to Sheikh Othman and spent the evening with them. It was a very interesting time. We walked out through the newly rising town, looked at the half-built enclosure wall round the piece of land he had taken for mission buildings, and talked over various plans . . . He looked well and strong, and little we thought how nearly his short course was run. We all knelt together before I left, and commended him and his work to the Lord.'[117] So they parted at Sheikh Othman in the very spirit in which they had first met in London, on their knees and in prayer, little dreaming that there were not years of useful service ahead.

'NOTHING FOR IT BUT PATIENCE'

On 9 February, Keith-Falconer and Cowen rode on camels for their second visit to Bir-Achmad. On his return the next evening, he had a slight fever; but he was still able to speak to a group of Somali women on the veranda at Sheikh Othman. Then he began to run a high fever, and on 13 February, Dr Colson was called out from Aden for his advice. Three days later, it began to abate. On 19 February, he was up for dinner; two days later, he could walk round to a neighbour's garden. On 22 February, he told his mother: 'I never felt so utterly miserable in all my life, but Colson declares that there is no danger in it.'[118] On 2 March, he and Mrs Keith-Falconer moved to Khor Maksar on the isthmus to stay with Louis Gordon, whose friendship they greatly valued. He went on to stay with Dr Jackson at Steamer Point, and after three weeks away, returned to Sheikh Othman greatly improved in health and free from all signs of fever. But he was far from rid of the trouble; during the next few weeks, he had a series of attacks. He was always hopeful, read a great deal, watched each development in the erection of the bungalow, wrote friendly comments on Hebrew grammar, and enjoyed Scott's novels. He kept three books by his bed all through his illness: his Bible, his Hebrew Old Testament, and his Hindustani grammar. On 4 April, he told Sinker: 'I am still weak and not fit for much . . . I have had five attacks in eight weeks. There is nothing for it but patience.'[119] On 1 May, he wrote of his seventh attack: 'This rather miserable shanty in which we are compelled to live is largely the cause of our fevers. It is all draughts . . . You need not have the slightest anxiety about us. At the present moment, we are distinctly better than we were after the first attack. We are not being gradually worn out.'[120] On 2 May, he wrote: 'I am better and stronger . . . Read Bonar's *Life of Judson,* and you will see that our troubles are nought.'[121] On 3 May, Colson found him looking pale and knocked up; yet he was bright and felt stronger than for some time. He wrote a large pile of letters for next day's mail and was full of eager expectation. 'Since February 10th until a day or two ago,' he said, 'I have been suffering from remitting fever; for twelve weary weeks, with a few short breaks, on my back a useless invalid. I hope and trust that I have shaken it off now.'[122] But that was not to be.

On Friday 6 May, he succumbed to fever again, but he was not depressed. His patience and brightness were marked by all who saw him, and his heart's desire was summed up in the last letter he wrote: 'The people are flocking to our dispensary', he said, 'and we keep a few in-patients. I long for health to be at them.'[123] Lady Hilda Keith-Falconer preserved the notes which were evidently written out by his wife: Lady Hilda herself noted that they were 'found in Grandmama's desk'; Lady Hilda's 'Grandmama' was Keith-Falconer's mother. They were dated 'Monday May 9th', and were a simple account of the conversation between husband and wife. 'When I was sitting with him early in the morning,' she wrote, 'he said to me, "I want you to thank God that I am so much better. I feel like a new man – do pray now." When I prayed, he repeated my words after me and added more, which I cannot remember . . . Then he said, "How I wish that each attack of fever had brought me nearer to Christ – nearer, nearer, nearer."' He said that he was not afraid to die, but he prayed that God would spare him from pain. He spoke about Dudley – how much he had suffered, and how joyful he was at the approach of death. In the afternoon, she tried to fan him, but he would not let her go on because Cowen had said she ought not to tire herself. 'In the evening, he said, "As soon as I get over this attack, we will go away for a change." I asked where to? He said, "We will go home."' The next afternoon his wife wrote, 'He asked me whether I thought he would get well'.[124] The notes broke off, and that evening he was very weak and restless until he fell asleep about 9:30 p.m. Cowen prayed for him with Mrs Keith-Falconer and left a nurse in charge at ten o'clock. The nurse said that he slept quietly most of the night and was breathing regularly at four o'clock in the morning. She then lay down herself and was asleep when Mrs Keith-Falconer called her just before six o'clock. Cowen also came at once and saw that it was the end. 'One glance told all', he wrote. 'He was lying on his back, with eyes half open and hands resting on the bed by his sides.'[125] He had died in his sleep not long before daybreak on 11 May 1887, only six months after he had sailed from England and while he was still no more than thirty years old.

Ion Keith-Falconer had thus laid down his life among those children of Islam for whom he had laboured with a love so perfect. He was buried on the evening of the same day in the bleak and desolate cemetery which is situated just beyond the crater: a wild and lonely site in a hollow among the gaunt hills and within sound of the waves that lap their rocks. His life had not been a long one, but it was long enough to do what he desired above all else to do: to pave the way for the proclamation of the gospel to the Arabs in the heart of Arabia. The Free Church of Scotland resolved to maintain the mission at Sheikh Othman, and the stipends for two missionaries were made available by gifts from his mother and his widow.[126]

Dr Cowen returned to Great Britain; but the Rev. W. R. W. Gardner and Dr Alexander Patterson went out to Sheikh Othman. Dr Patterson did not stay long; ill health compelled him to return. But in 1892, the

Rev. John C. Young, M.A., M.B., C.M., D.T.M., went out to work with the Gardners: he proved to be remarkable as a man and as a missionary in that torrid climate. Six days a week, he doctored the Arabs at Sheikh Othman, and on Sundays he exercised his ministry at Steamer Point where the Keith-Falconer Memorial Church was opened in 1897.

The small 'shanty' dispensary grew into a fully equipped hospital; nearly twenty thousand out-patients were treated each year. It was known for hundreds of miles beyond the fringe of Sheikh Othman; there were as well frequent visits by the missionaries to the immediate interior. Ion Keith-Falconer's faith and vision were not in vain; the seed that had fallen into the ground had sprung up and brought forth its fruit.[127] There were many vicissitudes, but the work was maintained for eighty years after his death. It was only when Aden became independent with a Communist government in 1967 that the mission had to close down and all missionaries were forced to leave. But his lonely grave still remains as a fitting emblem of those who strove long and valiantly to 'make straight in the desert a highway for our God' (*Isa.* 40:3).

Ion Keith-Falconer was one of the finest and most many-sided sons of Cambridge in the Victorian era. Alexander Somerville spoke for the Free Church of Scotland when he described him as 'one of the most chivalrous, distinguished, and beloved of our missionaries'.[128] Dr Robert Rainy summed up the case in the tribute which he offered after his death: 'His university distinction, his oriental learning, his position in society, his means, the bright morning of his married life, I may add his physical vigour – he brought them all to the service; he did so the more impressively because he did it with no fuss.'[129] His gifts and his career were of such an order that they cannot fail to invite both contrast and comparison with the life of Henry Martyn. Keith-Falconer's life knew little of the pathos which so pervades that of Henry Martyn, for he had what Henry Martyn had not in so many respects. He was the son of a Scottish noble, brought up partly in the Highlands, partly in the south of England, amidst the love and care of a devoted family. He had his own private income and was free from material anxieties. He moved with ease in the highest social circles, and he excelled in cycling and shorthand as the recreations of young manhood. His life was crowned with the love of a bride, and he entered on his work at Aden with his wife at his side. And he was so bright and sunny that the introspective moods of Henry Martyn were quite foreign to his nature. There was nothing comparable to these factors in the case of Henry Martyn; but they had so many points in common at the deeper levels of life that they might have been twins in the divine purpose. They were amazingly alike in their brilliant capacity for all language study and in their special love for the oriental vernacular. They were alike in their family history of frail health and in the delicate element which lurked in their constitution. They were alike in their longing to convey the gospel to the Arab in the heart of Arabia. Henry Martyn, who had berthed at Muscat and thought of the interior, was a true forerunner of Ion Keith-Falconer at Aden and Sheikh Othman. Henry Martyn had to complete his work in the lonely isolation of Shiraz, and he died in even greater solitude at Tokat; Keith-Falconer ran his course at Aden and laid down his life in the midst of friends at Sheikh Othman: yet they were both alike in that each died on the threshold of the thirties and was buried in a lonely grave and a far country. And now? 'Beyond the golden veil, west of the sunset shining trail',[130] they dwell in that city where 'the Lord God giveth them light, and they shall reign for ever and ever' (*Rev.* 22:5).

BIBLIOGRAPHY

1. Lady Hilda Keith-Falconer, *Keiths of Long Ago; 9th and 10th Earls of Kintore, 1844–1918.* (This is a manuscript at Keith Hall; it has as a whimsical sub-title the words: 'Notes collected by H. K. F. for "History of the Keiths" never written by S. C. K.!' It is one of fifteen volumes [or more] dealing with the Keith family and prepared by Lady Hilda Keith-Falconer, who died in 1967.)

2. 1888 – Robert Sinker, *Memorials of the Hon. Ion Keith-Falconer.*

3. 1891 – George Smith, *A Modern Apostle, Alexander N. Somerville.*

4. 1899 – Eugene Stock, *The History of the Church Missionary Society.*

5. 1900 – S. M. Zwemer, *Arabia, The Cradle of Islam.*

6. 1900 – George Smith, 'The Hon. Ion G.N. Keith-Falconer' (Chapter Ten in *Twelve Pioneer Missionaries).*

7. James Robson, *Ion Keith-Falconer of Arabia.*

8. 1953 – J. C. Pollock, *A Cambridge Movement.*

9. 1955 – J. C. Pollock, *The Cambridge Seven.*

I am deeply grateful to the late Dowager Countess, Lady Kintore, who allowed me to visit Keith Hall in July 1968 and to examine the records of the Keith family in the Muniment Room, and especially the Ion Keith-Falconer material so beautifully arranged by his niece, Lady Hilda Keith-Falconer.

It is unfortunate that none of his correspondence with his mother, his wife, or Lady Sydney Montagu, quoted by Robert Sinker, has survived.

In 1938, I was able to visit Aden and Sheikh Othman; in 1950, I preached in the Keith-Falconer Memorial Church and saw his grave in Aden; and in 1972, I visited Sana and Yarim, Hodeidah and Jedda.

Notes

[1] Sir Walter Scott, *The Lord of the Isles,* Canto Sixth, Stanza xii.

[2] Lady Hilda Keith-Falconer, *Keiths of Long Ago.* But *Burke's Peerage,* 1967, says 'before July 1548'.

[3] Ibid., but a later note suggests that he was the fifth son.

[4] John Park, 'At the Back of Ben-na-chie' (see Robert Sinker: Memorials of the Hon. Ion Keith-Falconer, p. 8.)

[5] Lady Hilda Keith-Falconer, ibid.

[6] His sunny and unselfish childhood may be compared with that of Her Majesty, Queen Elizabeth, the Queen Mother. Cf. David Duff, *Elizabeth of Glamis, the Queen Mother.*

[7] Sinker, ibid. p. 13. For Arthur Watson at Harrow see G. K. A. Bell: *Randall Davidson*, pp. 14, 17.

[8] G. W. E. Russell, *The School Days of Ion Keith-Falconer (see* Lady Hilda Keith-Falconer, ibid.)

[9] Sinker, ibid. p. 22.   [10] Sinker, ibid. p. 17.

[11] Ibid. p. 18. For Edward Bowen, see David Newsome: *Godliness and Good Learning*, p. 223.   [12] G. W. E. Russell, ibid.

[13] Sinker, ibid. pp. 17–18,   [14] Sinker, ibid. pp. 20–21.

[15] Ibid. p. 14.   [16] G. W, F. Russell, ibid.

[17] Sinker, ibid. p 16.   [18] G. W E. Russell, ibid.

[19] Lady Sydney Montagu, second daughter of the sixth Earl of Manchester, married Algernon Hawkins Keith-Falconer on 14 August 1873. He succeeded as Earl of Kintore in 1880.

[20] Sinker, ibid. p. 26.   [21] Ibid. p. 15.

[22] Ibid. p. 23.   [23] Sinker, ibid. p. 29.

[24] Ibid. p. 31.

[25] Lady Hilda Keith-Falconer, ibid.

[26] Lady Hilda Keith-Falconer, ibid.   [27] Sinker. ibid. p. 48.

[28] Ibid. p. 57.   [29] Ibid. p. 47.

[30] G. W. E. Russell, ibid.

[31] George Smith, *The Hon. Ion N. G. Keith-Falconer,* p. 210.

[32] G. W. E. Russell, ibid.   [33] Sinker, ibid. p. 19.

[34] Ibid.

[35] Cf. D. P. Thomson, *Eric Liddell, The Making of an Athlete and the Training of a Missionary.*

³⁶ Sinker, ibid. p. 37.   ³⁷ Sinker, ibid. p. 62.   ³⁸ Ibid. p. 63.

³⁹ Cf. J. C. Pollock, *A Cambridge Movement*, p. 43.

⁴⁰ One of the traditions in the Mowll family concerns a visit by Keith-Falconer to their Dover home at Chaldercot when he was rebuked by William Rutley Mowll's father for having too much mustard on his plate (Letter from John Mowll, 13 February 1939).

⁴¹ Sinker, ibid. p. 80.   ⁴² Cf. Sinker, ibid. p. 85.

⁴³ Sinker, ibid. p. 88.   ⁴⁴ Ibid. p. 90.

⁴⁵ James Robson, *Ion Keith-Falconer of Arabia*, p. 45.

⁴⁶ Sinker, ibid. p. 94.   ⁴⁷ Ibid. p. 99.

⁴⁸ The Rev. P. W. Minto (see Lady Hilda Keith-Falconer, ibid.).

⁴⁹ Sinker, ibid. p. 107.   ⁵⁰ Ibid. p. 110.

⁵¹ Sinker, ibid. p. 112.   ⁵² Ibid. p. 28.

⁵³ *The Christian*, June 3rd 1887 (see Lady Hilda Keith-Falconer, ibid.)

⁵⁴ Sinker. ibid. p. 114.   ⁵⁵ Ibid. p. 178.

⁵⁶ Sinker, ibid. p. 184.   ⁵⁷ Ibid. p. 245.

⁵⁸ Ibid. pp. 116–117.   ⁵⁹ Ibid. p. 123.

⁶⁰ Sinker, ibid. p. 124.   ⁶¹ Ibid. p. 133.

⁶² Sinker, ibid. p. 135.   ⁶³ Ibid.

⁶⁴ Sinker, ibid. p. 153.   ⁶⁵ Ibid. p. 154.

⁶⁶ Letter from A. F. Walls, 25 June 1968.

⁶⁷ The Rev. P. W. Minto (see Lady Hilda Keith-Falconer, ibid.).

⁶⁸ Sinker, ibid. p. 138.

⁶⁹ W. R. Moody, *The Life of D. L. Moody*, p. 308; J. C. Pollock, *A Cambridge Movement*, p. 63.

⁷⁰ J. C. Pollock, ibid. p. 70.   ⁷¹ Ibid. p. 82.

⁷² J. C. Pollock, ibid. p. 85.   ⁷³ Ibid.

⁷⁴ J. C. Pollock, *The Cambridge Seven*, p. 71.

⁷⁵ Sinker, ibid. p. 229.   ⁷⁶ Sinker, ibid. p. 239.

⁷⁷ S. M. Zwemer, *Arabia, The Cradle of Islam*, p. 333,

⁷⁸ Sinker, ibid. p. 184.

⁷⁹ John G. Paton, *Autobiography*, Part Two, p. 436.

⁸⁰ F. Allison Pears, *Ramon Lull*, pp. 30–31.

⁸¹ George Smith, *Henry Martyn, Saint and Scholar*, pp. 563–564.

⁸² Sinker, ibid. p. 146.

⁸³ I climbed this peak in October 1950 with Dr Alan Fawdry whose guest I was for several days; my first visit to Aden was in February 1938.

⁸⁴ Sinker, ibid. p. 174.

⁸⁵ See Gordon Waterfield, *Sultans of Aden*.

⁸⁶ Sinker, ibid. p. 166.   ⁸⁷ Sinker, ibid. p. 167.

⁸⁸ The Rev. P. W. Minto (see Lady Hilda Keith-Falconer, ibid.).

⁸⁹ Sinker, ibid. p. 179.   ⁹⁰ Sinker, ibid. p. 175.

⁹¹ George Adam Smith, *The Life of Henry Drummond*, p. 241.

[92] Sinker, ibid. p. 185.
[93] The Rev. P. W. Minto (see Lady Hilda Keith-Falconer: ibid.).
[94] Sinker, ibid. p. 176.   [95] Ibid. p. 179.
[96] Ibid. p. 180.   [97] Sinker, ibid. p. 186.
[98] Ibid.
[99] George Smith, *A Modern Apostle, Alexander N. Somerville*, p. 162.
[100] Ibid. p. 307.   [101] Ibid. p. 311.
[102] Ibid. p. 323.
[103] George Smith, *The Hon. Ion G. N. Keith-Falconer*, p. 216.
[104] Ibid. p. 204.   [105] Sinker, ibid. p. 203.
[106] Ibid. p. 209.   [107] Ibid. p. 211.
[108] Ibid. p. 212.   [109] Ibid. p. 217.
[110] Ibid. p. 100.
[111] The Rev. P. W. Minto (see Lady Hilda Keith Falconer, ibid.).
[112] Sinker, ibid. p. 222.   [113] Ibid. p. 228.
[114] Ibid. p. 233.   [115] Ibid. p. 233.
[116] Ibid. p. 236.   [117] Ibid. pp. 241–242.
[118] Ibid. p. 244.   [119] Ibid. p. 248.
[120] Ibid. pp. 251–252.   [121] Ibid. p. 252.
[122] Ibid. p. 253.
[123] George Smith, *The Hon. Ion G. N. Keith-Falconer*, p. 227.
[124] Lady Hilda Keith-Falconer, ibid.
[125] Sinker, ibid. p. 257.
[126] Keith-Falconer's widow married Major Frederick Ewart Bradshaw on 15 December 1894; she died on 24 October 1937, fifty years after Keith-Falconer's death.
[127] Keith-Falconer's Bible was a treasured possession of the Scottish Mission at Sheikh Othman.
[128] Sinker, ibid. p. 260.
[129] Ibid. p. 261.
[130] W. C. White, *Canon Cody of St Paul's Toronto*.

The Mission Hospital at Sheikh Othman – this photograph was probably taken in the 1930s.

Appendix

A Select Bibliography of the Published Writings of Marcus L. Loane

Oxford and the Evangelical Succession (London: Lutterworth, 1950).

Cambridge and the Evangelical Succession (London: Lutterworth, 1952).

Masters of the English Reformation (London: Church Society, 1954; repr. London: Hodder & Stoughton, 1983; repr. Edinburgh: Banner of Truth, 2005).

Archbishop Mowll (London: Hodder & Stoughton, 1960).

Makers of Puritan History (Grand Rapids: Eerdmans, 1961; repr. Grand Rapids: Baker, 1980).

Pioneers of the Reformation in England (London: Church Society, 1964).

Makers of Our Heritage: A Study of Four Evangelical Leaders (London: Hodder & Stoughton, 1967).

They Were Pilgrims (Sydney: Angus & Robertson Ltd, 1970; revised, Blackwood, South Australia: New Creation, 1984; repr. Edinburgh: Banner of Truth, 2006).

Hewn from the Rock: Origins and Traditions of the Church in Sydney (Sydney: Anglican Information Office, 1976).

John Charles Ryle, 1816-1900 (London: James Clarke, 1953; enlarged edition, London: Hodder & Stoughton, 1983).

Men to Remember (Canberra: Acorn Press, 1987).

These Happy Warriors: Friends and Contemporaries (Blackwood, South Australia: New Creation, 1988).